Southern Africa
Since the Portuguese Coup

Other Titles in This Series

Ethnicity in Modern Africa, edited by Brian M. du Toit

Botswana: An African Growth Economy, Penelope Hartland-Thunberg

Zambia's Foreign Policy: Studies in Diplomacy and Dependence, Douglas G. Anglin and Timothy Shaw

South Africa into the 1980s, edited by Richard E. Bissell and Chester A. Crocker

The Arab-African Connection: Political and Economic Realities, Victor T. Le Vine and Timothy W. Luke

An African Experiment in Nation Building: The Bilingual Cameroon Republic Since Reunification, edited by Ndiva Kofele-Kale

African Upheavals Since Independence, Grace Stuart Ibingira

Regionalism Reconsidered: The Economic Commission for Africa, Isebill V. Gruhn

Bibliography on African International Relations, Mark W. DeLancey

Africa and the West, edited by Michael A. Samuels

Alternative Futures for Africa, edited by Timothy M. Shaw

Westview Special Studies on Africa

Southern Africa Since the Portuguese Coup
edited by John Seiler

The April 1974 coup in Portugal markedly shifted political relationships in Southern Africa, forcing, among other outcomes, a clearer emergence of intractable differences within the region. The contributors to this volume present a careful exposition of events since the coup and an analysis of their implications. Reflecting divergent values and coming to differing conclusions, they confirm that no easy solutions to the regional conflict are at hand and that Southern Africa will for some time remain a focus for international attention.

John Seiler was formerly an associate research fellow at the Center for Strategic and International Studies, Georgetown University.

Southern Africa
Since the Portuguese Coup
edited by John Seiler

Westview Press / Boulder, Colorado

Westview Special Studies on Africa

Published in 1980 in the United States of America by
  Westview Press, Inc.
  5500 Central Avenue
  Boulder, Colorado 80301
  Frederick A. Praeger, Publisher

Library of Congress Cataloging in Publication Data
Main entry under title:
Southern Africa since the Portuguese coup.
  (Westview special studies on Africa)
  Includes index.
  1. Africa, Southern—Politics and government—Addresses, essays, lectures. 2. National liberation movements—Africa, Southern—Addresses, essays, lectures. 3. Portugal—History—Revolution, 1974—Influence—Addresses, essays, lectures. 4. Africa, Southern—Relations (general) with foreign countries—Addresses, essays, lectures. I. Seiler, John.
DT746.S62   968.06'2   80-11996
ISBN 0-89158-767-5

Printed and bound in the United States of America

For Miriam

Contents

PART 1
THE TRIGGERING EVENT

PART 2
THE INTERNATIONALIZATION OF REGIONAL CONFLICT:
ANGOLA AND ITS AFTERMATH

PART 3
TERRITORIES IN TRANSITION? ZIMBABWE RHODESIA AND
SOUTH WEST AFRICA/NAMIBIA

Maps

The Contributors

Donald G. Baker, professor of political science, Southampton College, Long Island University

David F. Gordon, assistant professor of government, The College of William and Mary

Maurice Halperin, professor emeritus of political science, Simon Fraser University

Noel C. Manganyi, professor of psychology and dean of the faculty of arts, University of Transkei

Ali A. Mazrui, professor of political science, University of Michigan

Keith Middlemas, reader in modern history, University of Sussex

John Seiler, associate research fellow, Center for Strategic and International Studies, Georgetown University (1978–1979)

Mary Simons, lecturer in African government, University of Cape Town

Roger J. Southall, senior lecturer in government and administration, National University of Lesotho

Christopher Stevens, research officer, Overseas Development Institute

Gerhard Tötemeyer, professor of political science, University of Transkei

C. Munhamu Botsio Utete, associate professor of political science, Montclair State College

Douglas L. Wheeler, professor of history, University of New Hampshire — Durham

Crawford Young, professor of political science, University of Wisconsin — Madison

Preface

Toward the end of 1975 I decided to edit a collection of essays on political developments in Southern Africa. At that time, I was teaching political science at Rhodes University in South Africa. Regional events since the Portuguese coup in April 1974 had already made an enormous impact, first suggesting the possibilities of peaceful accommodation between South Africa and its neighbors, but then demonstrating the destructive impact in Angola of widespread international intervention (in the latter half of 1975). From 1975 to the present, events in Southern Africa have neared center stage in international attention, but, as these essays will show, outstanding regional differences are no closer to peaceful resolution in late 1979 than they were in early 1976.

In my invitations to contributors, I consciously looked for a variety of viewpoints but asked that in expressing their viewpoints they avoid jargon and polemic. Despite my deep respect for and dependence on a number of journalists writing about Southern African affairs, all the contributors were drawn from the academic field because I wanted detailed descriptions of recent events to be related to long-term patterns.

Three acknowledgments are in order. First, to the contributors themselves for their patient acceptance of my editorial preferences. Second, to the Group Chairman's Fund of the Anglo American Corporation for a grant that enabled me to hold a workshop on the subject of this book at Rhodes University on 24–25 June 1976. Preliminary versions of a few essays were given; and black and white discussants from South Africa and North America took part in a general discussion of some of the central themes of this volume. This informal meeting would have been unusual in South Africa at any time, but its setting just after the beginning of the Soweto student riots gave it special poignancy.

Finally, my thanks go to my wife, with whom I shared many South African experiences from 1972 to 1977.

J. S.

Introduction

In what way was the April 1974 coup in Portugal a decisive and irreversible turning point in the political development of Southern Africa?

Before April 1974, Southern African regional political and economic relations were remarkably stable. This stability rested on a regional white hegemony based on unchallenged white rule in South Africa, Rhodesia, and the Portuguese colonies of Angola and Mozambique. External pressures presented no substantial threat to this hegemony. To the contrary, the net impact paradoxically enhanced white domination of the region.

The economic sanctions mounted against Rhodesia after its declaration of unilateral independence in November 1965 not only failed to topple Ian Smith's regime, but in fact strengthened the Rhodesian economy (until the aftermath of the 1973 Yom Kippur war and the Arab oil boycott produced a sharp cost increase for a great variety of commodities imported by Rhodesia) through the forced expansion of its secondary and tertiary components.

As for South Africa, after the 1966 International Court of Justice ruling disallowed to Liberia and Ethiopia legal standing to present the case against the South African mandate in South West Africa, its government moved with increasing confidence to solidify South African regional economic primacy and even made tentative (although naive and eventually unsuccessful) moves to gain political acceptance from its Black African neighbors.

Portugal fended off fitful U.S. pressure to accelerate modernization of its colonial policies. The Angolan nationalist movements were dormant and Frelimo contained. Only in Guinea-Bissau were its pacification efforts failing.

In short, despite the prolonged rhetorical internationalization of Southern African issues at the United Nations, in various UN-related agencies, and in the Organization of African Unity (OAU), Southern African developments, in fact, were effectively regionalized — controlled essentially by the three white regional governments. This regionalization was enhanced by de facto support from the governments of those major Western countries (the United States, the United Kingdom, France, and the Federal Republic of Germany)—countries that might have pressed for more rapid social-political change, but that instead applied only equivocal and occasional pressure while at the same time expanding trade and investment ties.

All this ended with the April 1974 Portuguese coup. Not all the implications for the region are certain yet. But the end of white hegemony is sure no matter what residual role or power whites may keep in Zimbabwe Rhodesia, South West Africa/Namibia, and South Africa itself. Less sure is the extent of effective long-term international involvement. Such involvement peaked during the 1975 Angolan civil war but has subsided considerably since, perhaps because the outcome of a renewed multisided international intervention elsewhere in the region remains too unpredictable and therefore poses a discernible threat to overall international stability.

The conflicts themselves—most directly over the immediate future of the three white-dominated territories—remain unresolved. Their outcomes seemed less clear at the end of 1979 than in the first months after the April 1974 coup when the white regimes and their black opponents both paradoxically shared a general optimism about the speedy and peaceful resolution of major regional conflicts. As the pervasiveness of polarized views about the region's future became more apparent, however, that optimism almost entirely disappeared. At first it was replaced by pessimism about the prospects for any early resolution of regional conflict and a growing sense that widening regional conflict, perhaps involving renewed international military intervention, would have great costs in human lives, in social stability, and in prospective economic development. But since the unexpected December 1979 ceasefire in Zimbabwe Rhodesia achieved by the U.K. government, hope has revived for regional stability based on the acknowledgment by regional governments of the destructive potentiality of renewed regional war.

The essays collected in this book speak directly to the basic conflicts in the region. In their divergent and sometimes-polarized perspectives and assumptions, they reflect the underlying normative sources of much regional conflict. Not all possible views are represented on any given topic nor are all possible topics addressed. That effort would entail an encyclopedic work.

The structure of the book reflects my appraisal of the present state of regional developments. Attention goes, in turn, to the immediate impact of the Portuguese withdrawal, the implications of the internationalization of the Angolan civil war, and the evolving character of regional conflict over the future of Zimbabwe Rhodesia, South West Africa/Namibia, and South Africa. The length of the section on South Africa strongly suggests that what happens there will be decisive in a variety of ways for the resolution of conflict throughout Southern Africa. Furthermore, the emphasis on South African official policies and white attitudes is an acknowledgement of the continued centrality of white power, although in addition some attention is given to changing black South African attitudes and political behavior. In the last section the role of various Black African states in Southern African conflicts is examined and the conclusion is drawn that their present significance remains indirect, rather than decisive.

John Seiler

Part 1

The Triggering Event

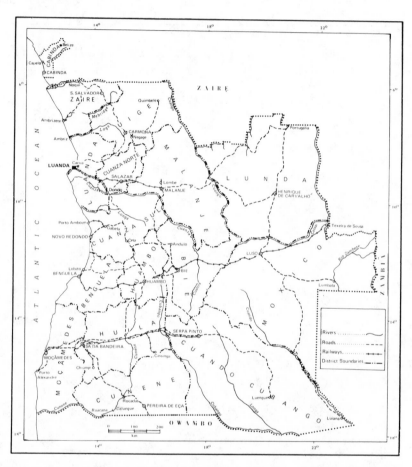

Map 1.   Angola. Source: The Africa Institute of South Africa, from *Bulletin* 14, no. 3, 1976, p. 55.

1
Portuguese Withdrawal from Africa, 1974–1975: The Angolan Case

Douglas L. Wheeler

*The felicity of a people cannot ever be built upon a heap of cadavers and inno-
cent victims.*

—General Silva Cardoso,
Portuguese High Commissioner in Angola,
interview, *Expresso* (Lisbon), 17 May 1975.

*The [African nationalist] movements have the duty to assume their responsi-
bility before history.*

—Foreign Minister Melo Antunes,
Luanda press interview, reported
in *Diario Popular* (Lisbon), 18 July 1975.

*The truth is, we are all puppets here, we are as much as are the three [African]
movements.*

—Admiral Leonel Cardoso,
last Portuguese High Commissioner in Angola,
9 November 1975 interview,
Veja (Sao Paulo), 19 November 1975.

Portugal's decolonization after the military coup of 25 April 1974 produced an unusually mixed result. In Asia by early summer 1975, Timor was
involved in a civil war, and the People's Republic of China evinced no im-

An earlier version of this chapter was presented on 2 March 1976 to a seminar on Portugal at the
School of Advanced International Studies, The Johns Hopkins University. It was published in
pamphlet form, along with other seminars, in a series edited by Professor Riordan Roett, *Pro-
ceedings of a Series of Seminars Conducted in Cooperation with the Assistant Secretary of
Defense (International Security Affairs) on National Security Policy Issues and Contemporary
Portugal* (Washington, D.C.: The Johns Hopkins University, 1976). The author is grateful to
Professor Roett for the invitation to participate in the seminar and for permission to use a revised version of the original seminar paper in this book.

mediate interest in supporting Portugal's offer of independence for Macão. In Africa, Guinea (Bissau), Mozambique, Cape Verde Islands, and São Tome–Principe Islands were rapidly granted independence (respectively, on 10 September 1974, 25 June 1975, 5 July 1975, and 12 July 1975). At the same time, Angola, the imperial prize, was embroiled in a civil war. It became the first sub-Saharan African country to begin independence deeply mired in a bloody, internationalized conflict.

This chapter will emphasize certain political factors that influenced Portugal's role in Angola from April 1974 to 11 November 1975, when the sixth provisional government, refusing to recognize any legal Angolan government, withdrew and. handed over sovereignty to "the people of Angola." Why was Portugal unable to contain the African nationalist power struggle in Angola? What links were there between politics in Portugal and the civil conflict in Angola? At what points during 1974–1975, through repeated attempts to enforce cease-fires and to prevent a civil war, were there "master events," after which it would have been difficult, if not impossible, to alter the course of events? Finally, what actions by Portugal, the three rival African nationalist parties, and external powers, given the circumstances, might have changed the course of events?

The Evolution of Portuguese Policy and of the Civil War

The military situation in Portuguese Africa on 25 April 1974 was varied and complex. Although a good case can be made to show that Portuguese forces were losing in Guinea (Bissau) and were under severe but relatively new pressure in central Mozambique, the overall war was not lost militarily.[1] In Angola, where insurgency had existed longest, the war had reached a stalemate not unfavorable to the Portuguese. Large sectors of the east and central parts of the territory supposedly "liberated" by the MPLA (Movimento Popular de Libertação de Angola) experienced little or no fighting. Civilians not involved in the conflict could travel from one end of this area to the other in safety and without incident.[2] Partisan claims to the contrary, no one nationalist group dominated even one-third of the vast territory, and the level of nationalist efforts against the Portuguese armed forces varied greatly. Indeed, once independence was in sight after March 1975, the three rival parties—the MPLA, the FNLA (Frente Nacional de Libertação de Angola), and Unita (União Nacional para a Independência Total de Angola)—fought each other with much greater intensity, and at greater cost in lives, than they had fought the Portuguese during thirteen years of ephemeral insurgency.

Although the war was not lost militarily, the coup in Lisbon brought political factors to the forefront. The MPLA intensified its insurgency in order to bid for negotiation of rapid independence with the new Portuguese regime dominated by the left-leaning MFA (Movimento das Forças Armadas—the armed forces movement).³ Until July 1974 it was not clear if this new regime would grant independence or if it would fight on for better terms for settler and economic interests. A power struggle in Lisbon involving the MFA leadership and the newly surfaced leftist political parties determined the initial course of decolonization.

Between 14 May and late June 1974, numerous pronouncements from President António de Spínola and several ministers led observers to believe that the regime would try to execute Spínola's Lusitanian Federation plan. Under the provisions of that plan, each territory would vote whether or not to remain in a federation that would guarantee the rights of Portuguese settlers and give Portugal certain powers in the economic and military fields. Leftist junior officers prevailed against the plan, and Premier Palma Carlos resigned on 9 July when he failed to obtain guarantees for the present or future power of President Spínola. On 19 July, the government published a law that included independence in the definition of "self-determination."⁴ It was announced that Guinea (Bissau) would be given independence soon. The stages of evolution toward independence for Angola and Mozambique would be monitored by the United Nations. Spínola's 27 July speech ruled out referendums. Instead, independence settlements would be negotiated with a selected one (or group) of the African nationalist parties involved in the struggle against Portugal.⁵ In the Lusaka Agreement, signed 7 August 1974, a major step was taken to clarify the decolonization process. The MFA program's vague language about a "political solution" to the overseas wars was made precise. Mozambique's future was settled. There would be no referendum there. Only Frelimo would be granted status and effective control of the transition government. After first withdrawing all Portuguese armed forces, Portugal would grant Mozambique independence on 25 June 1975.

The Angolan problem remained. The MFA's leadership moved steadily toward the left during 1974 and into 1975, and with this shift leftist demands for immediate decolonization were reinforced. As the political parties prepared for the 1975 elections, their congresses and published programs discussed decolonization. The PCP (Partido Comunista Português—the communist party) and its electoral ally the MDP (Movimento Democrático Português) strongly emphasized immediate decolonization, which they claimed would strengthen Portuguese democracy at home.⁶ More radical leftist views prevailed once again—General Spínola resigned as president on 30 September 1974, and with him went any possibility of pressure from the top for even partial implementation of his plan for a Lusitanian Federation and a more gradual decolonization process with some guarantees for the safety and property of the over 350,000 Portuguese settlers.

The turbulent, somewhat confusing, and surprising events in Portugal in the months after the April coup obscured those factors that traditionally would have supported a more conservative solution to decolonization. The size of the settler population, the economic stakes, and the fact that Portugal's economic weakness and dependence precluded a neocolonial comeback in Angola might have become significant factors; but the surface volatility and the "noise" of the dominant leftist forces obscured the undercurrent of center and rightist opinion on these issues. The Portuguese public was never given the opportunity to debate the colonial question freely.

Moreover, there is evidence that a substantial portion of the Portuguese population, especially those living in central and northern Portugal—north of the Tagus river—no longer subscribed fully to Estado Novo (New State), Luso-Tropical colonial rhetoric, but sought instead to protect relatively definable material interests. Indeed, well before the 1974 coup, Premier Marcello Caetano shifted his defense of Portuguese colonial policy from an emphasis on the major economic interests and Portugal's "historic mission" to a concern with the protection of the settlers' lives and property.[7] Thus, the opinions of Angolan settlers—an important Portuguese group, with their relatives and connections in Portugal and Brazil and further afield in other Portuguese-speaking communities—mattered both in the waning days of the Estado Novo (1968–1974, when Caetano "signaled left but turned right") and during the postdictatorship era.[8] Their opinions must also have been shared, at least in part, by numbers of black and brown Angolans who joined the white settlers as refugees in Portugal during 1975–1976.[9]

Kenneth Maxwell suggested in a recent article that Spínola's plan for a Lusitanian Federation was "twenty years too late."[10] On the contrary, such a plan might have been carried out in 1969–1970, although with considerable difficulty, since there had been no real preparation for self-government among either the Africans or the Portuguese settlers and since the settlers' political and racial attitudes were even more reactionary than they were in 1974–1975. Indeed, it would be more realistic to argue that the Lusitanian Federation was ten to twenty years too early. Of course, its implementation would have required a strong, liberal Portuguese government pursuing a gradualist decolonization plan according to a precise schedule. Such a strong government, like that of the United Kingdom in Northern Ireland, would have to have been willing to pay a high price politically and economically to maintain a lawful, orderly transition. The weakening of the Estado Novo system, the sudden opening to the left after 25 April 1974, and the subsequent power struggle among political groups in both Africa and Portugal precluded this possibility.

Negotiations between Portugal and the African nationalist parties of

Angola began in earnest in October 1974. They were slow, tedious, and complex. The two strongest and oldest parties, both recognized at one time or another by the OAU (Organization of African Unity), were the MPLA and the FNLA. Each maneuvered to get the upper hand. Zaire put pressure on Portugal to exclude the MPLA from any settlement and to ensconce its client, the FNLA. In Portugal, the radical leftist parties, especially the PCP and its allies, campaigned to have the FNLA excluded from a settlement. MFA moderates prevailed temporarily as the Portuguese government and African heads of state managed to get the major nationalist leaders to negotiate. When serious negotiations proceeded and the sessions moved to Mombasa in December 1974, a breakthrough was at hand.

By 5 January 1975, the Portuguese had worked out a basic agreement as a foundation for a final settlement. Three parties were assigned status as the only "legitimate" representatives of the Angolan people: the MPLA, the FNLA, and Unita. Unita's addition at the last minute was a compromise designed to balance ethnic representation among the parties and to offset the historic enmity between the two older parties. Unita was recognized by the OAU as a legitimate Angolan group only two days before the secret decolonization negotiations were moved into their final phase in Portugal on 10 January 1975.

At Alvor, in the Portuguese Algarve district, the Alvor Agreement was negotiated and agreed to by the four signatories. This extraordinary agreement set up a transitional stage between colony and independent state. The Alvor Agreement appeared to be a diplomatic masterpiece, a Portuguese and African compromise that successfully balanced divergent forces and interests. Independence was scheduled for 11 November 1975. The parties agreed to honor previously negotiated cease-fires, to remain within their own lines as established when the insurgency war ceased, and to cooperate in building an Angolan national army to be composed of Angolans drawn from the guerrilla forces of the FNLA, the MPLA, and Unita.

Portugal granted power to an Angolan transition government, which entered office in Luanda on 31 January 1975; equal roles in this government were assigned to each of the three nationalist parties. Portugal intended to negotiate further with the transition government on the future rights of Europeans, economic holdings, property transfers, and the control of mineral and infrastructural resources.

The transition government included an unusual executive college of three presidents, one each from the three parties. This executive college, together with a cabinet having posts distributed equally among the three parties and the Portuguese high commissioner, was to run the government until independence. Three areas of responsibility were delegated to other institutions: Portugal would handle foreign affairs, while a national defense committee would control external defense and internal security. This committee was crucial because it was meant to supervise the Portuguese armed forces, the police, and the nationalist forces. Its membership included the high commissioner (as chairman and effective military commander), the executive college, and a unified general staff.[11] The committee was intended to carry out military policy, to safeguard the existent territory and frontiers of Angola (including the Cabinda enclave), to guarantee peace and security and law and order, and to promote the safety of persons and property.[12]

One important clause of the Alvor Agreement stipulated that Portugal would maintain some armed forces in Angola until late February 1976—more than three months after independence. (Later, as the civil war intensified, Portugal accepted the MPLA demand to evacuate all Portuguese troops before independence.) Another important clause called for elections in October 1975 to elect a government and design a constitution before independence.

Optimism about the transition government was shattered by the bloody civil war that began in late March 1975 with clashes between the FNLA and the MPLA. The complex machinery of the transition government, including the key national defense committee, never worked properly. As the civil war became internationalized, the violence intensified and no elections were held before final independence on 11 November 1975.

Why was Portugal unable to contain the pressures that eventually exploded into a civil war and undermined the Alvor Agreement? There were two fundamental areas of concern: authority and security. The transition government was ineffective, and as violence escalated it lost all authority. Neither were the Portuguese government and armed forces able to exercise effective authority. As the violence of the power struggle among the African parties increased, no one could guarantee the safety of citizens of any race and insecurity became general.

Which armed forces were involved and to what extent was the military situation responsible for the breakdown of the Alvor Agreement and the evolution of the civil war? Table 1.1 outlines the changes in size and composition of the various military forces present in Angola. Most of the figures are estimates based on journalistic reports because official figures (for what they are worth) are not yet available.[13] Table 1.1 includes armed militants and mercenaries who came to Angola beginning in late January 1975 to support the various parties. The MPLA got aid from Portuguese leftists, East Europeans, and possibly some Brazilian "advisors." Mercenaries were important for both the FNLA and Unita—anti-Castro Cubans and Americans recruited in the United States, as well as French, British, Belgian, and South African citizens. The MPLA usually had twice as many foreign soldiers as did its opponents.[14]

Table 1.1   Changing Troop Levels in Angola.

Date	Party	Size of Force	Allies, etc.
April 1974	Portugal	70,000	30,000 Africans
	MPLA	10,000?	
	FNLA	10,000?	a few European
	Unita	2,000?	mercenaries
15 January 1975--Alvor Agreement, stipulated levels	Portugal	24,000	
	MPLA	8,000	
	FNLA	8,000	
	Unita	8,000	
15 January 1975--actual levels	Portugal	40,000	Africans demobilized
	MPLA	10,000?	Cubans?
	FNLA	15,000?	1,000-2,000 Zairoise
	Unita	5,000?	
1 July 1975	Portugal	24,000?	
	MPLA	15,000	300-500 Cubans
	FNLA	20,000	1,000-2,000 Zairoise
	Unita	8,000	
1 November 1975	Portugal	3,000-4,000	
	MPLA	27,000 (A)	2,000-3,000 Cubans
	FNLA	22,000	1,000-2,000 Zairoise
	Unita	8,000-10,000	4,000-5,000 South Africans
2 January 1976	Portugal	0	
	MPLA	27,000 (B)	8,000-10,000 Cubans
	FNLA	21,000	2,000 Zairoise, Portuguese
	Unita	9,000-12,000	4,000-5,000 South Africans, plus white mercenaries

A. Le Monde (12, 13 November 1975) reported that Mozambique dispatched 250
    Frelimo troops to the MPLA.

B. In addition to its regular troops and the Cuban units, the MPLA also
    apparently could use some 12,000 "part-time" guerrillas and 6,000 pro-
    MPLA former Katangan mercenaries and gendarmerie. Estimates of MPLA
    Soviet advisors ranged from 200 to 2,000. See Christian Science Monitor,
    2 January 1976, and 18 February 1976.

While the transition government broke down frequently, in part because
of the tripartite structure that precluded the exercise of power by any individual member of the executive, the military situation worsened steadily.
The power struggle began with an outbreak of fighting between MPLA and
FNLA soldiers in early March 1975 at a training camp north of Moçâmedes.
During the week of 22–28 March there was intense fighting between MPLA
and FNLA troops in and around the capital city, Luanda. Available evidence
points to provocation by FNLA troops through the murder or execution of
fifty to sixty MPLA soldiers. By 28 March a fragile truce was established in
Luanda, but only after several hundred deaths, partly the result of armed attacks by MPLA civilian militants, some armed with *catanas* (Angolan
machetes), in Luanda townships.[15] The Portuguese high commissioner and

his forces enforced curfews, established patrols using mixed forces, and attempted to confine the feuding troops to barracks. But the March bloodbath was only the beginning of a spiraling, if ephemeral, series of battles in Luanda and in major northern towns, including Caxito, Malanje, and Carmona. The possibility of a peaceful, constitutional transition to independence was further undermined by three separate, devastating bursts of full warfare: 28 April–3 May; early June; and finally 9–15 July — what might properly be termed "The Battle of Luanda."

The March FNLA-MPLA killings released the pent-up hatreds, fears, blood-feud memories, and mob instincts in the Luanda African shantytowns (*os muceques*), in the greater Luanda area, and in an area east of Luanda on a line to Malanje. Each wave of violence began with a single incident; further, there is strong evidence that the first three bursts of civil war between the FNLA and the MPLA were provoked by the FNLA to defeat the MPLA in its ethnic-regional base area.[16] A major FNLA objective was apparently to win over the Mbundu-dominated Luanda *muceques* and to drive MPLA forces from Mbundu towns east and north of Luanda.

The price of the breakdown of civil order was appalling. By 10 July 1975, probably 40,000 Africans were dead and twice that number injured. "Ceasefires" were invariably arranged following each burst of mayhem. At least until June the Portuguese armed forces, despite their war-weariness, fear, and strong desire to leave Angola, acted as mediators between FNLA and MPLA troops. But they were unable to prevent the killings; end the atmosphere of excessive tension, fear, and insecurity; or construct an effective, substantial Angolan national army.

The fighting had serious social repercussions. Work stoppages and strikes by African workers in industry, the ports, and farming paralyzed the economy. Food became scarce, services broke down, famine spread in rural areas, medical resources were hopelessly inadequate, and a massive displacement of people took place. Most of the Portuguese population began to flee by air, by ship, on foot, or in convoys of cars and trucks overland to South West Africa/Namibia.[17] Even larger and more significant was the displacement of Africans from towns and rural areas in northern Angola as the fighting escalated. Also, thousands of Africans fled Luanda — toward the south, if they were Ovimbundu; toward the north, if they were Bakongo. The resultant reduction of ethnic heterogeneity in the Luanda area helped to ensure greater MPLA dominance there. By June 1975, northeastern Angola was gripped by wartime conditions, and the International Red Cross had established emergency medical teams in some sections of the country.[18]

The Portuguese failure to enforce the Alvor Agreement, or even to honor its central stipulations, was caused by the combination of the Portuguese military situation, the behavior of the nationalist forces, and the massive external intervention in 1975. The most serious failures of the Portuguese armed forces were their inability to disarm various African civilian and military groups, to build a national Angolan army, and to prevent the MPLA "coup" of 9–15 July 1975, when MPLA forces drove the FNLA from its Luanda installations and conquered the city. The Portuguese military was at a serious disadvantage outside Luanda because it lacked the troops (and perhaps the equipment) to enforce peace. The last Portuguese high commissioner said the "basic error" was to fix Portuguese military strength at 24,000 men while the three African parties increased their forces (Unita may be an exception) well beyond their stipulated limit of 8,000 each.[19] Only in Luanda did the Portuguese retain some authority, although not enough to prevent the decisive MPLA takeover. Moreover, the Portuguese were unable to keep their forces at full strength. By independence day, 11 November 1975, only 2,000 Portuguese troops remained to embark from Luanda.

Politicization and favoritism within the Portuguese armed forces contributed to the problems of control. Some Portuguese units were pro-MPLA, some were neutral, some favored the FNLA and Unita. The Portuguese military commanders and high commissioners soon learned that their powers were highly influenced by Lisbon politics. The Portuguese government was pressed by political groups in Portugal and in Angola to keep or dismiss officials on the basis of their actions and attitudes to the Angolan nationalist parties. High Commissioner Admiral Antonio Rosa Coutinho was considered strongly pro-MPLA and apparently favored strengthening the MPLA with arms. High Commissioner Silva Cardoso (January–August 1975) was considered "neutral" by the FNLA and Unita but "hostile" by the MPLA's Agostinho Neto.[20] Until July 1975 a number of Portuguese military units favored the MPLA, channeling support from the dominant leftist parties in Portugal. When some Portuguese units turned on the MPLA in Luanda in early July to revenge a shooting incident, the MPLA leadership realized that the Portuguese military's attitude might soon reflect the political shift to the center and right that emanated from northern Portuguese rural areas and was beginning to sweep Portugal.

Another factor making Portuguese control difficult involved the actions of the nationalist parties, their followers, and their allies. The crucial battleground was the Luanda area. The FNLA made a concerted attempt to win over, both by propaganda and by intimidation, the pro-MPLA population of the Luanda *muceques*. They were unable to dislodge the pro-MPLA groups, who had been given arms by the MPLA, by their allies in the Portuguese political parties, and by some Portuguese military personnel. The MPLA was also better organized politically. By the first months of 1975, it had organized the *muceques* and surrounding towns into committees that used the slogan of *poder popular* (people's power). These groups, only some of which were ethnically Mbundu, sustained losses in the FNLA attacks but then struck back. At times they operated without effective control from the MPLA and simply went on the rampage with either guns or machetes. Both the MPLA and the FNLA were guilty of arming civilian militants. These murderous outbursts, more than the FNLA-MPLA fighting, caused the 1975 Portuguese exodus.[21] Ironically, Agostinho Neto worked to prevent this massive emigration, which was burgeoning even as he signed the Alvor Agreement in January 1975.

The internationalization of the Angolan civil war is discussed at length in other chapters. All that needs to be said here is that the ready availability of arms and advisors to both the MPLA and its FNLA-Unita opponents in the months after March 1975 made the Portuguese effort to control the conflict impossible.

The MPLA "coup" of 9–15 July 1975 in Luanda was a major turning point, even a point of no return. The MPLA drove FNLA forces from their headquarters and all their installations. The FNLA troops panicked and most of them fled, leaving only a few pockets of resistance in several industrial sectors of the city and in an old fort-prison, which FNLA soldiers held until August. The MPLA probably reasoned that—besides avenging the earlier FNLA attacks—the taking of Luanda would strengthen their subsequent negotiating position, if anything of the Alvor Agreement could be saved. In any case, after taking the capital with minimal Portuguese resistance, the MPLA would have a stronger position if and when elections were held. By early August, all FNLA and Unita forces had withdrawn from the Luanda area and a massive airlift of Portuguese refugees was underway with international support. Holden Roberto of the FNLA declared "war" on the MPLA, promising to capture Luanda within weeks. The prospects for the transition government and for peace were ended.

The Portuguese government, beseiged by political upheaval at home, was now helpless. It could not even enforce orders given its own troops, as President Francisco da Costa Gomes admitted after the abortive 25 November 1975 coup.[22] On 14 August, interim High Commissioner General Ferriera Macedo assumed "control" of the transition government, which had effectively disbanded due (Macedo suggested) to the "incapacity" of its three members to continue. On 29 August the Alvor Agreement was officially abrogated. While nationalist troops increased in number, the Portuguese military dwindled in size. The Portuguese troops were needed at home, no matter what emergency plans might have existed for their deployment to Angola, and, in any case, some soldiers refused to board planes taking them to Angola.

Given the MPLA occupation of Luanda, the exacerbating impact of international interventon, and Portuguese domestic disunity and even passivity about Angola, Portugal could have done little to prevent the continuation of civil war. Perhaps coincidentally, massive Soviet-Cuban assistance for the MPLA began to have an impact in Angola in early September 1975, when the pro-MPLA Vasco Gonçalves government fell from power in Lisbon. On 22 October 1975, Agostinho Neto made clear the unilateral nature of MPLA aims:

> We conquered that right to independence and the recognition of Portugal of our right to independence came only after fourteen years of struggle. We feel that we deserve it and we are going to declare it. Whether Portugal wants it or not, we will be independent on the 11th November. It is not Portugal, however, who comes to offer us the instruments of power. We are going to create them and to assume our responsibility.[23]

It was evident at this point that Portugal had failed to carry out its decolonization plan for Angola and that the much discussed "spirit of Alvor" was no more than a memory.

Explaining the Failure of Portuguese Policy

On 10 November 1975, some hours before the official independence of Angola, the last Portuguese troops and officials left Luanda. The high commissioner, Admiral Leonel Cardoso, left without recognizing any legal government. He claimed that Portugal granted sovereignty to "the people of Angola." In an interview given just before leaving, he stated that powerful international groups hankered after Angola's rich resources and that external forces manipulated both the Portuguese and the nationalist movements like puppets. Despite his government's refusal to recognize the MPLA's "People's Republic of Angola," Cardoso concluded that "no government in Angola could last more than a week without the support of the MPLA."[24]

What were the exact connections between political conflicts in metropolitan Portugal and Portugal's inability to prevent the Angolan civil war? The central point needs reiteration: Portugal's ability to act decisively in Angola was seriously limited by the political battles in Portugal. As Major Melo Antunes, then Portuguese foreign minister, stated in an 18 July 1975 Luanda interview:

> Portugal has tried to avoid, at all costs, direct intervention in the armed confrontations of the two movements . . . except when it is absolutely necessary. . . . Unfortunately, during these months, national public opinion was not sufficiently sensitive concerning decolonization problems, namely the problem of Angola, which was the most serious of all. Partisan groups have made it worse with their acts, their press and public opinion have done a disservice . . . Por-

tugal cannot support simultaneously this decolonization and a process of profound political, social, and economic change now occurring in the country.[25]

One feature of partisan politics in Portugal was a press campaign strongly biased in favor of the MPLA. Except for a handful of newspapers, most of the Lisbon press (the most influential medium in the country) openly favored the MPLA and bitterly attacked the FNLA and Unita.[26] When the MPLA's propaganda campaign against the FNLA entered a more explicit phase in July and August 1975, numerous Lisbon press reports attacked the FNLA as racist, tribalistic, savage, and "primitive." On the basis of unconfirmed reports of the finding of bodies and parts of human organs during the MPLA capture of the FNLA's Luanda installations, the nondemocratic left's Lisbon newspapers launched a barrage of attacks on 11 July—the day that Mario Soares resigned from the provisional government.[27] These attacks were followed in August by MPLA claims of extensive FNLA atrocities, including cannibalism, presented at an international "nonaligned" conference in South America.[28]

Whatever the truth of such claims and allegations, the MPLA propaganda was disconcerting, if not totally effective. There is considerable irony in the strong resemblance between the tone and language of the MPLA propaganda and that of propaganda used in 1961 by the Salazar regime to arouse political support for the war effort against the first nationalist attacks.[29] This MPLA campaign, designed to smear and discredit the FNLA and to gain enough political advantage to win Portuguese diplomatic recognition by 11 November, might have been designed deliberately to appeal to a relatively unsophisticated Portuguese audience in both Angola and Portugal. The FNLA propaganda was less ruthless and less persuasive.[30]

In the context of escalating political struggle in Portugal, many political observers realized the implications for Angolan policy of a move from the left toward the center and right. Those leftist parties—including the PCP, MES (Movimento de Esquerda Socialista), and MDP—that supported the Vasco Gonçalves government throughout the "hot" summer of 1975 also supported the MPLA and attacked the FNLA and Unita and the support given them by any Portuguese party.[31] Some leftist writers attempted to link the Socialist party's resignation from the provisional government and its campaign to win support from moderate MFA elements with the FNLA attacks in Luanda.[32]

Although it remains difficult to document in detail the political impact of Portugal's withdrawal from Angola and its failure to maintain the Alvor Agreement, some immediate and long-range consequences may be suggested. The most obvious immediate problems emerge from the exodus of between 300,000 and 400,000 Portuguese from Angola that began in 1974.

Some emigrated to South Africa, Brazil, Gabon, South West Africa/ Namibia, the Portuguese Atlantic islands, the United States, and Canada, but most landed in Portugal. This massive influx posed enormous difficulties for the provisional Portuguese government: increased unemployment; the cost of housing, feeding, and maintaining this uprooted and disoriented group; and an increased security problem caused by the proliferation of private firearms.[33]

The provisional government, even when able and anxious to aid these *retornados* (returned ones), was threatened with armed conspiracies from several rightist factions—especially the ELP (Exército de Libertação Português) and the MDLP (Movimento Democrático de Libertação de Portugal) —which fed on the discontent of the Angolan refugees. Other partisan forces, including the CDS (Centro Democrático Social), gained political support from refugees.[34]

In effect, events in Angola and the arrival of the refugees helped to polarize further an already divided and tense Portuguese population. As more refugees arrived, there was a corresponding tendency for public opinion and government policy to move toward the right. Typical of this phenomenon was the government instability between 11 July 1975 (when Mario Soares left the government) and 25 November 1975 (when a radical nondemocratic leftist coup attempt failed). The Azevedo Pinheiro government, successor in September to the Gonçalves government, was under severe pressure form the refugees, their allies, and public opinion about the disastrous turn of events in Angola. A conspiracy theory—"a stab in the back in Angola"—emerged among certain Portuguese rightist factions and perhaps among some centrist groups. The adherents of this theory attacked the government for its failure to protect Portuguese lives, jobs, and property in Angola; to arrange for return transportation to Portugal in an adequate and timely manner; and to maintain the refugees properly once they reached Portugal.

Angolan issues—the status of refugees; the status and future of Portuguese property, jobs, and capital in independent Angola; and diplomatic recognition of the MPLA government—received considerable attention in the campaigns preceding the April 1976 parliamentary election and the June 1976 presidential election. Although center and rightist parties gained strength in the elections, the Angolan factor was apparently less significant than a range of domestic issues.

The Portuguese government's attitude toward the MPLA remained equivocal into early 1976. In February, while recognition of the MPLA was still a minority cause in the sixth provisional government, a pro-MPLA government official—Minister for Interterritorial Cooperation Vito Crespo —made a revealing, if questionable, argument for recognition: it was the only choice, given Portuguese interests in Africa and elsewhere in the developing world. Further, Crespo said,

> The MPLA has the vocation to defend and to realize in the future a policy of nonalignment. The Soviet support for MPLA was somewhat forced by the circumstances. There was, in fact, an initial involvement of the U.S. with FNLA and Unita, through South Africa, which obliged the MPLA, in danger of near destruction, to get help for itself from its friends.[35]

Communication between Portugal and the People's Republic of Angola began to improve in late February 1976; on 22 February Portugal officially recognized the MPLA government. Negotiations opened on the questions of Angolan debts in Portugal, the capital and property claims of Portuguese citizens in Angola, diplomatic arrangements, and Portuguese aid to Angola. In early 1977 Portuguese diplomats were posted to Luanda. In the next months, Angola's Foreign Minister paid an official visit to Lisbon to discuss questions of mutual concern. The publication of Angola's new law of citizenship opened another question: what rights would Portuguese-born residents have in Angola and how would the remaining settlers in Angola be handled by the new regime? One provision permitted all individuals who had lived in Angola for ten years or more to obtain Angolan citizenship; it was a much less radical approach than that adopted in independent Mozambique.[36]

As of early 1977 relations between Portugal and Angola had improved but were not yet normal, despite the resumption of diplomatic relations and regular air service between Luanda and Lisbon. Two serious questions of a financial nature remained: the claims of refugees (both white and black) from the civil war; and the amount of technical and monetary aid Portugal could or would give and the amount Angola would accept. Whatever the needs of the crippled Angolan economy, it was clear that (at least for the immediate future) Cuban and East European personnel—not Portuguese— would dominate the skeletal cadres that kept the country operating. It was also clear that the manner in which Portugal withdrew authority, people, and equipment from Angola would have an impact upon the new Angola for years to come.

The aftermath of the civil war remains clouded in a vigorous propaganda war involving various groups in Portugal, the Soviet Union, Cuba, Angola, Zaire, South Africa, and Zambia.[37] Nonetheless, it seems logical that the new Angolan government has three priorities: to establish political unity within the MPLA; to establish general control and security throughout Angola; and to revive a war-torn economy, including the Benguela railway, crucial to Zairian and Zambian exports. As late as September 1979 none of these goals had been achieved. An abortive coup had taken place in Luanda, led by several radical ideologues. The MPLA had launched several major attacks in southern Angola to crush Unita but had apparently failed to do so. And, partly because Unita still cut portions of the line, the Benguela railway was not yet in operation.

The nature of decolonization also had a basic impact on Portuguese politics. The nondemocratic left had argued that immediate decolonization would strengthen Portuguese democracy. On the contrary, the abrupt (if not immediate) collapse of Portuguese colonial authority and the absence of a legitimate transitional regime severely tested Portuguese democracy. Ironically, the nondemocratic left was itself seriously weakened and center and rightist parties strengthened. More significantly, the various problems growing out of the refugee influx will not be easily solved, and the armed forces' leadership has shifted from its position as the dominant decision maker to that of a moderating power, the historic *poder moderador* symbolized in Portugal's constitutional past by the monarch or the president of the republic.[38]

Conclusion

What might have prevented the Angolan civil war from developing beyond its early stages of fighting? One answer might be armed intervention by either the United Nations or the OAU. But even if these bodies had been able to agree on such a plan and to launch an expeditionary force, there is little guarantee that their actions would have been effective. Unless the Soviet Union and the United States had agreed to back the force, the plan would not have been feasible. Moreover, the Angolan nationalist movements were consistently opposed to such international intervention.

Given Portugal's incapacity to contain the Angolan power struggle and to prevent the civil war, some other interested government with sufficient power would have been required to back the provisional government's plans and objectives for Angola. Even if the U.S. government had been able to gain congressional support for a massive, decisive backing of the Portuguese army in Angola, the question must be asked: Would the Portuguese government and party leadership have been able to accept or utilize such aid during the struggle for power in Lisbon? Economic aid from Western European governments was feasible, but a large amount of U.S. aid would probably have been rejected. In the summer of 1975 the nondemocratic left was attacking the Socialist and Popular Democratic parties for their presumed association with U.S. and international capitalist interests. U.S. aid, although crucial for the maintenance of an orderly transition in Angola, would probably have weakened or even defeated the MPLA. Knowing this, the nondemocratic left would have fought it tooth and nail.[39]

Nonetheless, there was a period when decisive preventive action might have been taken—the six months before the Luanda events of 9-15 July 1975. Portugal might have had a better chance to enforce the Alvor Agreement had it insisted upon two preconditions before any final decolonization settlement: the measures necessary to prevent the arming of Angolan civilians; and the disarming of the Angolan nationalist forces and their civilian partisans, as a first step toward building an Angolan national army.

A vicious circle confronts analysis at this point. The Angolan nationalist forces were intact in April 1974. The Portuguese wanted to cease fighting. The nationalist troops insisted on staying armed against the day when they would struggle for power with their rivals. This insistence contributed to the failure to organize an integrated Angolan army. Hence, once fighting began among the nationalists, nothing but massive outside intervention—which the Portuguese government was unable to provide—could end it.

The Angolan civil disorders, civil war, and subsequent insurgency amount to one of the greatest human tragedies in the history of modern Africa. The loss of life alone must rank with the losses sustained in the Congo civil war, 1960-1964, and in the Nigerian civil war, 1967-1970. Repercussions in Portuguese domestic affairs and in international affairs remain significant. In the internationalization of the Angolan civil war there is a strong message to political leaders who value human life above ideological commitments—internationalization had a murderous impact upon the people of Angola. As with that oddly similar conflict—the Spanish civil war, 1936-1939—international intervention, unless carried out in the interest of conciliation and peace, may lengthen the conflict and will surely increase the human cost.

Notes

1. Keith Middlemas states in *Cabora Bassa, Engineering and Politics in Southern Africa* (London: Weidenfeld & Nicolson, 1975), p. 319: "The war was not lost. Given adequate backing, the army could have held Mozambique for years more, as Frelimo privately acknowledged. Subversion and actual fighting never reached the scale of the war in Algeria in the 1950s." Middlemas's study and its conclusions represent one of the most accurate and realistic works on the subject.

2. Personal conversations with U.S. officials serving in the Luanda consulate-general in 1973-1974; a survey of the international press.

3. See Portuguese press, especially *O Século, Diário de Notícias, Expresso, A República*, 1 May-1 July 1974. See also the interesting reports by Brazilian correspondents in Angola, in the weekly magazine *Veja* (São Paulo), during this period.

4. See texts of these documents and speeches in *Textos Históricos Da Revolucão*

(Lisbon: Diabril Editora, 1975), pp. 41ff.

5. Ibid., pp. 46ff.

6. Douglas L. Wheeler, "Portuguese-speaking Africa's Rocky Road to Self-Rule," *Christian Science Monitor*, 9 September 1974. For MFA program published just after the 25 April 1974 coup, see *Textos Históricos Da Revolucão*, pp. 41–46; see also Kenneth Maxwell, "The Hidden Revolution in Portugal," *New York Review of Books*, 17 April 1975. For party programs: see Cesar Oliveira, *MFA E Revolucão Socialista* (Lisbon: Diabril Editora, 1975) for views close to the MES; see also Edicões Avante, PCP, *Programma E Estatutos Do PCP. Aprovados no VII Congresso (Extraordinário realizado em 20/10/74)*, Lisbon, 1974; MDP, *Programma E Estatutos*, Lisbon, December 1974, pp. 33, 34—"Descolonizacão."

7. Douglas L. Wheeler, "Portugal in Angola: A Living Colonialism?" in Christian P. Potholm and Richard Dale, eds., *Southern Africa in Perspective* (New York: The Free Press, 1972), pp. 172–182.

8. Douglas L. Wheeler, "Thaw in Portugal," *Foreign Affairs* 48, no. 4 (July 1970), pp. 769–781.

9. My personal observations while visiting the Lisbon area during 4–25 July 1975, including a visit to one of the Angolan refugee camps at Costa da Caparica, lead me to conclude that perhaps thousands of black and brown Angolans accompanied fleeing Portuguese in the summer of 1975.

10. Kenneth Maxwell, "The Thorns of the Portuguese Revolution," *Foreign Affairs* 54, no. 2 (January 1976), p. 252.

11. See my testimony before the U.S. Senate Subcommittee on Africa, 16 June 1975, later published in *Issue 5*, no. 3 (Fall 1975), pp. 21–23.

12. For the text of the Alvor Agreement, see *Angola: The Independence Agreement* (Lisbon: Ministry of Mass Communication, 1975). Texts were also published in the Portuguese press during the week of 15–20 January 1975.

13. Sources for this table include Douglas L. Wheeler, "African Elements in Portugal's Armies in Africa, 1961–1974," *Armed Forces and Society* 2, no. 2 (Winter 1975); *Jornal Novo* (Lisbon), 21 June 1975, p. 17; *New York Times*, 1–20 November 1975; *Economist*, 22 November 1975, pp. 47–51; *Christian Science Monitor*, 2 January 1976 and 18 February 1976. Michael Kaufman estimated that the FNLA had no more than 10,000 fighting men and that it was the "largest of the armies"; this seems a severe underestimation (*New York Times*, Sunday Magazine, 4 January 1976).

14. *Christian Science Monitor*, 2 January 1976 and 18 February 1976. I have not taken into account the evidence that Cuban aid was being funneled to the MPLA via Portugal before the large Cuban buildup began in October 1975.

15. *Expresso*, 28 March 1975.

16. *Expresso*, 19 July 1975.

17. *Expresso*, *Veja* (São Paulo), *New York Times*, *Christian Science Monitor*, all for period 12 July–1 November 1975; *Le Monde* August–December 1975, made available by Rene Pelissier.

18. Personal correspondence with the Boston branch of the International Red Cross, November 1975.

19. Interview published in *Veja*, 19 November 1975.

20. *Expresso*, October 1974–August 1975, and other Portuguese newspapers, including *O Século* and *Diário de Notícias*.

21. *Veja*, 23 July 1975, p. 27. This report suggested that the incident that led to the "Battle of Luanda" was an FNLA attack on a funeral for a female MPLA member. See also *Expresso*, 7, 12, 19 July 1975; *A Capital*, 21 July 1975; and *Jornal Novo*, June 1975, July 1975.

22. *A Republica*, 6 December 1975; cited in *Varias* (Lisbon), no. 1, 13 December 1975, p. 13.

23. *Expresso*, 22 October 1975.

24. *Veja*, 19 November 1975.

25. *Diário Popular* (Lisbon), 18 July 1975, p. 17.

26. Namely the weeklies *Expresso*, *Jornal Novo*, and *O Tempo*.

27. Author's survey of Lisbon press, 11–25 July 1975.

28. *Le Monde*, 26 August 1975.

29. Author's observations, documented by newspaper collection for 1961–1962 (Lisbon, Oporto press) and survey of government literature. Also, observation of government trucks with mobile "atrocity picture shows" parked at country fairs in Algarve province, July 1962.

30. *Veja*, 25 June 1975, p. 34. FNLA hired a Brazilian public relations firm to work in Luanda. Among other projects, it printed and circulated posters in FNLA colors proclaiming "Angola, love it or leave it." See also FNLA press releases in Lisbon newspapers in this period.

31. See "Angola O CDS, A Unita E O MPLA," *Vida Mundial* (Lisbon), no. 1871, 24 July 1975.

32. "Angola's Capital Liberated From FNLA Mercenaries," *A Republica*, 15 July 1975, p. 16.

33. See various issues of *Expresso* throughout 1975; also "O drama cruel dos refugiados," *O Tempo*, 19 June 1975. The government established a special refugee body, A Comissao dos Deslocados do Ultramar.

34. Strongly conservative views on the Angolan issue appeared also in Portuguese emigrant publications; one, *Portuguese Times* (New Bedford, Massachusetts), contained much news of Angolan events, about refugees, and views expressed in numerous, often lengthy, letters to the editor.

35. *Expresso*, 7 February 1976, p. 1.

36. "Nationality Law," Article 3, in Angola, *Documentos Da Independencia* (Lisbon, 1976), p. 76.

37. For recent Portuguese literature on the Angolan civil war, Portuguese policy, and the international intervention, see Raúl Valdes Vivo (translation of a Cuban book), *Angola: Fim Do Mito Dos Mercenários* (Lisbon: Africa Editora, 1976); Valdemiro de Sousa, *Angola: A Guerra E O Crime* (Lisbon: Editorial Formacão, 1976); Amadeu José de Freitas, *Angola: O Longo Caminho Da Liberdade* (Lisbon: Moraes Editores, 1975); Georges Lecoff, *Angola: L'independance empoisonnée* (Paris: Presses de la Cité, 1976); Pompílio da Cruz, *Angola: Os Vivos E Os Mortos* (Lisbon: Intervencão, 1976). For recent reports on MPLA internal struggles, see *New*

York Times, 30 May–6 June 1977, and *Expresso,* 4 June 1977, pp. 1R–2R.

38. For an analysis of the role of the executive and *poder moderador* in Portuguese history, see Douglas L. Wheeler, *Republican Portugal: A Political History, 1910–1926* (Madison: University of Wisconsin Press, 1977), Chaps. 2, 6–13.

39. See Kenneth Maxwell, "The Hidden Revolution in Portugal," *New York Review of Books,* 17 April 1975, p. 34; and his "The Thorns of the Portuguese Revolution," *Foreign Affairs* 54, no. 2 (January 1976), pp. 266–268; see also Jane Kramer's article on Portugal, *New Yorker,* 15 December 1975.

Part 2

The Internationalization
of Regional Conflict:
Angola and Its Aftermath

2

The Cuban Role in Southern Africa

Maurice Halperin

Cuba's massive—and decisive—intervention in the Angolan civil war resulted in a victory for the Soviet Union and a sharp setback for the United States and China. There is little doubt that Cuba's subsequent role in bolstering the impoverished and vulnerable regime of Agostinho Neto earned the Kremlin's gratitude. Fidel Castro's personal efforts to mediate the territorial dispute between the Soviet-supported regimes in Somalia and Ethiopia were obviously encouraged by the Soviet Union and were intended to strengthen Soviet interests.[1] Elsewhere in Africa, without exception, Soviet and Cuban policies have coincided to a remarkable degree for a number of years.

Which of the two governments is the prime mover in the implementation of this common policy? It would be palpably absurd to cast Cuba, a small, dependent state heavily subsidized by the Soviet Union, in this role. It would be equally absurd to argue that the Soviets are promoting Cuban geopolitical power in Africa rather than their own. Thus, however Castro may explain the Cuban role in Angola and elsewhere in Africa, practically speaking (or "objectively," to use Marxist terminology) Cuba has been no more than a Soviet surrogate or auxiliary, depending on the particular situation.

This much conceded, to call the Cuban troops in Angola (and, by extension, Cuban personnel elsewhere in Africa) "mercenaries" (as the Chinese and others have done) still is an oversimplification. It implies that Cuban services were "purchased," that Castro took orders from Moscow, and that there was no other motivation for the Cuban presence in Angola or elsewhere in Africa. This explanation ignores the long history of Cuban involvement in Africa, the dynamics of the Cuban Revolution, and the singular character of Fidel Castro, Cuba's maximum leader.

The Origins of Cuba's African Involvement

Castro's interest in Africa antedates his relations with the Soviet Union.

On 2 March 1959, precisely two months after his triumphal entry into Havana, *Revolución* reported that representatives of the then hard-pressed Algerian National Liberation Front, on a Latin American tour to gather support for their cause, had stopped in Havana and presented Castro with a medal. In the newspaper's words, it was "the first given by this heroic people, and the first accepted by the leader of the Cuban Revolution." More than likely, Castro had made a sizable financial contribution, in addition to promising strong political support for the Algerian revolution.[2] This was the first recorded contact between the new Cuban regime and the African continent. For Castro, at that time, the contribution was essentially a matter of anti-imperialist principle, consistent with his conception of the Cuban Revolution's commitment to end U.S. neocolonial domination of Cuba.

Three months later the first Cuban emissary reached Africa. In mid-June, Che Guevara, accompanied by three aides, met with President Nasser in Cairo. It was the start of a three-month globe-circling tour, in which the countries visited—with the exceptions of Japan, a major consumer of Cuban sugar, and Yugoslavia, a leader of the nonaligned bloc—were former colonial possessions in North Africa and Southeast Asia. Cuba was demonstrating that, for the first time in its history, it had become an independent actor on the international scene, even beyond the confines of the Western Hemisphere. At the same time, it signaled its intentions to identify with the Third World. This choice was dictated not only by anti-imperialist principle, but by practical considerations as well: to lessen its dependency on trade with the United States and, more urgently, to secure political support in what was clearly becoming a major confrontation with the United States. Principle and realpolitik were joined, and they remained inseparable from then on. Principle, to be sure, was always asserted, but realpolitik (and not uncommonly, its offspring, opportunism) lurked in its shadow. This combination—to which must be added Castro's personal risk-taking proclivities and his enormous and indefatigable ego—set the style of Cuba's international relations which still persists.

Shortly after Che's return to Havana, Raúl Roa, Castro's foreign minister, addressed the Fourteenth General Assembly of the United Nations. His speech on 24 September 1959 placed Cuba in a position without precedent among Latin American governments. It amounted to a forthright "declaration of independence." Roa proclaimed Cuban neutrality in the cold war, supported the Algerian liberation struggle, and in general allied Cuba with the Third World. By the time Castro appeared in New York a year later to attend the Fifteenth General Assembly, Cuban foreign policy had further crystallized. A formal break with the United States was imminent. Cuba had established close relations with the Soviet Union, and as a result of this step, had become the target of the U.S.-sponsored anticommunist "Declaration of San José" at the August 1960 meeting of the OAS (Organization of American States). Castro immediately compounded his heresy in U.S. eyes by extending diplomatic recognition to the People's Republic of China in September.

Castro used the UN forum to play the role of a fearless anti-imperialist David confronting the U.S. Goliath. Ostentatiously taking up quarters in a Harlem hotel, he was just as ostentatiously visited there by Khrushchev, Nasser, and Nehru. At the United Nations, Tito and Nkrumah, among others, made a great display of cordiality toward him. His September 1960 General Assembly speech skillfully blended a defense of Cuba's position vis-à-vis the United States with an appeal for support from the Third World. "The situation confronting Cuba," he said, "is the same as that of the Congo, Egypt, and Algeria." On his return to Havana, his speech was issued in a fat pamphlet along with speeches by Nkrumah and Nasser.[3] Clearly Castro saw some promise in his relations with these African leaders.

The continuing growth of Cuban influence and prestige in the Third World was demonstrated by the Cuban participation in the first conference of heads of state of nonaligned countries, held in Belgrade during September 1961. Fresh from its stunning Bay of Pigs victory, Cuba was the only Latin American country among twenty-five voting delegations, of which eleven were African. Significantly, among the conference's resolutions was one asserting "the right of Cubans . . . to freely choose their political and social systems" and another acknowledging that "the North American military base at Guantánamo, Cuba . . . affects [Cuba's] sovereignty and territorial integrity."[4]

Algerian independence in 1962 marked the beginning of a new period in Cuban-African relations. In mid-October the Algerian prime minister, Ahmed Ben Bella, visited Havana after addressing the UN General Assembly and meeting in Washington with President Kennedy. Because it was the eve of the missile crisis and Cuba was already in a state of great alarm about a U.S. intervention, Ben Bella's visit was seen as an extraordinary gesture of solidarity. Castro organized a tumultuous welcome, unparalleled until Brezhnev's January 1974 visit. In an airport speech, Ben Bella declared that "just as Cuba gave unstinting support to Algeria, so Algeria supports and will support Cuba." The joint communiqúe issued at the end of the one-day visit declared that Cuba and Algeria were engaged in "socialist construction" and were joined by "indestructible bonds of brotherhood."

The evening the Ben Bella visit ended, Castro spoke to a group of Cuban medical students and called for fifty doctors to volunteer for service in Algeria. This first step in Cuban technical aid to Africa was both a magnanimous gesture in response to Ben Bella's visit and a political investment. It consolidated Castro's ties with the dynamic leader of this new

African state. It also created an image of unstinting, self-sacrificing "internationalism." As time went on, Castro would promote and embellish this image with considerable success among his own people and his admirers in other parts of the world. After the Cuban intervention in Angola, the Havana press spoke of "international solidarity at its most daring, generous, and heroic."[5] That such intervention often was also self-serving went unmentioned, as did the fact that it was made possible by diverting resources — with or without Soviet consent — from the Soviet subsidy originally intended to keep the Cuban economy and society intact. Indeed, as Cuban doctors departed for Algeria, Soviet doctors, equipment, and supplies continued to flow into Cuba.

After Ben Bella's visit, something akin to a Cuban-Algerian alliance emerged. For Castro, the relationship assumed special importance. He had been humiliated during the October missile crisis, when Khrushchev agreed to withdraw Soviet missiles from Cuba without consulting him. An active African role would repair his injured pride, demonstrate his renewed determination to conduct his own foreign policy, interfere with U.S. interests outside the Western Hemisphere, and help him to develop potential bargaining power vis-à-vis the Soviets.

Beginning early in 1963, Algerian news became a staple of the Cuban press, while considerable traffic of people developed between the two countries. Statements of mutual admiration and support were common. An Algerian military mission was conspicuous among the foreign guests at Havana's 1963 May Day festivities. On 3 July, the first anniversary of Algerian independence, Che Guevara appeared in Algiers with a delegation that included military specialists. A clue to the relationship appeared in the 29 May issue of *Revolución,* which included a feature story quoting Ben Bella: "We are helping revolutionary movements in Africa."[6] There was reason to suspect Castro was doing likewise. For example, on 15 February 1963 *Revolución* reported the story of a Congolese student in Cuba who had come "with the noble purpose of being more useful in the struggle for the definitive liberation of his people: the people of Patrice Lumumba."

In mid-October 1963, fighting broke out on the Algerian-Moroccan frontier. In Havana, the clash was front page news under the banner heading "Algeria Invaded by the Moroccan Army" (*Revolución,* 15 October 1963), followed by the statement that members of the Cuban medical team in Algeria had enlisted to fight the Moroccan aggressors. What went unreported for nearly two years was Castro's decision to rush a sizable shipment of men and weapons to Algeria. He revealed this act in a speech on 26 June 1965, in which he excoriated Colonel Lahovari Boumediène for overthrowing Ben Bella.[7] At a time of general disillusionment with both the Soviets and the Chinese for their failure "to take all necessary risks" to defend North Vietnam against U.S. aggression, and a time of special concern for Cuban security because of the U.S. intervention in the Dominican Republic, Castro was shocked by the coup against the leader of a socialist state who was also a close friend and ally.

Against this background, Castro decided to reveal an example of the Cuban model of quiet, unheralded, self-sacrificing international solidarity:

> At a moment of crisis for Algeria, for the Algerian Revolution, when they needed our help, men and arms from our country, crossing the Atlantic in record time, arrived in Algeria ready to fight side by side with the Algerian revolutionaries! . . . Nor did distance prevent us from being the first to arrive. [An allusion to Egypt, followed by a critical allusion to the Soviet Union and China.] Proleterian internationalism in fact, with deeds and not the mouthing of cheap words! Small country that we are, constantly threatened by the imperialists, we gave part of our most important weapons and sent them to the Algerian people.[8]

Castro had obviously taken an enormous risk, probably without consulting the Soviets—although they had originally supplied Cuba with the weapons sent Ben Bella—and almost certainly without Soviet permission. If a major war had developed, its international escalation and dimensions would have been unpredictable and hazardous to Soviet interests. Fortunately for Castro—and for all concerned—the original conflict was resolved by arbitration after only a few skirmishes, in which very likely neither Cuban men nor arms were involved.

First Contacts in Sub-Saharan Africa

While the Castro regime almost from its inception voiced its full support for Southern African liberation movements, there is no conclusive evidence of a Cuban presence in that region (aside from limited, open diplomatic contacts) until the end of 1964. Che Guevara's extended tour, from mid-December 1964 to early March 1965, marked the first substantial Cuban regional involvement—but even then only at the margin of the region.

Guevara's objective (it later transpired) was to prepare the way for Cuba's direct military intervention, under his personal command, in the Congo civil war. The Congo was then the focal point for confrontation between Marxist-oriented governments and other governments concerned with the direction of African political development. Castro had several compelling reasons to take an initiative there. He was increasingly apprehensive about U.S. intentions and, simultaneously, was skeptical about the Soviet policy of peaceful coexistence with the United States. The steady deterioration of Sino-Soviet relations cast a deepening shadow over the "unity of the socialist camp," which he deemed vital for Cuban security. The start of the U.S. bombing of North Vietnam in August 1964 and the failure of both the Soviet Union and China to challenge this aggression against a "sister republic" gave concrete evidence that neither the Soviet commitment to defend Cuba nor the rhetoric of Marxist-Leninist international solidarity was sufficient guarantee against military attack.

At the same time, Castro had reason to be discouraged by Latin American developments. Cuban-supported guerrilla operations had been largely ineffective. In April 1964 Brazil's left-leaning Goulart government was overthrown by a military coup and in August Castro's socialist friend, Salvador Allende, failed to win the Chilean presidential election.[9] Thus Castro turned to Africa as an area in which to launch a bold political-military offensive. As Guevara later explained, from a military point of view Africa enjoyed an advantage over Latin America "because of its greater distance from the U.S. and its greater possibilities for logistical support [from Algeria and Egypt]."[10] In short, if his Congo operation was successful, Castro reckoned it would enhance his international prestige and give him much needed leverage with both the United States and the Soviet Union.

After heading the Cuban delegation to the Nineteenth General Assembly of the United Nations, Guevara flew from New York directly to Algiers, arriving on 19 December 1964. His itinerary included stops in the seven "anti-imperialist" African states: Algeria, Mali, Guinea, Ghana, Egypt, Congo (Brazzaville), and Tanzania. This tour was interrupted by a visit to Peking and apparently included a secret excursion into leftist-held territory in the eastern part of Congo (Leopoldville). Guevara returned to Havana on 14 March 1965. Shortly thereafter he disappeared from public sight and a veil of secrecy covered his whereabouts.

In retrospect, it is astonishing that the widespread speculation about his whereabouts did not include the possibility of Guevara fighting in the Congo. Even before he left New York, the Cuban press had given increasing attention to the Congo civil war, emphasizing the unflinching struggle against U.S. and Belgian imperialism. After Guevara reached Africa, he gave several interviews that more than hinted at this prospect. In Algiers, he told Josephine Fanon, widow of Franz Fanon, that "Africa is one, if not the most important, among battlefields against imperialism."[11] In Algiers he spoke of "combining our resources . . . to resist imperialist aggression, for example in the Congo."[12] In that same interview, he said that in Cuba "we were always conscious of the African character of our popular culture. . . . Cuba and Africa are relatives. . . . this bond is more visible in the Congo: it is possible to observe ethnic — even physical — similarities."[13]

This theme had previously been restricted to academic writings, but it was subsequently revived, amplified, and broadcast worldwide in 1975 to celebrate the "visible bonds" between Cuba and Angola.[14] In Dar es Salaam, Guevara "spoke with representatives of African movements of national liberation . . . to whom he expressed full moral support by Cuba," and he said, "After completing my trip through seven African countries, I am convinced that it is possible to create a common front in the struggle . . . against imperialism."[15]

Very little has been revealed about Guevara's Congo campaign. It appears that he left Cuba in April 1965, that in July he took command of some two hundred well-armed Cuban combat veterans, that despite their assistance the Congolese rebel forces disintegrated, that Guevara then withdrew in disgust, and returned to Cuba with an unknown number of his troops toward the end of that same year. What little is known comes primarily from Guevara's remarks to a visitor at his Bolivian guerrilla base in early 1967. Guevara reportedly said, "The human element failed. There was no will to fight. The leaders are corrupt. In a word, nothing could be done."[16] The Cubans subsequently faced similar difficulties in Angola.

Some additional details come from a defector who had worked in the intelligence department of Cuba's Paris embassy, where he had talked with a Cuban survivor of the Congo operation. According to his source,

> the Cubans had endured severe privations. . . . They were busy trying to keep the tribes from fighting among themselves. . . . There were angry arguments. . . . Guevara and his Cubans had to flee through the jungles, pursued by enemy troops and their former allies. It took a month to get to safety. . . . The Russians had been against Guevara's African adventure. . . . Fidel Castro had not agreed, and there had been friction between him and the Russians over the matter.[17]

This disaster did not enhance Guevara's revolutionary stature or Castro's political judgment, which may explain why the presence of Guevara and the Cuban detachment in the Congo remained a "nonevent" for more than a decade in the voluminous accounts of Guevara's exploits and virtues. Only in January 1977, in a Castro-approved account of the Angolan intervention, was there Cuban acknowledgment of Guevara's earlier Congo campaign. This brief, sanitized version was designed to associate Guevara's image with a military excursion of an entirely different order, to bolster Castro's claim that Cuban involvement in Africa had always been motivated by high moral purpose. As the document put it, Guevara's presence in Africa had "planted a seed that no one could uproot."

Guevara's discreet withdrawal from the Congo occurred on the eve of the Conference of Solidarity of the Peoples of Africa, Asia, and Latin America— commonly known as the Tricontinental—which took place in Havana during the first two weeks of January 1966. If the news of Guevara's failure had not been suppressed, it would have cast a pall on the conference generally and more particularly on the credibility of the leadership role that Castro had assumed. As it was, this conference was the successful culmination of several years of Cuban lobbying at meetings of the Organization of Afro-Asian Solidarity. Over five hundred delegates took part, representing several score Third World liberation movements, semiofficial delegations from several leftist-governed African and Asian countries, and Soviet and Chinese contingents. The meeting was a triumph of Castro's virtuosity in manipulating contending factions to reach agreement on resolutions in support of the Cuban Revolution and the primacy of armed struggle in Latin America —a thesis Castro promoted vigorously in opposition to Soviet views and those of Moscow-oriented Latin American communist parties.

Unpredictably, the major benefit for Castro—and the Soviets, who, it is safe to assume, footed the largest share of conference costs—only came a decade later. The Tricontinental organization set up at the meeting soon withered away, and a second conference, scheduled for Cairo in two years, was not held. What did survive were connections between Castro and those African liberation movements that took part in the Havana meeting. The MPLA and the PAIGC (Partido Africano da Indepêndencia da Guiné e Cabo Verde) had been the only organizations invited from Angola and Portuguese Guinea, respectively, due to Soviet influence in screening prospective invitations. Both Agostinho Neto and Amilcar Cabral had made favorable impressions. Cabral's speech was singled out as "one of the most significant" at the conference and was the subject of a lengthy commentary in the official Cuban report of the meeting.[18]

A Self-Constrained African Involvement

From the very beginning of his regime, as was to be expected, Castro gave priority to Latin America in his search for allies against the powerful pressure exerted on him by the United States. Following the missile crisis and the subsequent Soviet–U.S. détente, his determination to develop his own leverage against the United States in Latin America was reinforced. Even while he sought to build a network of support in the rest of the Third World, his attention was never distracted from Latin America. In fact, one of his major objectives at the Tricontinental was to secure uncontested leadership of revolutionary insurgency in Latin America.

At the same time, Guevara's defeat in the Congo must have convinced Castro that his African opportunities were meager, and his personal contact at the Tricontinental with the largely ineffective African delegations probably reinforced this conviction. Presumably, Cabral, a realist with whom he spent much time, gave him sober advice on this point. In any case, his resources were limited. After the Tricontinental, Castro gave his full attention to Latin America, the end result of which was the Guevara guerrilla force in Bolivia; and African interests were relegated to a back burner. However, they were not permitted to cool entirely, as Castro sent modest and discreet military training and technical assistance missions to selected regimes already, to some extent, in the Soviet sphere of influence.

Thus, news of Cuban activities in Africa continued to surface from time to time. In June 1966 a mutiny in the Brazzaville garrison that threatened to overthrow the Massemba-Debat government was foiled by a Cuban-led elite corps.[19] The Cubans were still in Brazzaville when the MPLA established its headquarters there in 1968 and Brazzaville was the staging point for the Cuban-MPLA incursion into Cabinda in late 1975. A Cuban presence in Portuguese Guinea was revealed in November 1969, when Captain Pedro Rodríguez Peralta was captured by the Portuguese during a clash with PAIGC guerrillas.[20] With the 1974 independence of Guinea-Bissau and São Tomé and Principe, Cuban military and technical personnel assumed a prominent role in organizing their security cadres and providing social services. Cuban relations with Sékou Touré's Guinean regime, which had been cordial even before Guevara's 1965 visit, were further strengthened by the appearance of Cuban military and other specialists.[21]

Until the Angolan civil war, it is a matter of conjecture whether and to what extent these Cuban interventions were the result of consultation with the Soviet Union. Before the Tricontinental, it is a fair assumption that Castro acted mainly on his own. In the three years following the Tricontinental, when Soviet-Cuban relations reached their nadir, the same assumption is even more compelling. In fact, soon after the Tricontinental, Castro embarked on a course of action that blatantly challenged the Soviets on three fronts. With the active collaboration of North Korea and the blessing of North Vietnam, he unleased a virulent propaganda campaign against the Soviets for their failure to "take all the necessary risks" to defeat the United States in Vietnam. At the same time, he defied the Soviet claim to revolutionary leadership in Latin America by setting up a new Havana-based Latin American Solidarity Organization, undermining the region's Soviet-oriented communist parties, and (completely at cross-purposes with Soviet policy) intensifying Cuban-subsidized and -directed guerrilla warfare in a number of Latin American countries. Finally, he embarked on an ultra-leftist course in domestic affairs, abandoning much of the Soviet model of economic planning and management, expropriating what remained of small private commercial enterprise, and promising the imminent establishment of a pure, money-free, morally impeccable communist society.

The first public sign that Castro was reassessing his critical posture vis-à-vis the Soviet Union came in August 1968 when, to the astonishment of his fellow countrymen and his "new left" following elsewhere, he issued a statement supporting the Soviet invasion of Czechoslovakia. Guevara and his band had been wiped out in Bolivia, and other Latin American guerrilla operations had all but collapsed. Cuba itself was gripped by increasing austerity, while Castro militarized the work force to meet a 1970 sugar production quota of 10 million tons, double the usual harvest. Castro solemnly staked his honor and that of the Cuban Revolution on meeting that commitment. In the meantime, all open criticism of the Soviet Union ceased and the "armed struggle" thesis for Latin American revolution was quietly abandoned.

Castro's hopes to reduce his growing dependency on the Soviet Union were demolished when 1970 sugar production fell short of its goal by 1.5 million tons. The unsuccessful effort had required the diversion of resources from other sectors of agriculture and industry. The economy was effectively ruined. Castro had no choice but to relinquish the Cuban road to communism, negotiate a new agreement for huge, long-term Soviet aid, and—as part of the deal—reorganize Cuban society in conformity with Soviet economic, political, and ideological norms. This reorganization was fully under way by 1974 and essentially completed by the end of 1976.

As a result, Cuba was transformed from an unstable Soviet client into a dependable Soviet satellite. However, unlike Czechoslovakia or Bulgaria, Cuba was hyperactive on the international scene, intent on playing the role of a junior partner rather than a mere subsidiary to the Soviet Union. The situation could hardly be otherwise given Castro's personality. Having renounced his earlier heresies and unconditionally accepted the Soviet Union's leadership of international communism, he became a zealous apostle of his newfound faith.

This time in complete harmony with Soviet policy, he re-emerged on the international scene as the foremost champion of the Third World. He aggressively supported the "new economic order" in Latin America and the Caribbean, black liberation in Africa, the struggle against "Zionist imperialism and racism" in the Middle East, and "internationalist proletarian solidarity" wherever infant Marxist-Leninist regimes needed assistance to survive. When necessary, he publicly defended the Soviets from their detractors in matters of human rights or Marxist-Leninist doctrine and echoed the Soviet attack on the Chinese for shameless complicity with imperialism.

Nonetheless, to assume that Castro was acting under Soviet orders, or simply paying back part of his enormous debt to the Soviets, fails to account for a significant factor in his motivation. The revival and expansion of Cuba's (and Castro's) world role, unprecedented among small Third World states, was its own reward. Castro's sensitivity on this score, expressed in an East Berlin speech in April 1977, is revealing and understandable: "There are Cubans working in Asia and Africa. . . . We aren't doing it for national prestige or out of vanity to play a role on the international scene. We're doing it out of a sense of internationalism."[22] It is in this light that Castro's dispatch of a Cuban army to Angola in the latter half of 1975 must be considered.

The Cuban Intervention in Angola

The only extensive account of the Cuban intervention in Angola was written by the Colombian novelist Gabriel García Márquez, an outspoken admirer of Castro and of the Soviet Union. The eight-thousand-word chronicle, a skillful blend of information and propaganda—but nonetheless a convenient point of departure for unraveling the chronology of events and assessing the Cuban impact on the civil war—was published in January 1977.[23]

As the prospects for a viable coalition among the three Angolan nationalist movements dwindled during early 1975, the Cubans became deeply involved in preparing the MPLA for the coming armed struggle over control of the country. García Márquez provides some hitherto unreported details. In May 1975 the MPLA's leader, Agostinho Neto, and a high level Cuban military delegation met in Brazzaville. They agreed that urgent military assistance was required. On 16 July, during a Havana visit by Colonel Otelo de Carvalho, then a leftist member of Portugal's ruling junta, Castro asked him "to arrange Portuguese permission for Cuban aid to Angola [the MPLA]. Carvalho promised to see to it but his answer did not arrive." Nevertheless three Cuban troop ships reached Angola in early October—on the fourth, seventh, and eleventh. They docked "without anyone's permission—but also without anyone's opposition." The ships arrived a month before the Portuguese withdrawal from Luanda on 11 November, at which time the MPLA seized control of the capital and proclaimed itself to be the government of Angola.

García Márquez relates further that the Cubans immediately set up "four training centers" located strategically north, east, and south of Luanda. The southern one on the coast at Benguela, midway between Luanda and the Namibian border, was attacked and overrun quickly by the South Africans on 3 November. By this time things were going badly for the Cuban-MPLA forces on all fronts. García Márquez explains that while the MPLA had "a broad popular base [actually much less than Unita's poorly organized forces] . . . it was nonetheless the one in the weakest military position. It had Soviet arms, but lacked people trained to use them." From other sources it appears that the Soviets began to supply the MPLA with large quantities of military equipment as early as April 1975.[24] It is hard to imagine that the Soviets would fail to send a sizable military contingent to instruct the MPLA in the equipment's use, since much of it was highly sophisticated.

In another context, García Márquez provides a clue to the Soviet problems in training the MPLA. In describing the Cuban "difficulties of December," when the Cuban army was still mainly on the defensive, he wrote,

> They were due to the miserable conditions and cultural backwardness left by half a millenium of soulless colonialism . . . [which] posed the greatest obstacle to a decisive integration between the Cuban troops and the armed people of Angola. . . . Old superstitions not only complicated daily life, but also hindered the war effort. The Angolans had been convinced that the bullets would not penetrate white skin, they feared the magic of airplanes and refused to go into the trenches because tombs were only for the dead. . . . [It] was a dirty war in which [Cubans] had to watch out as much for snakes as for mercenaries, as much for cannibals as for cannonballs. A Cuban commander, in the midst of a battle, fell into an elephant trap. At first, the black Africans, conditioned by generations of resentment against the Portuguese, were hostile to the white Cubans. Many times, especially in Cabinda, Cuban scouts felt betrayed by the primitive telegraph of the talking drums, whose thumping could be heard for as much as twenty miles.

However, despite the "difficulties of December," the Cuban situation improved sufficiently so that on

> 22 December, at the closing of the [first Cuban Communist] party congress . . . Fidel Castro reported that the invaders in Cabinda had been defeated in seventy-two hours; that on the northern front the [FNLA] troops, who had been only fifteen miles from Luanda on 10 November, had been forced to retreat to more than sixty miles away; and that South Africa's armored columns, which had advanced more than four hundred miles, had been blocked more than one hundred and twenty miles from Luanda.

Soon the "unstoppable offensive of the MPLA on all fronts turned the tide, once and for always, in its favor. . . . In January it was conducting operations originally planned for April."

What García Márquez describes as an MPLA offensive was in fact a Cuban offensive, even though he intended to give the impression that the MPLA and the "Angolan people" conducted the war, with the Cubans in a supportive role. However, it is clear from his own account that the Cuban military planned and executed the military operations on all fronts, using Soviet weapons and other equipment.[25] Castro himself "was keeping up to date on the smallest details of the war . . . in constant contact with the battlefield high command," and at times issuing tactical orders. The Cuban military chief of staff "went to Angola personally at the end of November—anything was possible then, except losing the war." Elsewhere, he describes the death in battle of the Cuban "commander of international operations." Clearly, once the struggle for control of Angola flared into the open, the war was directed and fought by Cubans, with the MPLA playing at best an auxiliary role. When the South Africans halted their advance and began their withdrawal in December 1975 (there is no documented evidence that they were defeated in battle), the modern army of 12,000 Cubans made short shrift of its FNLA and Unita opponents, who were in a similar or worse state of backwardness than the MPLA:

> In the north, the leader of a mercenary [FNLA] column directed operations from a Honda sports car, beside a blonde who looked like a movie actress. They advanced as if they were on a holiday, with no scouts ahead. . . . [a] rocket . . . blew the car into bits. In the woman's overnight case, there was only a party dress, a bikini, and an invitation to the victory party Holden Roberto was already planning in Luanda.

The South African press reported in a similar vein that "Roberto ignored South African advice not to attack Luanda. . . . Roberto's attack was extremely poorly coordinated and planned, with disastrous results." In addition, the South Africans could not persuade Unita's Jonas Savimbi to "engage in an all out struggle. He was interested only in controlling his traditional area."[26]

In his discussion of the Cuban decision to commit substantial military manpower to Angola, García Márquez suggests that this step was made only on 5 November. Two days later "a reinforced battalion of special forces, made up of six hundred and fifty men," left Cuba by air. The implication is that until then the Cuban presence in Angola was something less than genuine military intervention, which the Cubans repeatedly claimed was strictly in accord with international law since it was by invitation of the legitimate government headed by Agostinho Neto. Thus, Carlos Rafael Rodríguez, a deputy prime minister and Politburo member, claimed that the Cuban role was "legal in international law because we were asked for help by an established government."[27] García Márquez skirts this issue by failing to mention that the Portuguese remained the "established government" for Angola until their withdrawal on 11 November.

However, on the question of Cuban independence from Soviet control García Márquez was more forthright: "Far from what has so often been said it was an independent and sovereign act of Cuba. Only after the decision was made, and not before, was the Soviet Union informed." There is some truth in this assertion, just enough to conceal from the unwary the false impression it was designed to create. That the decision was a "sovereign act of Cuba" can be granted readily. That Castro could have made his offer of aid prior to a request from either the MPLA or the Soviets is entirely in character with his temperament and his aspirations for leadership of the Third World. When asked about Soviet pressure on the Cubans, one Soviet official credibly responded, "We did not twist their arms. We didn't even have to twist their arms. The Cubans wanted to go in."[28] Still, this is not the same as saying the Cubans made their decision without first consulting the Soviets. Before 1970 Castro occasionally made important decisions before informing the Soviets or even without informing them at all. But since 1970 the totality of Soviet influence on Castro's domestic and foreign policies made such independence unlikely. With both regimes committed to the MPLA even during the period of greatest tension between themselves, it is safe to assume that Soviet and Cuban military aid moved rapidly to full synchronization in early 1975. García Márquez obliquely confirms this by stating that "Cuba was sure it could count on solidarity and material aid from the Soviet Union."[29]

The Cuban role in Africa is not lacking in irony. Khrushchev's dangerous Caribbean gamble in 1960, the nearly catastrophic nuclear confrontation with the United States in October 1962, Soviet difficulty over the years in handling Castro's arrogant provocations in the bilateral relationship, the huge Soviet investment in creating Cuba's first-class military establishment, and the enormous costs of salvaging the Cuban economy finally all paid off—not in the Western Hemisphere, but in Angola. The Soviet Union made an important geopolitical and ideological gain without the risky commitment of its own troops. A willing, indeed eager, Cuban army—Soviet trained and equipped, consisting of many blacks and mulattoes, Spanish-speaking and therefore able to communicate with the Portuguese-speaking Angolans, and (most important, perhaps) perceived as a Third World force—was made to order to wrest control quickly for the Marxist contenders in the civil war.

The Implications of the Continuing
Cuban Presence in Angola

The Cuban military intervention proved to be only the beginning of the Cuban involvement in the Angolan crisis. Castro spoke of Cuba's continuing obligations in a Havana speech on 6 June 1976—some three months after the formal end of hostilities.

> What will be the period of time for the withdrawal of our forces? We describe it as follows, and this is the agreement we have reached with the Government of the People's Republic of Angola: the time which is strictly necessary to aid the defense of the Angolan people against any form of foreign aggression while the People's Army of Angola is trained, organized, and supplied. . . .

We, together with the Soviet Union, are helping to organize the Angolan army. We will spare neither resources nor cadres needed to organize that army. . . . We are at present increasing civilian aid to Angola. We are helping them try to put several sugar mills into operation, and we are aiding in medical programs and various other activities of an economic nature. . . . although the number of civilians will be much less than the number of fighters that were in Angola at one time.[30]

In mid-1977, a sizable Cuban military force remained in Angola, although there had been some troop rotation. The reason was not "foreign aggression" but the Neto regime's inability to consolidate its control in southern Angola coupled with dissension within the regime itself. Unita was waging a stubborn guerrilla war, which, while not an immediate threat to the Luanda government's survival, inflicted serious economic damage by disrupting the coffee harvest (a principal export crop) and halting the normal operation of the Benguela railway, and which therefore posed serious military and political challenges to the MPLA regime.[31] More than a year after the formal end of the civil war, Neto gave the Unita guerrilla campaign sufficient importance to urge MPLA militants "to complete the liberation of the [national] territory . . . as a top priority."[32] Internal dissension was most seriously reflected in the May 1977 coup attempt by a high-ranking associate of Neto, who had organized an ultra-leftist and "pure" black nationalist faction within the MPLA. This serious uprising, involving an armored brigade, came very close to success and was suppressed only by the intervention of Cuban troops, with many deaths.[33]

Castro also underestimated the number of Cuban civilians required to replace departed Portuguese technicians and other skilled workers and to train Angolan personnel. A sympathetic Yugoslav report, published in the Belgrade daily *Politika* in mid-May 1977, after painting an extremely bleak picture of life in Luanda, went on to describe the administrative situation:

Currently, Cubans can be seen everywhere. . . . working as advisors or experts in almost all ministries. They even sit [at] business desks as Angolan representatives when deals are negotiated with foreign firms. Besides the ten thousand to fifteen thousand Cuban soldiers, officers, instructors. . . . [Cubans] are present everywhere and very active. . . . [In considerably lesser numbers, but also visible, were] experts from the Soviet Union and other Communist countries. [That this large foreign presence, both military and civilian, would continue for a long time seemed evident.] Angola, once self-sufficient in food, now must import more than ninety percent. . . . A real crisis has resulted from the disruption of agricultural production which cannot be restored easily and from transportation problems because many bridges have been destroyed and roads are plagued by ambushes organized by . . . adversaries [Unita].[34]

This situation offered no comfort to Castro. Notwithstanding the Soviet payment of most costs, and quite apart from unavoidable expenses incurred by Cuba, Cuba's perennial labor shortage was aggravated by the ongoing commitment of some 10 percent of the Cuban army and perhaps several thousand technicians and skilled workers, posing a serious economic burden.

More morale problems might also arise. The fact that no casualty figures were released left the suspicion that they were not nominal.[35] In the beginning, losses were probably tolerable. Cubans had been conditioned by patriotic and missionary slogans calling for the liberation of the fraternal Angolan people and for struggle against the South African racists. Also, like any other people in similar circumstances (including, ironically, white South Africans), the Cuban population was undeniably buoyed by pride in what it was told was a military victory. However, continuing casualties endured in policing and pacifying an occupied country—for whatever noble purposes—could not be accepted so readily.

In addition, relations between the Cubans and their "hosts" were likely to become less than cordial as time wore on. The massive influx of foreigners, with no prospect of their early departure, would raise questions among many Angolans. As the Yugoslav report suggested, despite the recognized benefits of their aid, "these experts, Cuban and Soviet, bring along their experiences and also their attitudes, understandings, ideas, ways of organization, and they influence their surroundings." It would be an influence not easily assimilated, particularly by more militant and impatient Angolan nationalists who had pride in their own culture and were eager to take charge of their own destiny. No doubt the aborted coup of May 1977 was partly motivated by resentment against what seemed to be Neto's compliant acceptance of foreigners—and most conspicuously, Cubans—occupying key positions in his administration.

Castro revealed an awareness of these problems in a Luanda speech on 27 March 1977, during his first visit to Angola:

> There is a growing number of Cuban technicians working in Angola and I will now address them. I know how many sacrifices this effort entails; what a sacrifice it is to be away from your homeland, your families, your comrades, your loved ones. We know that sacrifices are involved [by] our technicians . . . as they can't bring their families. It would be very expensive for Cuba and for Angola. . . . This is why our cooperation with the Angolan people in times of peace as well as . . . war implies efforts and sacrifices. Today, the only thing I can say to my compatriots and ask of them is to keep on holding high your revolutionary principles, the banners of internationalism, humility, and modesty. Never let it be said that a Cuban revolutionary was self-sufficient or thought himself better than or superior to an Angolan.[36]

The nature of the Cuban involvement in Angola leaves a paradoxical situation. While prospects for an early departure of the Cubans seem remote, Cuban intervention at any significant level elsewhere in Southern Africa seems less likely than the original impetus of the Cuban intervention in Angola suggested was possible. There are additional constraints on Castro. He has a compelling interest in normalizing Cuban relations with the United States. His own Southern African interests must be worked out within the intricate complexities of overall Soviet-U.S. relations, in which Southern Africa plays only a minor, although perhaps growing, part. Finally, not to be discounted is the growing disenchantment of many African governments with imposed "solutions" to African problems. At the July 1977 OAU (Organization of African Unity) "summit" meeting dealing with Angola, the Egyptian delegate put the issue pithily: "The only issue that matters here is that of Soviet interference in Africa."[37] Significantly, in a meeting characterized by bitter divisions, one of the few resolutions adopted condemned foreign intervention "in terms widely interpreted as being directed toward Moscow and Havana."[38]

Senegal's president, Léopold Sédar Senghor, raised the question of the Cuban intervention in Angola in terms that some African leaders could not afford to accept, but that none could afford to ignore.

> Angola fills me with anguish, not because Neto is a Communist, not at all; we have good relations with most of the Communist states, but because Cuba has interfered in our internal affairs by sending its army to Africa. . . . And I think that it is a very bad example for Africa, because now when we have arguments or conflicts we will summon the foreigners. I believe that today our dependence on the foreigner is more serious than during the time of the colonial regimes. Under the colonial regime, we could protest, we had the people with us. Today, we are colonized and we lie to the people telling them that they are free.[39]

Notes

1. During his extensive African tour in March 1977, Castro met secretly in Aden with the Somali and Ethiopian leaders. Somali president Siaad Barre reported later that while Castro "did his best . . . our Ethiopian friends remained rigid in their colonialist attitude." (*Le Monde*, 17 May 1977) Later, he took a more negative position: "Castro was misled. He doesn't know Africa and is uninformed about the grass roots. . . . Ethiopia is neither Marxist nor Leninist, neither socialist nor democratic. They only know how to kill." (*Newsweek*, 27 June 1977, p. 45) Castro had previously claimed, in line with the Soviet view, that the Ethiopian revolution was comparable to the 1917 Bolshevik revolution. Somalia broke relations with Cuba in November 1977.

2. For events before 1971, additional references can be located in Maurice Halperin, *The Rise and Decline of Fidel Castro: An Essay in Contemporary History* (Berkeley and Los Angeles: University of California Press, 1972).

3. *Claman los Pueblos por Justicia y Paz* [The peoples cry out for justice and peace] (Havana: Imprenta Nacional de Cuba, 1960), p. 81.

4. *Facts on File* 21, no. 1080, 31 August–6 September 1961, p. 343.

5. *Granma Weekly Review* (Havana), 12 June 1977, p. 1.

6. Also see David Ottaway and Marina Ottaway, *Algeria: The Politics of a Socialist Revolution* (Berkeley and Los Angeles: University of California Press, 1970), p. 163.

7. This led to a de facto break in Cuban-Algerian relations; they were restored to normal only in 1967 when Castro conceded that Boumediène had proved his anti-imperialist mettle by sending troops to Egypt during the Six Day War and particularly by opposing the cease-fire.

8. These weapons included forty Soviet T-34 tanks, four MiG fighters, some trucks, and more than eight hundred tons of light arms, artillery, and ammunition. (Ottaway and Ottaway, *Algeria: The Politics of a Socialist Revolution,* p. 166) The number of Cuban troops remains undisclosed.

9. The winner was Christian Democrat Eduardo Frei. Allende won in 1970 and was overthrown by the military in 1973.

10. Daniel James, *Che Guevara: A Biography* (New York: Stein and Day, 1969), p. 159.

11. *Revolución* (Havana), 23 December 1964.

12. *Alger Ce Soir* (Algiers), 30 January 1965.

13. Ibid.

14. For example, in a eulogy for Cubans killed in Angola: "In Angolan soil, the soil of many of their ancestors, remain the bodies of the internationalist fighters killed in combat, followers of Che Guevara, eternal heroes of two homelands, giving new life to the Latin-African roots of which Fidel spoke. It was these roots which gave rise to this . . . tree . . . which is putting forth new flowers." (*Granma Weekly Review,* special supplement on Angola, 25 July 1976, p. 58)

15. *Prensa Latina,* 11 February 1965.

16. James, *Che Guevara: A Biography,* p. 159. This visitor was the Argentine journalist Ciro Roberto Bustos, who, along with Régis Debray, was arrested by the Bolivian military and gave them a long statement about his experiences in Guevara's camp.

17. Orlando Castro Hidalgo, *Spy for Cuba* (Miami, Fla.: E. A. Seemann Publishing, Inc., 1971), pp. 54, 55. While friction is credible, it would have been over tactics, not political-ideological considerations, because the Congolese insurgents were pro-Soviet and associated with supporters of the murdered leader, Patrice Lumumba, who was venerated in both Moscow and Havana.

18. Fernando Alvarez Tabío, "Primera Conferencia de Solidaridad de los Pueblos de Africa, Asia, y América Latina," *Política Internacional* (Havana), no. 13 (1966), pp. 36 ff. As for Neto, he had attracted Cuban attention as early as 1962, when *Revolución* featured a long interview with him just after his escape from a Lisbon jail.

19. Samuel Decalo, *Coups and Army Rule in Africa: Studies in Military Style*

(New Haven, Conn.: Yale University Press, 1976), p. 149.

20. *The Portuguese Revolution, 1974–1976* (Facts on File, 1976), p. 23. In 1973 eight Cuban soldiers were reported to have been killed by Portuguese marines in an engagement with PAIGC guerrillas. (*Area Handbook for Cuba* [Washington, D.C.: The American University, second edition, 1976], p. 482)

21. *New York Times,* 14 June 1976, cited a Pentagon source in reporting 310 Cuban military personnel in Guinea-Conakry. In 1977 a Cuban journalist wrote admiringly of the Cuban aid to Guinean development projects and of the fraternal sentiments between Cubans and Guineans. (*Granma Weekly Review,* 5 June 1977)

22. *Granma Weekly Review,* 17 April 1977.

23. García Márquez relates that he gathered his material during several visits to Cuba. The Mexican weekly *Proceso* published the entire work. Then, to ensure a much wider distribution, Prensa Latina, the official Cuban news agency, released several large extracts. An authorized English-language version of the extracts appeared in the *Washington Post* in three consecutive installments starting on 10 January 1977. The references herein are from that source.

24. *Support the Second Anti-Colonial Struggle of the Angolan People* (Toronto: Norman Bethune Institute, 1976), p. 30. A pro-Unita study, this describes the arrivals in April 1975 of three Yugoslav freighters and in May 1975 of one East German freighter and eight Soviet freighters, all carrying military equipment for the MPLA and unloaded with Portuguese consent. Some thirty Soviet transport aircraft landed in Brazzaville in this period with military equipment for the MPLA.

25. He noted that the first Cuban contingents arriving in November brought some of their own supplies with them (although all of this came originally from the Soviet Union), but he infers that the bulk was "Soviet material coming in through other channels demand[ing] a constant supply of personnel able to handle new weapons and teach others to use them."

26. *The Star,* weekly airmail edition (Johannesburg), 5 February 1977.

27. *New York Times,* 12 January 1976.

28. *New York Times,* 5 February 1976.

29. He credits Castro, rather than the Soviets, with an insightful analysis of the various constraints operating on the U.S. government that made major U.S. intervention in Angola improbable and justified the risk of the Cuban invasion.

30. *Granma Weekly Review,* 20 June 1976.

31. *New York Times,* 27 June 1977.

32. *Le Monde,* 29, 30 May 1977.

33. *New York Times,* 20 June 1977.

34. Associated Press dispatch, from Belgrade, 16 May 1977, reported in *International Herald Tribune* (Paris), 17 May 1977.

35. A Unita spokesman reported 3,000 Cuban casualties. (*New York Times,* 27 June 1977)

36. *Granma Weekly Review,* 10 April 1977.

37. *New York Times,* 4 July 1977, dispatch from Libreville, Gabon.

38. *New York Times,* 6 July 1977.

39. *Le Monde,* 26, 27 December 1976.

3

The Soviet Role
in Southern Africa

Christopher Stevens

Many students of Soviet-African relations were surprised by the Soviet Union's vigorous intervention on the side of the MPLA during the 1975 Angolan civil war. This action marked a major change in Soviet tactics toward Africa and even suggested that Soviet strategy might also have changed. Fears were expressed that the Soviet Union would support revolution elsewhere in the region, not only in Zimbabwe Rhodesia and South West Africa/Namibia, but against the black regimes of Zaire and Zambia as well. The 1977 Soviet intervention in Ethiopia reemphasized these fears.

Nonetheless, this chapter argues that some exaggeration is involved. Analysis of earlier Soviet activities in Africa suggests a different conclusion: the Soviets will raise a more subtle challenge to Western interests in Southern Africa, based on the continued ambivalence of Western regional policy and on the Soviet ability to take marginal advantage by relatively small amounts of aid to black nationalists. In short, the Soviet goal is political and diplomatic gain, rather than any immediate military-strategic advantage. The Soviet Union's previous African experience has provided little encouragement for the prospect of unlimited commitments or any assumptions of long-term success for its own political preferences.

Soviet Lessons from the 1960s

The Soviet Union became involved in Africa with high hopes. During the 1950s its policy of friendship and rapprochement with newly independent Asian and Middle East states seemed an outstanding success. After a tentative start in 1953 with its immediate South Asian neighbors, by 1958 the Soviet leadership could reflect with satisfaction on the collapse of the Baghdad Pact. But the policy of friendship with bourgeois nationalist regimes in the new states was not extended immediately to Black Africa, an area of minor strategic interest. Ghana's independence in 1957 stirred little Soviet comment. However, the dramatic independence of Guinea in 1958 provoked a more active Soviet interest in Black Africa, because the complete rupture with France left a vacuum and because Sékou Touré was known to the Soviet Union from his earlier involvement with the French Communist party and its trade union affiliate, the CGT (Confédération Générale du Travail).

The Congo crisis marked a high point for Soviet ambitions in Black Africa, though actual Soviet involvement was limited. The Soviet Union promised Lumumba military supplies and thirty transport planes, but even this meager offer — indeed, the very act of Lumumba's soliciting Soviet assistance — enraged the West and was crucial to Lumumba's downfall. The Soviet Union was unable to help him, and its effectiveness in the Congo ceased.

Nevertheless, the Soviet Union still retained high hopes for its African policies. If it could not win in an open confrontation with the West, perhaps it could improve its position by supporting friendly African regimes. It put three such governments — those of Ghana, Guinea, and Mali — into a special category. Their leaders were each awarded the Lenin Prize and each proclaimed scientific socialism to be his nation's goal. For its part, the Soviet Union gave them material support — trade, aid, and military assistance — as well as moral support. But on the whole, little was gained. Nkrumah in Ghana and Modibo Keita in Mali were overthrown by leaders less favorably disposed toward the Soviet Union, while Guinea became increasingly idiosyncratic in its world outlook.[1]

The Soviet Union learned several important lessons from its initial phase of African involvement. First, it was hazardous to assume that the first leaders of these new states (or, by implication, their immediate successors) could move their societies easily in any desired direction. On the contrary, severe limits existed on the amount of effective power they could bring to bear without losing control of important social forces and risking overthrow.[2] To the Soviets, as indeed to all other nations interested in enhancing influence in Africa, the lesson was clear. The advantages to be gained from close friendship with any particular regime were fewer than had been hoped. In fact, close ties could be harmful, given the increasing instability of African governments — the architects of successful coups often assumed that the allies of the deposed regime were automatically their foes.

In response to this changed outlook, and also because competition with the People's Republic of China became less important as the Chinese turned their energies inward during the Cultural Revolution, Soviet policy shifted from support of embryonic "socialist" regimes to low-key, businesslike relations with a wide range of African states, regardless of their ideological positions or the condition of their domestic political and economic systems.

Following this shift in emphasis, the Soviet Union became involved in its second major African conflagration — the Nigerian civil war. The Soviet approach was in marked contrast to its Congo involvement. At first Nigerian requests for military aid were met cautiously. The Soviet Union was unsure which side to support, but it also wanted to avoid a U.S. riposte to any action that it might take. Only after the United States indicated that it did not consider the conflict vital to U.S. interests did Soviet military aid reach a significant level.

The underlying characteristics of Soviet-African relations before the 1975 Angolan civil war are crucial to an understanding of the Soviet role in Southern Africa. First, the creation of friendships and alliances has often depended less on the Soviet Union than on its African partners. It is easy to assume that the Soviet Union, a superpower, could pick and choose its friends and that its own ideological considerations would be the only constraint. This has not been the case. The Soviet Union has shown itself willing to make friends with governments and factions of varying hues, particularly since its disappointments of the mid-1960s, and even before then. Not all African groups have responded to such advances, and it has often appeared as though the initiative for creating a friendship lay with the African partner. A second, related feature is that the Soviet Union has often found itself linked to weak allies because the strong governments and factions have found support elsewhere, usually in the West. Third, the Soviet Union has had difficulty in extricating itself from such weak friendships because it has a history of rarely changing partners. The Soviet switch from Somalia to Ethiopia in 1977 was the first major example of such a change. Finally, until Angola, the Soviet Union was not able to decisively influence domestic events in Africa.

The Soviet Role in Angola

Before Angolan independence, the pattern of Soviet support for the MPLA seemed very much like that in other African states. Although Soviet aid began after Agostinho Neto's first visit to Moscow in 1964, the total military aid until 1975 was only $54 million.[3] During 1972–1973 aid declined to a trickle. There is even some evidence that during the MPLA leadership clash between Neto and Daniel Chipenda the Soviet Union initially backed Chipenda, although it later reversed its position.[4] Partly because of this relatively low level of military support, but also because of chronic leadership dissension, the MPLA was by late 1974 considerably weaker than the FNLA, which had larger and apparently more effective forces.

Indeed, in the early months of 1975 as the FNLA advanced into Angola from the north, and even after mid-1975 when Unita and the South African forces began their concerted drive from the south, Soviet observers were obviously alarmed that the MPLA might be defeated.[5] The Soviet Union was not prepared to let this happen. During the remainder of 1975, it sent the MPLA military equipment worth over $200 million and several hundred military advisors, while at the same time it provided the logistical and economic support indispensable to the Cuban provision of some fifteen thousand troops.[6] The result was the fourth largest army in Africa (only those of Nigeria, South Africa, and Somalia were larger) and the third largest military expenditure (following that of Nigeria and South Africa).[7]

Unlike the case with Soviet involvement in the Congo, only modest rhetoric at first accompanied the major commitment of resources in Angola. Soviet commentators took a moderate line vis-à-vis the communist-supported Portuguese government, despite that government's policy of reconciliation among the Angolan nationalist movements. Only after the conflict between the MPLA and its nationalist rivals flared up did Soviet commentary become more aggressive. By contrast, Soviet action was bold on both diplomatic and military levels. It flouted the neutral position favored by the OAU at its June 1975 Kampala conference and tried crudely, but without success, to press Idi Amin (presiding at the conference) into public support of the MPLA.[8] On the military level, Soviet supplies began arriving in Angola during March 1975. On 25 March, thirty Soviet cargo planes arrived in Brazzaville, the nearest staging point for military shipments to the MPLA. The following month some one hundred tons of arms arrived in Dar es Salaam and were dispatched by sea to Angola. Shortly afterward, a Yugoslav freighter was turned away from Luanda and unloaded at Pointe-Noire, Brazzaville's port.[9] Strengthened by these supplies and even more by support in Luanda and other major cities, the MPLA drove its rivals from Luanda and then from a strip of territory running eastward to the Zambian border. By the beginning of September, aided by further substantial Soviet arms supplies, the MPLA controlled eleven of the sixteen district capitals, virtually the entire length of the country's seaboard, and held (in a loose way) more territory than its rivals. During October, the MPLA suffered reversals, as U.S. aid to the FNLA and Unita increased and the South Africans intervened. Then Soviet aid to the MPLA also increased substantially. Between early October and mid-December, the Soviet Union sent twenty-seven ships and thirty-forty planes with supplies.[10] Cubans also began to arrive in large numbers.

Did the Soviet-Cuban buildup occur before the South African intervention or was it in response to it? Although a Soviet-Cuban agreement to intervene existed as early as May 1975, and the first Cubans arrived in Brazzaville by July, there were still less than three thousand Cubans in Angola by mid-November.[11] What remains unknown is whether the buildup was part of a predetermined plan or occurred in reaction to events. The latter appears more likely. There is some evidence that elements in the Soviet foreign and defense ministries actually opposed the intervention on the grounds that it threatened détente with the United States and might also prove too expensive,[12] and there is also evidence that the Soviet decision in late 1974 to increase aid to the MPLA was probably more a reaction to increased Chinese support for the FNLA than an intended challenge to the United States. It was probably evident to the Soviet Union from its previous African involvements that a small show of force might be counterproductive. At the same time, its concern with the potential U.S. reaction argued for a modulated intervention in order to balance its commitment to the MPLA with the risk of open confrontation with the United States. For example, because of U.S. threats of retaliation, the Soviet airlift of Cubans was halted in early December 1975, only to be resumed on 24 December after the U.S. Senate voted to end covert aid to the FNLA and Unita.[13]

Angola was not the first occasion on which the Soviet Union supplied arms to African conflicts, and Soviet-trained pilots had flown in other engagements. Never before, however, had the Soviet Union or its allies supplied soldiers for active ground combat in Black Africa. Apart from the use of Cuban troops, the type (as distinguished from the level) of military aid was not novel. The T-34 tank had been supplied widely ever since Guinea first acquired it in 1960. It is of World War II vintage and relatively unsophisticated. The more modern and complicated T-54 tank had been supplied only to Somalia and Uganda before its appearance in Angola. MiG-17 planes date from 1953 and are fairly common in Black Africa. Guinea was given eight of them in 1960, and thirty-six were supplied to the Nigerian federal forces during the civil war. MiG-21s, which began production in 1956 and are considerably more sophisticated, were very recent imports to Black Africa. Only in mid-1974 did Somalia receive them; Uganda also has some. The only new weapon introduced during the Angolan war was the 122mm rocket launcher. This relatively unsophisticated weapon proved most effective in demoralizing FNLA and Unita opposition during the small-scale clashes characteristic of the war. It became a central element in Cuban military tactics, in which a disruptive rocket attack would be followed by a methodical tank advance.[14]

The Implications of Angola

Soviet policy in Angola involved both continuity and change: continuity in Soviet support for an old friend and a weak ally; change in Soviet willingness to use military force to overcome that weakness. The crucial question for developments in Southern Africa must be whether the aggressive Soviet posture in Angola is a harbinger of its regional policy in the future. Although any answer is speculative, it may help to narrow the range of possibilities to consider what the Soviet Union has gained from Angola and what it might reasonably hope to achieve elsewhere in the region.

The Soviet gains from Angola on the superpower and regional levels are linked. At the superpower level, it has demonstrated its superior resolve. The West insisted that Angola was a test of strength between the West and the Soviet Union; and, while this may have been a mistaken approach (especially since implementation rested on the South African intervention),[15] once the approach was adopted it demanded that Soviet aid to the MPLA be vigorously resisted. Instead, the United States and its allies equivocated about resistance and, as a result, incurred high losses with only minimal gains.

Also significant in superpower relations was the Soviet demonstration of its increased logistic capability to conduct a military operation far from its own borders. According to the report by the Colombian writer Gabriel García Márquez, regarded widely as a reliable source for official Cuban views, the United States made several ultimately unsuccessful attempts to halt the Soviet airlift of troops from Cuba to Angola. U.S. pressure shut down the first route via Barbados; then the Cubans tried to fly their troops via Cape Verde and, after U.S. pressure cut that transit, via Guyana. When that transit was halted as well, the Cubans were flown directly to Brazzaville.[16]

The Soviet arms airlift to Ethiopia, begun in November 1977, provided a second African example of this new capability. While that Soviet airlift raises the possibility of replication elsewhere in Africa, circumstances in the Somali-Ethiopian conflict favored the Soviet Union. In particular, the Somali invasion of the Ogaden was opposed by enough OAU members that no OAU action against the Soviet intervention was feasible. In addition, the West was unable or unwilling to intervene and court the disfavor of most Black African states.

Although the Soviet intervention in Angola has shifted superpower relations, that change need not be manifested in Southern Africa, or in Africa at all. The sequel could be played out in another region or in terms of some other aspect of U.S.-Soviet relations—trade, technology, or human rights, for example. If Southern Africa takes on greater importance for the superpowers, then one or both might use policy in these other areas to influence Southern African policy.

Political credibility is the Soviet Union's greatest gain in the regional context. After fifteen years of defeats, it finally achieved a political victory in its

African policy. Even more important, its position coincided with the OAU's, at least at the end of the conflict, while the West and China were identified with South Africa in support of the FNLA and Unita.

The Soviet Union made some immediate diplomatic gains with black regional governments as a result of its Angola intervention. The most dramatic change occurred in relations with Mozambique, where the rapid Soviet eclipse of the Chinese was startling. The February 1977 Frelimo party conference underlined this change by extending a welcome to fraternal delegations from the Soviet Union, Cuba, and several Eastern European states, but not to a Chinese delegation. The change in Mozambican policy seems to stem from a growing fear that the Zimbabwe Rhodesian conflict could develop into a conventional war, for which Chinese military aid would be inadequate, while the Soviet Union brought from Angola the image of an ally prepared to back its friends to the hilt. In fact, Soviet military aid to Mozambique seems modest. A recent estimate puts the total at thirty-five tanks (T-34s, T-54s, and T-55s), eight MiG-21 fighters, and a number of SA7-7 SAM missiles and 122mm howitzers.[17] By comparison, during the Nigerian civil war the federal forces received sixty-six Soviet and Czech planes as well as 122mm howitzers, but no tanks or SAMs.[18]

The symbol of the improved Soviet relations with African countries was President Podgorny's March 1977 tour, following hard on the heels of Castro's African visit, and bringing reminders of the historic Khrushchev and Bulganin visit to India in 1955. Podgorny arrived in Tanzania on the Soviet supersonic airliner TU-144, underlining his country's prestige and superpower status. From there he moved to Zambia and Mozambique, for the first visits by any senior Soviet leader. While in Mozambique, he signed a treaty of friendship and cooperation similar to those already concluded with Somalia and Angola.

Although the Podgorny tour highlighted the Soviet Union's new confidence in its African policy, the tour also illustrated the policy's basic weakness. The visit was not followed by any initiative, either to encourage negotiation or to increase military aid to the nationalists. Elsewhere in Africa, the Soviet Union has found itself backing weak allies because the strong factions have preferred the support of the West. The same applies in Southern Africa to the extent that the West has been given the first option to produce a settlement. However, the Western governments have to take account of their links with the white populations. In Zimbabwe Rhodesia and South West Africa/Namibia Western governments have tended to give greater weight to white interests than the Patriotic Front, SWAPO (South West African People's Organization), and the majority of "front-line" states could accept. Therefore, the possibility has been raised for the first time on any scale that the strong factions, having failed to obtain the Western support they seek, may turn to the Soviet bloc. This possibility, which will become increasingly likely the longer the nationalist struggle continues, was outlined clearly by Zambia's Kenneth Kaunda.

> If the West is afraid that the visits of President Podgorny and Dr. Castro are going to end up in Southern Africa being Communist-influenced, it is the West that is to blame. . . . The West not only refused to support us, they even refused to remove the cause of the conflict. . . . Why are President Podgorny and President Castro receiving such a hero's welcome? Because the masses of the people of Southern Africa realize . . . it is the people of the Eastern countries who are supporting them.[19]

The Soviet Union's position has been strengthened by the African willingness to accept foreign intervention against white regimes in Southern Africa. The OAU's endorsement of the Soviet-Cuban intervention in Angola marked an important change from previous practice. This new legitimacy granted to foreign intervention partly reflects the African tendency to see Southern African conflict as blacks versus whites. Thus it is significant how African opinion of the Soviet intervention in Angola changed after South Africa became involved. For example, Nigeria denounced Soviet intervention just three days before Angolan independence, but by the OAU meeting in February 1976 it had reversed its position.[20]

There is also considerable skepticism among Africans about the Western argument that the Soviet Union seeks a new hegemony in Angola. This skepticism may come in part from overexposure to cries of "Red menace" whenever the Soviet Union gains any advantage in its overall African relations. For instance, Nigeria was warned that acceptance of Soviet military aid during the civil war was very risky. Today the Soviet Union plays a very small role in Nigeria. As a result of this experience, the Nigerian foreign minister, Lt. Colonel Joseph Garba, argued that the Soviets would be easier to get out of Angola than an FNLA-Unita government, with U.S. and South African advisors who would remain indefinitely. It is ironic that the West, playing the part of the boy who cried wolf, has provoked this attitude, just when there is a chance that for the first time the Soviet Union has acquired dominant power in an African state.

Although the Soviet Union has an entree in Southern Africa that it lacks elsewhere in Black Africa, the West has some weapons to dissuade the Soviets from using that entree. Deterrent pressure can be exerted in arenas far removed from Southern Africa, and it is clear that such pressure is being exerted. In a speech to a London banquet during which he was sufficiently outspoken to provoke an Ethiopian walkout, David Owen, the U.K. foreign secretary, warned that Soviet and Cuban military involvement in Ethiopia placed "a large question mark over the future of détente" and that "even more serious complications for Africa and East-West relations would flow if there were any attempt to use Cuban forces to undermine current talks to bring peace and democracy to Rhodesia and Namibia."[21]

If similar deterrent pressure is renewed and Soviet leaders accept the premise that the United Kingdom and the United States have vital interests in Southern Africa, the result might be to constrain the Soviet Union to play a low-key regional role. The Soviet Union would, of course, make political capital from Western discomfort whenever possible, but without overcommitting itself. Only when black rule becomes imminent, with rival nationalist factions jockeying for power, might the Soviet Union become more seriously involved in support of its allies.

Joshua Nkomo's reluctance to commit his guerrilla forces to active fighting in Zimbabwe Rhodesia suggests that he expects violence between nationalist groups to take place and that he hopes for Soviet support for his organization. If the Soviet Union gave his group (or some other faction) such support to gain control of the Zimbabwean government, how much influence might it expect to gain?

While the Soviet experience in Angola affords some insight into the prospects of Soviet influence on Zimbabwe, it is very difficult to assess Soviet strength in Angola. Not only is Angola freshly independent, but nowhere else in Black Africa has a regime so clearly owed its position to continued Soviet support. Even in Guinea, which was kept afloat by Soviet and East European help in 1958, the ruling party achieved substantial national support before independence. Because of the repression and secrecy surrounding the operations of the MPLA and the other nationalist movements during the Caetano regime, the extent of their popular support at that time is unknown. During the period of very rapid decolonization, there was little opportunity for the nationalists to win public support by conventional political means. In short, when the MPLA took power, it held active allegiance only from people in the major towns. It was predictable that the new regime would subsequently alienate some of these supporters in its efforts to curb the economic chaos that existed at the end of the civil war.

The 27 May 1977 attempted coup led by Nito Alves grew out of urban discontent and demonstrated the MPLA dependence on Soviet and Cuban support. When the rebels seized the radio station and prison and tried to take the presidential palace, Soviet armored vehicles with Cuban drivers were instrumental in driving the rebels back and then in guarding public buildings and road junctions until government control was restored.[22] Although Alves was subsequently denounced as an anti-Soviet Maoist, there is some evidence that the Soviet Union had supported his earlier attacks on the MPLA leadership.[23] If so, this would be the second time in recent years that the Soviet Union had backed anti-Neto elements in the MPLA, only to switch support to Neto. It underlines the dependence of MPLA leadership on Soviet support.

However, even before the Alves coup attempt it was clear that the MPLA government relied on Soviet and Cuban military assistance to maintain its position. This reliance, in part a result of Unita's continued resistance, suggests that the Soviet role in Angola may differ markedly from its role elsewhere in Black Africa. No African government has been prevented from breaking its links with the Soviet bloc when it felt its interests required such action. Even Somalia, which achieved closer military collaboration with the Soviet Union than any other sub-Saharan government, was free to follow the path trod earlier by Egypt, Ghana, Mali, and Zanzibar. Only time will tell if Angola will be free to do so, if and when it wants to.

There are some obvious implications for any potential Soviet role vis-à-vis Zimbabwean nationalists. In Rhodesia, black political activities have been more open than they were in Angola before independence. There is a measure of popular support for one or another of the nationalist leaders, certainly in the towns, and to some extent in the rural areas. This support, taken together with the West's greater closeness to Nkomo than to Neto, suggests that a future Nkomo-led regime would be more independent from the Soviet Union than the MPLA has been to date. Of course, the West still might find any degree of Zimbabwean sympathy for the Soviet Union undesirable.

What would the Soviet Union gain from such sympathy? This depends on the extent and realism of its long-term regional motives. Observers usually suggest three motives, taken either separately or in some combination. The first involves Soviet control of Southern African minerals in order to deny them to Western users. The second suggests a Soviet desire for military bases to ensure regional strategic control. The third argues, more modestly, that the Soviet Union wants to increase its influence and prestige in the region, simultaneously making the West as uncomfortable as possible.

Underlying the first two explanations is a Western fear that may be based on a resurrection of the somewhat mechanical view of African power common at the start of the 1960s. Now, as then, in a period preceding the transfer of power, uncertainty is expressed whether the new black leaders can resist Soviet "penetration." Assurances on this score gained during the balance of the 1960s have been undermined by events in Angola.

It is true that the West depends on Southern Africa for a number of key minerals: Zaire is the source of 80 percent of U.S. cobalt imports; South Africa and Zimbabwe Rhodesia are, along with the Soviet Union, the major chrome producers for the industrialized world; and the region produces over half the world supply of diamonds, gold, and vanadium, and over one-third of the world supply of platinum-group minerals. This dependence on a handful of white minority and unstable black regimes has raised the specter of Soviet mineral manipulation intended, at the very least, to increase prices to the immediate and medium-term detriment of Western economies. There is some evidence that the supply instability for important minerals is causing concern in the West. Henry Kissinger's proposal for an international resources bank made at the 1976 UNCTAD conference (United Nations Conference on Trade and Development) in Nairobi was only one major manifestation of this growing concern, which is focused more on inadequate investment in mineral exploitation than on fears of Soviet competition or manipulation.

In fact, there is very little sign of any Soviet policy commitment to the manipulation of Southern African mineral prices. For such a policy to succeed, the Soviet Union would have to persuade African producers to supply it with minerals either voluntarily or through coercion. To obtain minerals by consent, the Soviet Union would have to pay the commercial rate in cash or use barter goods with a high foreign exchange value (for example, petroleum), or the African governments would have to be willing to sacrifice some part (probably a major part) of their foreign exchange earnings.[24] Since the Soviet Union is virtually self-sufficient in the minerals involved, and since even the most radical African nationalists have tended to put national interests above ideological considerations, neither prospect is imminent. To acquire the minerals by coercion would require a degree of political control the Soviet Union has never obtained in Black Africa. Even in Angola, the MPLA continues to sell Cabinda petroleum to Gulf Oil and diamonds to the De Beers mining organization, an offshoot of the Anglo American Corporation (a major South African firm). Besides, in the final analysis, if the Soviet Union intends to put serious pressure on the United States and its allies, there are cheaper, more flexible, and more effective ways to do so.

Is the Soviet Union seeking military bases in Southern Africa? The distinction must be made between a base — with its guaranteed physical security, storage for ammunition and supplies, and repair facilities — and berthing stations that are really no more than mooring buoys. The Soviet Union now has no permanent bases in Black Africa, and Soviet naval strategy does not require them. It does have berthing stations, and it is possible that more such stations in Mozambique and Angola will be sought. However, since it is able to purchase at reasonable cost most of the facilities available at its various berthing stations, there is little motivation to make the extra diplomatic and economic effort to win them as part of a binding bilateral agreement. Furthermore, Soviet use of regional naval facilities would not pose any immediate strategic challenge to Western security interests.[25]

Although a friendly Angolan regime would be a helpful adjunct to Soviet military policy, it is not of central strategic importance to the Soviet Union.

Most of Black Africa is of the same marginal significance. Soviet military aid to these governments can therefore best be interpreted as an exercise intended to bolster Soviet diplomatic stock and superpower status. However, the Horn and the eastern seaboard of Africa do hold strategic importance for the Soviet Union, and a future black-ruled South Africa might attract Soviet interest for this reason.

For the Soviet Union, increasing Soviet prestige and increasing Western discomfort are the crucial motives. Southern Africa is a growing embarrassment to the West. The issue of regional policy sharpens differences of opinion within Western countries and differences in interests among their governments. The implicit tension between the U.S. and U.K. governments over the use of economic sanctions is a case in point. The Soviet Union will have ample opportunities to increase its global status through diplomatic-political initiatives in Southern Africa (a region from which it has been largely excluded until recently), initiatives intended to champion the nationalists and the "front-line" states against the white regimes. Although the West may be able to exert pressure to deter the Soviet Union from providing large-scale support to the nationalists, it will have little success in halting Soviet gains in prestige.

The advance of Soviet influence is often linked to the political success of avowedly Marxist African nationalists, but the linkage is not straightforward. To talk of a "Marxist belt" across Southern Africa, linked by Frelimo and MPLA governments with the Zimbabwean Patriotic Front (PF), is simplistic.[26] Ideological labels applied to African nationalist groups must be treated with caution, since supposedly pro-Soviet or anti-Soviet tendencies have rarely been decisive in shaping a nationalist organization's actions after it gained power. Of course the spread of Marxist regimes boosts Soviet prestige, but it may pose difficult problems and embarrassments in subsequent relationships. Somalia is only the most recent instance of this recurrent dilemma for the Soviet Union. First, regimes proclaiming adherence to "scientific socialism" are not always stable. Even if they are, they may not favor the Soviet Union in either their domestic or foreign policies, and even if they do, they may become more a burden than an advantage to the Soviet Union.

One such liability is economic in nature. Pro-Soviet developing countries often seek amounts and kinds of Soviet economic aid that the Soviet Union is not well placed to provide. The Soviet Union has given worthwhile aid and in certain circumstances has been a valuable trading partner.[27] However, from the perspective of developing countries, it is better seen as an adjunct to the West than as an alternative. Its aid has been limited in size and scope and is subject to various technical problems. The main attraction of the Soviet Union as a trading partner is that a developing country exporter can use the existence of the Soviet market to improve its position in the Western market. In short, if the future black governments of Southern Africa want to maximize foreign exchange earnings, they will seek to maintain substantial commercial links with developed Western states.

Thus, the primary concern for the West should not be the professed Marxist orientation of these governments, but whether they set development priorities stressing austerity in consumption patterns and movement away from dependence on foreign exchange earnings, although of course the two characteristics are often linked. The Soviet Union's greatest success in Africa has come with such governments—those of Libya, Somalia, and Tanzania for example. Since prolonged guerrilla war tends to bring austere nationalist leaders to the fore, the Soviet Union tends to gain if nationalist groups are prevented from peaceful participation in national politics and must come to power by force of arms.

Soviet strength in Africa has always been inversely related to Western weakness. In Southern Africa, the West is weaker than it has been in other parts of Africa. Because of an ambivalence toward the whites, the West has been unable either to satisfy black demands or to take the opposite course and bolster white power. The West's problems have been exacerbated by errors of judgment. The Soviet Union, for its part, has taken advantage of its opportunities and shown that, despite appearances in the early 1970s, it retains a lively interest in Black Africa and is more nimble in pursuing that interest than it used to be. The lessons of Angola and the Horn are that the Soviet Union's ability to detect and take advantage of Western weakness has benefited from its twenty years of experience in African affairs. This combination of unusual Western weakness and enhanced Soviet capacity to exploit that weakness makes Southern Africa different from the rest of Black Africa.

Notes

1. For further historical detail, see Christopher Stevens, *The Soviet Union and Black Africa* (New York: Holmes & Meier Publishers, Inc., 1976), pp. 4–27.

2. Ibid., pp. 11 and 133. Also see Aristide Zolberg, *Creating Political Order: The One-Party States of West Africa* (Chicago: Rand McNally, 1966), p. 159.

3. Peter Vanneman and Martin James, "The Soviet Intervention in Angola: Intentions and Implications," *Strategic Review* (Summer 1976), p. 93.

4. Colin Legum and Tony Hodges, *After Angola: The War Over Southern Africa* (London: Rex Collings, 1976), p. 11.

5. For further details, see Christopher Stevens, "The Soviet Union and Angola," *African Affairs* 75, no. 299 (April 1976), pp. 137–151. Also see David L. Morison, "The Soviet Union's Year in Africa," *Africa Contemporary Record, 1975–1976* (Lon-

don: Rex Collings, 1976), p. 103.

6. Vanneman and James, "The Soviet Intervention in Angola," put the value of Soviet military support at $300 million and the number of Soviet advisors at 400.

7. *The Military Balance, 1975–1976* (Boulder, Colo.: Westview Press, 1975), pp. 42–44.

8. Legum and Hodges, *After Angola,* pp. 17 and 23.

9. Ibid., pp. 19, 20.

10. Ibid., p. 57.

11. Ibid., p. 21.

12. Vanneman and James, "The Soviet Intervention in Angola," p. 97.

13. Henry Kissinger's testimony to the U.S. Senate Foreign Relations Committee, Subcommittee on African Affairs, 29 January 1976; *Financial Times* (London), 30 January 1976; also, *The Times* (London), 4 February 1976.

14. Stephen Larrabee, "Moscow, Angola, and the Dialectics of Detente," *World Today* 32, no. 5 (May 1976), p. 181.

15. J. E. Spence, "Detente in Southern Africa: An Interim Judgement," *International Affairs* 53, no. 1 (January 1977), pp. 11, 12.

16. *The Times* (London), 11 January 1977. During the Cuban missile crisis of 1962, U.S. pressure was successful in achieving the Guinean refusal of refueling rights to Soviet planes flying to Cuba.

17. *The Military Balance, 1977–1978* (Boulder, Colo.: Westview Press, 1977), p. 45.

18. Stevens, *The Soviet Union and Black Africa,* p. 185, footnote.

19. *Africa Research Bulletin: Political Series* 14, no. 3 (April 1977), p. 4377.

20. Legum and Hodges, *After Angola,* pp. 29, 30.

21. *Financial Times* (London).

22. *Africa Research Bulletin: Political Series* 14, no. 5 (June 1977), pp. 4429, 4430.

23. *Le Monde* (Paris), May 1977, cited in *Africa Research Bulletin: Political Series* 14, no. 5 (June 1977), p. 4431.

24. For further discussion of the value of Soviet barter trade, see Stevens, *The Soviet Union and Black Africa,* Chap. 2, pp. 28–67; and his "In Search of the Economic Kingdom: The Development of Economic Relations Between Ghana and the USSR," *Journal of Developing Areas* 9, no. 1 (October 1974), pp. 3–26.

25. Vanneman and James, "The Soviet Intervention in Angola," p. 96.

26. *The Times,* 7 February 1977.

27. For further details, see Stevens, "In Search of the Economic Kingdom," and his *The Soviet Union and Black Africa,* Chaps. 2 and 3, pp. 28–100.

Part 3

Territories in Transition?
Zimbabwe Rhodesia and
South West Africa/Namibia

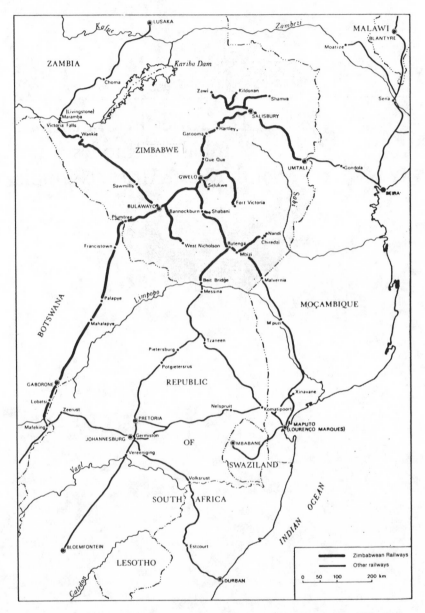

Map 2.   Zimbabwe: Rail Links to South Africa and Mozambique. Source: The Africa Institute of South Africa, from G.M.E. Leistner, editor, *Rhodesia: Economic Structure and Change*, 1976, p. 168.

4

Zimbabwe and
Southern African "Détente"

C. Munhamu Botsio Utete

Introduction

The victories of the armed liberation movements in the former Portuguese colonies of Angola, Guinea-Bissau, and Mozambique during 1974–1975 had a discernible impact on liberation struggles elsewhere in Southern Africa and particularly on the struggle in Zimbabwe. These victories disproved the notion once entertained by, among others, the U.S. government, to the effect that Southern African liberation movements could not hope to "gain the political rights they seek through violence. . . ."[1]

As far as the Zimbabwe liberation movement is concerned, the Frelimo victory was the most directly relevant. It opened new strategic possibilities in the northeastern and eastern borders of the country, now accessible to freedom fighters penetrating from Mozambique. Moreover, as became clear soon after Mozambique reached independence on 25 June 1975, the Frelimo regime appeared determined to provide both rear bases and unwavering political support to the Zimbabwean freedom fighters.

The Frelimo victory was also significant in providing a Mozambican model for the postcolonial socioeconomic reconstruction of Zimbabwe and the rest of white-dominated Southern Africa, although, in the final analysis, each victorious liberation movement works on the basis of its own ideology, experiences, and its perception and self-definition of its country's socioeconomic realities.

From the vantage point of the South African regime (the major regional actor and the most determined foe of regional liberation), the Portuguese colonial liberation led to a rethinking of the substance and tactics of South African regional policy. Before 1974 that policy had centered on the cultiva-

Portions of this chapter have already been published as part of Chapter 7 in C. Munhamu Botsio Utete, *The Road to Zimbabwe: The Political Economy of Settler Colonialism, National Liberation, and Foreign Intervention* (Washington, D.C.: University Press of America, 1978).

tion of the newly independent regional black states, but without sacrifice to the security, viability, and interests of South Africa's Portuguese and Rhodesian allies. Its basic objective had been to assure the survival of the apartheid system at home and South African military and economic domination of the region. With the collapse of Portuguese rule, South Africa pursued these same goals with greater determination under a new — and somewhat misleading — rubric: "détente."

The problem of Zimbabwe was central to the diplomatic efforts toward regional détente begun after April 1974. Four aspects receive extended attention in this chapter: South Africa's regional policies; the response of Black African states — especially the "front-line" states — to this policy; the internal politics of the Zimbabwean liberation movement and its response to the détente exercise; U.S. and U.K. efforts since early 1976 to achieve a settlement and the apparent failure of these efforts to persuade the backers of a Rhodesian "internal settlement" to accept a constitutional solution involving all parties in Zimbabwe.

South Africa and Zimbabwe:
"Détente" — Phase One

The historical links between South Africa and Southern Rhodesia are well known. These can be traced back to the 1880s, when the representatives of British imperialism in South Africa, especially Cecil John Rhodes and his British South Africa Company, were involved in a determined effort to construct a greater South Africa incorporating lands to the north of the Limpopo River, including Zimbabwe. The "origins of Rhodesia" — to borrow the title of Samkange's book[2] — cannot be fully understood without reference to the South African connection.[3] From the very beginning, British imperialists saw Southern Rhodesia as logically destined to become part of South Africa — hence the involvement of the Rhodesian settlers in the 1909 negotiations leading to the formation of the Union of South Africa. Although the Rhodesian settlers were reluctant to join the union immediately, provision was made nonetheless in the union constitution for the eventual incorporation of the territory as a fifth province of South Africa. Rhodesian settlers rejected incorporation in a 1922 referendum, but the original conception of Southern Rhodesia as somehow part of South Africa was never entirely abandoned in London or Pretoria. While the settlers themselves could, for a time, pretend that they went their separate way, the economic and (later) strategic realities of Southern Africa never left them independent of South Africa in any significant sense.

South Africa had always been a major trading partner for Rhodesia, but Rhodesian dependence on South Africa became heavier after the 1965

Unilateral Declaration of Independence (UDI).[4] In 1965, 9 percent of Rhodesian exports went to South Africa, making that country the third-largest market for Rhodesian goods after Zambia and the United Kingdom. In the same year, 22.9 percent of Rhodesian imports came from South Africa, then the second-largest import source after the United Kingdom.[5] Within a few years after UDI, South Africa replaced the United Kingdom as Rhodesia's main trading partner. In 1972, about 20 percent of Rhodesian exports were directed to the South African market. The Rhodesian regime's effort to nullify UN-imposed sanctions proved successful largely because of South African willingness and capacity to keep Rhodesia's beleaguered economy afloat. Thus, in 1972, 67 percent of Rhodesian exports—valued at $470 million—were channeled to the outside world through South Africa. In the same year, 40 percent of Rhodesian imports came directly from South Africa and most of the rest were funneled through South Africa. With the March 1976 closure of the border with Mozambique, arising from Frelimo's commitment to assist in the liberation of Zimbabwe, the Rhodesian regime became totally dependent on South Africa.

Rhodesia's trade dependence on South Africa was paralleled by the penetration of South African capital into the territory's economy, a pattern that became more pronounced after UDI. South African corporations, some large enough to be classed as multinationals, penetrated the Rhodesian economy with significant volume in various sectors. The Anglo American Corporation, Charter Consolidated, Hullets Sugar Corporation, Rhodesian Steel Sales Company, Rhodesian Eagle Insurance, and the Netherlands Bank were involved to an extent that—even in the absence of precise figures on the book value of the investment—implied a significant dependence relationship. Because Rhodesia had also depended on South African military assistance since 1967, including troops and equipment (with the paramilitary South African Police units withdrawn only in 1975), it is clear that post-UDI Rhodesia emerged as a de facto South African dependency.

The collapse of Portuguese colonialism disrupted South Africa's carefully conceived regional strategy, which had been based on two logically contradictory premises:

1. White minority regimes would survive into the indefinite future in Mozambique, Angola, and Zimbabwe, with South African efforts to bolster them economically and militarily.
2. The black-ruled states of Southern Africa, although opposed to racism and white minority rule, might nonetheless be brought into the South African orbit—if they were not already in it—through offers of aid coupled with threats of military retaliation for participation in anti–South African military activities.

Malawi immediately and enthusiastically accepted South Africa's hand of "friendship." Others were initially more timid in expressing the same attitude; but when the OAU met in its 1971 annual conference, nearly one-third of the membership adopted Malawi's attitude.[6] South Africa's regional policy (then called "dialogue") was somewhat successful in splitting the OAU, despite the absence of perceptible political change in any of the colonial or racist territories of Southern Africa. Although South African policy failed to the extent that the majority of OAU members refused to abandon the strategy of armed struggle, it did break unified African support for the anticolonial and antiracist struggle.

The collapse of Portuguese rule and the escalation of the Zimbabwean armed struggle (which had begun at the end of 1972) immediately and dramatically brought the Zimbabwe question to the foreground of the overall Southern African crisis. From the Vorster regime's perspective, Rhodesian white settler rule was no longer a viable proposition. UDI was untenable because, with Mozambican independence, the guerrilla war centered in northeast Zimbabwe would quickly be extended along the entire border area. Rhodesia could not contain this higher level of warfare without a deeper commitment of South African money, materials, and even troops. Hence Vorster's October 1974 statement in the South African House of Assembly: "I believe that Southern Africa has come to the crossroads. I think that Southern Africa has to make a choice. I think that the choice lies between peace on one hand or an escalation of strife on the other."[7]

Peace was the implied South African preference. But peace on what terms? The diplomacy of "détente" would be the key to unlock the peace package, and Zimbabwe would be the chosen arena for playing out this South African strategy. The principal players would be South Africa vis-à-vis Zambia and its allies, acting as surrogates for the Smith regime and the Zimbabwe nationalists, respectively. The underlying assumption was that an agreement among the principals on the general framework of a Zimbabwean settlement would be accepted by Smith and the nationalists, who would then meet to flesh out the framework into a constitutional basis for speedy transition to black rule.

As far back as 1968 Vorster engaged Zambian president Kenneth Kaunda in secret correspondence about the Southern African situation.[8] The correspondence did not lead to any substantive results, especially regarding South African domestic policies to which Kaunda expressed continued opposition, but apparently there was enough encouragement from the correspondence and from secret discussions between Kaunda and various South African emissaries to suggest that a basis existed for a mutual exploration of the Zimbabwean problem in 1974.[9] Within six months of the Portuguese coup, South Africa reestablished contacts with the Zambian government. The upshot was intense diplomatic activity starting toward the end of 1974, which in its high level, its air of expectancy, its sense of high drama, and its urgency approximated Henry Kissinger's just begun Middle East "shuttle diplomacy."

The substance of this regional diplomacy emerged by December 1974; its primary focal point was a set of agreements on Zimbabwe. Four main points of presumed agreement were announced, following meetings in Lusaka involving South Africa, Zambia, Botswana, Tanzania, the Rhodesian regime, and the four leaders of the divided Zimbabwean nationalist movement (Bishop Abel Muzorewa, Joshua Nkomo, Ndabaningi Sithole, and James Chikerema):

1. The Smith regime would release all of the 400 African political prisoners held in jails and detention camps.
2. The Zimbabwean liberation organizations would merge into a single African National Council (ANC) under Bishop Muzorewa's leadership, pending an ANC congress to be held within four months.
3. A cease-fire would be declared in northeast Zimbabwe, where ZANU (Zimbabwe African National Union) had mounted sustained military operations since late 1972.
4. A constitutional conference would be held in early 1975, before Mozambican independence on 25 June 1975.[10]

None of these four points was achieved fully. Understanding this failure is central to understanding the shortcomings of the Vorster-Kaunda "détente" exercise.

First, only a few political prisoners were released. Smith was impelled to release Nkomo and Sithole and some of their senior aides in order to achieve nationalist unity and a cease-fire as preconditions to the proposed constitutional discussions. Even this step rankled for Smith, and he found an early excuse in March 1975 to redetain Sithole, using the patently groundless charge that he had plotted to murder his political rivals and sabotage the proposed cease-fire. South Africa felt forced to intervene, because Sithole's continued detention would scuttle "détente," and South African foreign minister Hilgard Muller flew to Salisbury to urge Smith to release Sithole. For his part, Smith was humiliated by his public disavowal under palpable South African pressure of the charges against Sithole.

Most of the detainees were not released, because Smith insisted that first all "terrorist activities" cease. In short, the detainees became pawns to Smith's aim of sabotaging those aspects of the "détente" exercise that he judged inimical to the survival of his regime and to settler colonialism in Zimbabwe.

The second point of the agreement—unifying the nationalist movement —will be discussed more fully later in this chapter. Here only the failure to fully involve the guerrillas in the Lusaka discussions and the highhanded imposition of "unity" by the senior partners in the discussions need be noted as contributory factors to continued nationalist disunity.

As for the cease-fire, it never took hold. The nationalist leaders never admitted that it was unconditional, while the Smith regime took it to mean the immediate surrender and disarming of all guerrillas. To Smith, this point was central to the agreement. Cease-fire on these lines would effectively cripple the armed struggle, remove the necessity for further diplomatic discussions, and leave Smith free to deal with the guerrillas as criminals rather than as war combatants. Although the cease-fire never took place, guerrillas in northeast Zimbabwe were cut off for awhile from essential supplies of weapons, ammunition, food, and medicine because of political machinations in Lusaka and elsewhere.[11]

The constitutional conference was held, starting on 25 August 1975, aboard a South African Railways train parked symbolically on the midpoint of the Victoria Falls bridge between Rhodesia and Zambia. Because of the failure to achieve the first three points of the earlier Lusaka agreement, this conference was doomed to futility, in spite of the last-minute personal interventions by Kaunda and Vorster. Afterwards, Smith and Nkomo (who had broken away from the Muzorewa-led ANC to lead his own faction) began a series of exploratory talks toward the end of 1975; full-scale constitutional talks between them started in December 1975.[12] These had failed by March 1976 because the Rhodesian government would not entertain the possibility of a rapid transfer of political power to the African majority. This failure was a severe setback to the "détente" exercise, although Henry Kissinger's April 1976 Lusaka speech revived its prospects, albeit under extraregional initiative and control.

The African States and "Détente"

Two aspects of the role of the "front-line" states—especially Zambia, Mozambique, and Tanzania—need further attention: their perspectives on the strategy of political struggle in Southern Africa, particularly in Zimbabwe;[13] and the domestic bases of their regional policies.

The OAU has never pursued a consistent approach to liberation struggles in Southern Africa. It has vacillated about which liberation movements to recognize and which means of struggle to give full backing. This lack of a consistent policy is perhaps inevitable, given the ideological heterogeneity of the organization and "national interest" considerations that must occasionally impinge on the organization's processes of policymaking.

However, it is possible to discern some pattern in the OAU's posture on the liberation struggle. The organization has generally preferred peaceful solutions to armed struggle, if such solutions seem possible. Armed struggle has been espoused only as a last resort, forced upon the Africans by the stubborn, uncompromising tenacity of colonial authorities. But even then armed struggle is viewed only as a tool to nudge these authorities into a more accommodative stance. In short, it serves as a tactical component of a negotiating strategy, in itself only setting the stage for negotiations. Armed struggle is not a strategic requirement dictated by the concrete social and political conditions of the target state, nor is it seen as the essential element of a more authentic national liberation process that amounts to a social revolution. Rather, in the OAU perspective, armed struggle is merely a more violent expression of nationalist political struggle. It is the analogue of the worker strikes and mass demonstrations that were a stock-in-trade of the anticolonial political struggles that set the stage for the decolonization of much of the African continent.

In the application of this analysis to Zimbabwe, the African states assumed by early 1975 that even if the Smith regime could not be persuaded that its collapse at the hands of guerrillas was imminent, South Africa might be so persuaded. According to this argument, since South Africa was effectively the colonial authority in Rhodesia, a South African commitment to negotiation would be sufficient to successfully complete the armed struggle there. The April 1975 Dar es Salaam Declaration reflected this viewpoint, stating:

> In the consideration of Africa's objectives in Rhodesia, it is important properly to evaluate the role of South Africa in that territory. South Africa has troops in Rhodesia which help to maintain the white minority rule. South Africa has frustrated the efforts of the international community by being the major sanctions buster. Both in its military and economic support of the Smith regime, South Africa continues to defy Africa's and the United Nations' opposition. The apartheid regime must put an end to the military and economic support.
>
> While Africa accepts helping [by South Africa] in genuine negotiations in order to facilitate the transfer of power to the African majority, it must remain absolutely vigilant and undertake the necessary preparations for the intensification of the armed struggle should peaceful solution to the Rhodesian conflict be blocked.[14]

This view of South Africa as the effective colonial authority in Rhodesia was also stated vehemently by Vernon Mwaanga, then Zambian foreign minister, in reply to critics of Zambian participation in the détente exercise: "If South Africa is the colonial authority as we believe she is in Zimbabwe and Namibia, what is wrong with talking to a colonial authority about granting independence to the people that she oppresses or to the people that are under her colonial domination?"[15]

The strategic perspective of the majority of OAU states derives not so much from an inadequate perception of the political problems of Southern Africa — although this has been evident in some of the actions taken or proposed — but from an ideological commitment to a purely nationalist solution to these problems. In general, African states — with the notable exceptions of Angola, Mozambique, and Tanzania — are as apprehensive as major Western powers about the potential radicalization of liberation movements. The possibility of the emergence of radical regimes in Southern Africa — regimes committed to a neo-Marxist social policy — is seen as a destabilizing influence by political elites in countries like Zambia and Zaire.[16]

As for the "front-line" states themselves, although they remain committed to majority rule in Zimbabwe the Southern African conflict places their economic, political, and security interests in serious jeopardy. This is especially true for Zambia, a country that has suffered heavy economic losses since Rhodesian UDI because of its geographic position and its regional policies.[17] For Zambia, the liberation of Zimbabwe could not come too soon. In addition to the heavy material and security costs incurred in active support for the liberation struggle, there have been serious political costs. The Zambian regime formulated and pursued its regional policy against the background of considerable domestic political disunity within UNIP (United National Independence Party) and the nation at large. This disunity, although not a product of Zambian foreign policy actions, impinged increasingly on foreign policy. By the early 1970s a number of influential Zambians concluded that the protracted regional liberation process was too burdensome for their country.[18] They took a "national interest" view, emphasizing Zambian needs and priorities rather than the seemingly elusive goal of liberation beyond the country's borders. President Kaunda was aware of these opinions. As one observer put it, "Zambia will support the Zimbabwe liberation struggle so far and for as long as the alternative not to do so is politically too costly to its leadership."[19]

Given the dangers and costs of supporting the liberation struggle, Zambia settled on a double-pronged strategy. On the one hand, it condemned the continuation of repressive racist regimes in Southern Africa and, making full use of all available diplomatic outlets, it energetically championed the cause of regional liberation movements. On the other hand, it maintained some contacts with such regimes (especially with South Africa), including both trade and secret diplomatic contacts.

For Mozambique, despite its much shorter period of independence, the Zimbabwe struggle has been even more costly and disruptive. Frelimo's

March 1976 decision to close its Rhodesian border—to cut Rhodesia's road and rail links with the Mozambican ports of Beira and Maputo—clearly contributed to the further weakening of Mozambique's financial and economic position and deterred vital economic reconstruction needed after ten years of warfare. Above all, Mozambique's unreserved support of the Zimbabwean armed struggle exposed it to retaliatory raids by the Rhodesian military on a scale not then faced by either Zambia or Botswana. In August 1976 Rhodesian troops moved across the frontier, destroyed the Nyazonia camp inhabited by hundreds of Zimbabwean refugees, and killed some six hundred and seventy of them on the claim that they were "terrorists" poised to attack northeast Rhodesian border settlements.[20] Incidents of a similar kind, although on a smaller scale, took place more frequently during 1976. For instance, on 31 October 1976 Rhodesian troops invaded Mozambican territory on a "hot pursuit" operation that lasted two days and resulted in large casualties among Mozambican civilians, Zimbabwean refugees and guerrillas, Mozambican soldiers, and the invaders themselves.[21] These preemptive attacks continued until late 1979.

Because Tanzania is far from the center of fighting, it is the only "frontline" state with significant immunity from reprisal attack. As its president, Julius Nyerere, stated in February 1976: "Tanzania is now free with the freedom of Mozambique, but Mozambique is not free without the freedom of Zimbabwe. Botswana is not free without the freedom of Zimbabwe. Of the four 'front-line' presidents, I am the only free one. I can sleep soundly at night. They can't because they are not free."[22] Tanzanian involvement in Southern African liberation, then, can be considered primarily a matter of principle, motivated by solidarity with both oppressed African majorities and with fellow "front-line" states closer to the arena of conflict.

This is not to suggest that Tanzania has absolutely no material interests in the regional conflict. First, Tanzania, like all other regional states but to a lesser extent, stands to gain economically from a postliberation regional economy in which there might be significant intraregional trade. Second, the liquidation of colonialism or similar forms of rule in any part of the world increases Tanzanian international stature and legitimacy. Nyerere has expressed this well: "Anything which strengthens the acceptance of the principle of national independence is of importance to us; anything which weakens it is of concern to us."[23]

Zimbabwe Nationalist Politics

The collapse of the August 1975 Victoria Falls conference led to the emergence of two nationalist organizations, each claiming the name African National Council. Bishop Muzorewa led the more popular United ANC, while Joshua Nkomo led the ANC/ZAPU. Both claimed guerrilla support. The UANC's support was impossible to ascertain, partly because its leaders were denied access to guerrilla camps in Mozambique, Tanzania, and Zambia after 1975.

The ANC/ZAPU (Zimbabwe African People's Union) guerrilla force amounted to no more than a thousand men by 1976. These guerrillas raided into Zimbabwe from Zambian bases and their movements had full support from the Zambian government. This force, formally called the Zimbabwe People's Revolutionary Army (ZPRA), briefly established an alliance with ZANU's force, the Zimbabwe African National Liberation Army (ZANLA), in November 1975. The alliance, headed by an eighteen-man high command (nine men from each side), took the name the Zimbabwe People's Army (ZIPA) and undertook to coordinate and direct the overall armed struggle independent of civilian political control. ZIPA high command argued that nationalist factionalism should not be imported into the guerrilla forces, lest it slow or even cripple the armed struggle.

Nonetheless, by mid-1976—less than a year after its formation—ZIPA was disintegrating amid recriminations and even bloodshed in some of its camps. According to the ZPRA commander, Albert "Nikita" Mangena, the split arose from a basic disagreement over the relationship of ZIPA and the existing Zimbabwean nationalist parties and their leaders. Mangena suggested that ZPRA contingents in ZIPA remain loyal to ZAPU leadership, but some ZANLA elements saw ZIPA as an independent political force.[24] In confirmation of this latter view, a ZIPA spokesman, Dzinashe Machingura, explained ZIPA's nature and status in September 1976: "ZIPA is not in negation to the former traditional nationalist organizations in Zimbabwe. What ZIPA aims at is assimilating, synthesizing, and espousing the progressive revolutionary content of these former organizations."[25] This argument was flawed in one profound respect: neither ANC/ZAPU nor ZANU was willing to lose its identity in the ZIPA alliance.

ZANU itself suffered a serious split. Robert Mugabe, its secretary-general, left Zimbabwe in early 1975 to revamp ZANU's political and military organization in Mozambique and elsewhere abroad. ZANU had suffered near-paralysis during an internal crisis in late 1974 and early 1975 that culminated in the March 1975 assassination of Herbert Chitepo, the party's national chairman and a principal architect of its increasingly successful guerrilla campaign.[26] The assassination had a profound effect on ZANU, which Mugabe, among others, sought to repair in order to restore momentum to the organization. Mugabe's efforts led to ZANU dominance of the ZIPA command by mid-1976.

For awhile Sithole adhered to the Lusaka declaration of unity. After Nkomo split away from the momentarily united ANC, Sithole kept his own ties with the residual Muzorewa faction. However, in September 1976, he announced his resignation from the UANC and the "resuscitation" of ZANU with himself as president. Sithole's moves were not coordinated with Mugabe and other senior ZANU figures active in ZIPA. In fact, Sithole denounced ZIPA as a creature of the "front-line" states, owing allegiance to them, with no political base in Zimbabwe and no connection with the recognized Zimbabwean nationalist leaders.[27]

Thus, four main nationalist groups crystallized by the end of 1976: Muzorewa's UANC, Nkomo's ANC/ZAPU, Mugabe's ZANU, and Sithole's ZANU. In addition, an alliance was formed in October 1976 between the Nkomo and Mugabe groups; called the Patriotic Front, it claimed control of all guerrilla forces based in Mozambique and Zambia. In January 1977 the Patriotic Front was recognized by the five "front-line" presidents as Zimbabwe's representative nationalist movement to which they pledged "full political, material, and diplomatic support. . . ."[28]

The recurrent divisions in the Zimbabwean nationalist movement derive from sources as complex as the political situation of Zimbabwe, but some factors are readily apparent. At first, little seemed to separate the four leaders on an ideological plane. All were apparently committed to majority rule — Africa rule — in Zimbabwe. In general, none of them initially seemed to be committed to the demolition and subsequent restructuring of Rhodesia's socioeconomic structure. To put it differently, divisions among the recognized leaders of the Zimbabwean liberation movement did not, on the surface, reflect a Fanonesque split between a national bourgeoisie and a determinedly socialist faction.[29]

However, as the military and political struggle intensified, elements of ideological polarization became discernible. One focus was the appropriate definition of majority rule. Another involved the state's economic role.

Those leaders associated with the March 1978 internal agreement accepted a heavily-qualified political franchise that left much power in white hands. At the same time, they spoke cautiously about economic change, stressing the need to keep a productive white involvement in both the agricultural and industrial sectors of the economy.

The Patriotic Front rejected any political settlement that left effective veto power in white hands. While Nkomo was somewhat vague about his economic program, Mugabe espoused a socialist, populist economy. He called for considerable state intervention, especially in the redistribution of agricultural land among the peasantry and the provision of a wider range of social services. Mugabe's reputation for radicalism stemmed in part from this commitment to a fuller *reform* of the present socioeconomic order.

In addition to differences of ideology and about tactics, personality differences among the four men and their competition for power were also significant factors, especially from late 1974 when the escalation of factional politics partly reflected the perception that African control of Zimbabwe was imminent.

It seems that another aspect of ideological cleavage in the Zimbabwean movement lies not merely among these four leaders but between them and their supporters among the "traditional" nationalist leaders, on the one hand, and the guerrilla fighters and their officers, on the other. Training, fighting, and reflection on the Zimbabwean situation from a very different vantage point had radicalized many guerrillas. Some of them saw their struggle in terms akin to Frelimo's view of Mozambique: a social revolution rather than merely an anticolonial struggle. The political and ideological orientation of independent Zimbabwe would depend on which group gained preponderance in the first government—these guerrilla fighters or the "traditional" nationalist leaders.

A further division emanated from actions of the "front-line" presidents based on considerations only peripherally related to Zimbabwean liberation. For example, in late 1974 they successfully urged the unification of the nationalist movement. A year later, they disavowed this stillborn aim to favor a unified guerrilla command not affiliated with any political party. By early 1977 they switched to formal recognition of the Patriotic Front. This attempt by the "front-line" presidents to control the strategy of the Zimbabwean struggle could only have a demoralizing impact. For instance, the premature calls for negotiation with Smith in 1974 and 1975, accompanied (in some cases) by actions subversive of the continuation of armed struggle, could not help but accentuate nationalist divisions.[30]

"Détente" — Phase Two

Henry Kissinger's 1976 diplomatic activities in the region rekindled "détente" and led directly to talks among Kissinger, Vorster, and Smith in Pretoria in September 1976. On 24 September 1976 Smith announced his government's acceptance of a new formula for peaceful resolution of the Rhodesian dispute.[31]

The formula contained two major points: the achievement of majority rule in two years; and the establishment of a transitional government, both to implement normal legislative and executive duties and to lay the groundwork for independent Zimbabwe's constitution. As Smith described it, the transitional government would consist of a Council of State and a Council of Ministers: the former would have both legislative and administrative powers, equal black-white membership, and a white chairman; while the latter, with a black majority and a black chief minister, would be subordinate to the first body and limited to administrative matters. Smith announced also that the United States, together with other major Western powers and South Africa, would establish a trust fund to "buy out" white Rhodesians unwilling to live under majority rule and to provide guarantees for those willing to stay but concerned about their property and pension rights. The fund would be available also for capital investment in the transition period and after independence.[32]

The first reactions to this formula from the "front-line" presidents and Zimbabwean nationalist leaders were relatively favorable, with the exception of Frelimo and ZIPA, which both denounced the plan.

Within three days of Smith's announcement, opposition became concerted. While nationalist concern focused on specific aspects of the transitional government's structure, functions, and procedures, its underlying concern was that the substance of power would remain in white hands. Why else should the Smith regime accept political suicide—the onset of long-dreaded majority rule within two years?

The Rhodesian Front's acceptance of these terms is best explained by the interplay of two factors. First, some "concessions" were required to avoid the inevitable total defeat that would come in time from a prolonged guerrilla war. Second, these apparent concessions were designed to confer the appearance of political power on the African majority while reserving its substance for the white minority. Whites would maintain effective control over both government administration and the economy. In particular, the privileged position of white farmers—the social stratum most directly threatened by Zimbabwean nationalism—would be protected.

Smith's "divide and stall" strategy was already well known to the nationalist leaders, so none trusted his willingness to make genuine changes. Thus, it was not surprising that all the nationalist delegations at the October-December 1976 constitutional conference in Geneva rejected the transition formula. U.K. efforts to revive the conference failed in January 1977 because Smith refused to move from the September 1976 formula, announced his opposition to any further talks involving the Patriotic Front, and renewed his efforts to find an "internal settlement." First, he encouraged Senator Chief Chirau (who had recently been appointed a member of the Rhodesian government to deal with African matters), along with some other senior chiefs, to form a moderate African political party. Then he tried, without success, to entice Bishop Muzorewa into bilateral talks on an "internal settlement." During 1977 Smith also announced "important" socioeconomic changes, wrenched from the strong resistance of the Rhodesian Front right wing. In fact, they involved marginal improvements in African opportunities to buy farms in white areas and in African access to government posts and to private (but not government) schools.

Thus, nothing was done by Smith to change the Zimbabwean nationalist leaders' belief in Smith's cunning intransigence and his wide support among white Rhodesians.

Yet with an escalating and seemingly unwinnable war on his hands, Smith was under pressure to somehow meet African demands. In doing so, divisions among the Zimbabwean nationalist factions enabled him to choose negotiation partners with the aim of preserving a good deal of white power and privilege in an independent Zimbabwe. In early December 1977 the Smith government began negotiations with delegations from three African political parties: Muzorewa's United African National Council, Sithole's African National Council, and Chief Jeremiah Chirau's Zimbabwe United People's Organization. Two important political developments preceded the negotiations. First, Smith won a strong victory against an extreme right-wing splinter group in the 31 August legislative election. Then, on the next day, the U.S. and the U.K. governments together announced a constitutional and administrative plan for transition to majority rule. Despite personal intervention by U.K. Foreign Secretary David Owen and U.S. Ambassador Andrew Young, Smith rejected the plan. He took special exception to two points: the plan's imposition of a U.K. resident commissioner in place of the present Rhodesian government and its provision for a Zimbabwean national army that would include elements from both the guerrilla forces and the existing Rhodesian army.

On 3 March 1978 the negotiations between Smith and the three African political groups reached fruition. A formula was announced that outlined the broad principles upon which the constitution of an independent Zimbabwe would be based. The structure of the transitional regime — responsible for administration of the country, preparation of the constitution, and the organization of preindependence elections — was set forth.

The "internal settlement" laid out the basic elements of the future constitution. All adults eighteen years or older would be eligible to vote. The legislative assembly would have seventy-two African members (elected by all voters) and twenty-eight white members. Of the whites, twenty would be elected by white voters, while the remaining eight would be elected by a multiracial electorate from a list of sixteen candidates drawn up by white members of the Parliament. These terms could be amended only after the first ten years of independence. Provision was also made for a constitutional bill of rights, with resort to the judiciary, that guaranteed human rights, property rights, public service job security, and pensions.

This agreement provoked uproar in many quarters, including outright condemnation by the Patriotic Front and the UN Security Council. Critics saw it as conceding far too much power and influence to the white minority in both the transitional period and after independence. They regarded Smith's acceptance of adult suffrage and an African parliamentary majority as insufficient, in light of the power held by the twenty-eight white legislators to block any constitutional amendments tending to "infringe" upon their "protected rights," including property, pensions, and public service employment.

Subsequent events did nothing to allay this criticism. First, the constitutional plan was submitted for approval only to a white voters' referendum. The transitional government was effectively dominated by Ian Smith, despite the unwieldy formal mechanism of a rotating executive chairmanship among Smith, Muzorewa, Sithole, and Chirau. The military tightly controlled the day-to-day administration of the war, so that the responsible black co-ministers had no impact on this central policy area. In general, the scheme of co-minister, one white and one black, made little impact on departments altogether controlled by white officials. When one black co-minister, Bryan Hove, called for civil service reform to right this imbalance, he was rebuked by Muzorewa and dropped from the government. For these reasons, and because the transitional regime made very little progress in ending discriminatory practices and none at all in the provision of socio-economic programs aimed especially at blacks, it did nothing to build black support for those black leaders who risked participation in it.

The April 1979 election was successful from Muzorewa's point of view, but not surprisingly, since the combined coercive resources of the army, "auxiliaries," officials, and employers were brought to bear in favor of Muzorewa's party. First, 64 percent of the estimated eligible voters turned out. Second, Muzorewa's party won more than 40 percent of the vote and fifty-one of the seventy-two African seats in the legislative assembly, although seven members subsequently defected from his party leaving him with a minority government. Muzorewa took office as prime minister soon after the election, and on 1 June 1979 the independent state of Zimbabwe Rhodesia came into existence.

The problems facing Muzorewa have become increasingly difficult. The guerrilla fighting has increased, and with it massive disruption of services and life in general throughout much of rural Zimbabwe Rhodesia. The white emigration rate increased sharply toward the end of 1978 and throughout 1979, with immediate impact on military officer strength and a more subtle impact on the economy.

Muzorewa's basic quandary is the growing impact of a war which his government can neither win nor end peaceably with its own resources. Thus he is altogether dependent on the U.S. and U.K. governments. Their initial reluctance in June 1979 to offer him any measure of support, until such time as he demonstrated more thorough black support and black control of the government, led him in frustration to request South African economic and military aid, which was apparently pledged. Then, Margaret Thatcher's apparent reversal in August from a public admission of eventual ending of sanctions to a call for a Muzorewa–Patriotic Front conference in London must have been puzzling and even more frustrating.

Muzorewa will take part because even he recognizes that he has absolutely no other political alternative. Because of this recognition, and despite the enmity between Muzorewa and Patriotic Front leaders, it seems probable — indeed, inevitable — that this conference will succeed, unlike so many predecessors (perhaps after one or two false starts), and Zimbabwe will finally secure legally recognized independence and (even more important) authentic self-government for its people.

Notes

1. Mohamed A. El-Khawas and Barry Cohen, eds., *The Kissinger Study of Southern Africa: National Security Study Memorandum 39 (Secret)* (Westport, Conn.: Lawrence Hill & Co., 1976), p. 105.

2. Stanlake Samkange, *Origins of Rhodesia* (London: Heinemann, 1968).

3. L. M. Thompson, *The Unification of South Africa, 1902–1910* (Oxford: The Clarendon Press, 1961); Eric Walker, *A History of Southern Africa*, 4th ed. (London: Longmans, Green and Co., 1965); and C. Munhamu Botsio Utete, "South Africa and Independent Africa: Continued Confrontation or Peaceful Coexistence?" (Ph.D. diss., Carleton University, 1971), esp. Chap. 2.

4. C. Munhamu Botsio Utete, "South Africa's Neocolonialist Strategy in Zimbabwe," international seminar on imperialism and liberation, University of Dar es Salaam, 17–19 January 1975.

5. Leonard T. Kapungu, *The United Nations and Economic Sanctions Against Rhodesia* (Lexington, Mass.: D. C. Heath Co., 1973), p. 74.

6. C. Munhamu Botsio Utete, "Crisis in the Organization of African Unity," *Black World* 20, no. 12 (October 1971), pp. 23–31.

7. *The Guardian* (weekly), 4 January 1975, p. 5.

8. Republic of South Africa, *House of Assembly Debates,* 33 (1971), cols. 4929–4940.

9. Republic of Zambia, *Details of Exchanges Between President Kaunda and Prime Minister Vorster of South Africa,* Lusaka, April 1971.

10. Neal Ascherson, *Daily Nation* (Nairobi), 18 April 1975.

11. Interviews, Dar es Salaam, January-June 1975.

12. See the useful, but tendentious, unsigned article, "Smith/Nkomo-Oppenheimer-Vorster/Kaunda: Deceit, Danger," in the right-wing journal, *Property and Finance* (Salisbury), November 1975.

13. See the 1969 *Lusaka Manifesto* and the *Dar es Salaam Declaration* of April 1975; also, United Republic of Tanzania, *African Strategy in Southern Africa* (Dar es Salaam: Tanzania Publishing House, 1971); Nathan Shamuyarira, "A Revolutionary

Situation in Southern Africa," *The African Review* (Dar es Salaam) 4, no. 2 (1974), pp. 159–179; and C. Munhamu Botsio Utete, "NATO and Southern Africa," *The Black Scholar* (Sausalito, Calif.) 7, no. 8 (May 1976), pp. 36–46.

14. See note 20.

15. *Daily News* (Dar es Salaam), 13 April 1975, p. 7.

16. Ernest Harsch and Tony Thomas, *Angola: The Hidden History of Washington's War* (New York: Pathfinder Press, 1976).

17. Richard L. Sklar, *Corporate Power in an African State: The Political Impact of Multinational Mining Companies in Zambia* (Berkeley and Los Angeles: University of California Press, 1975), Chap. 5.

18. Private communication.

19. Masipula Sithole, "Dynamics of Foreign Interest in the Liberation of Zimbabwe: An Assessment of Current Trends," second annual conference, Southern African Research Association, University of Maryland, 2 October 1976.

20. *Africa* (London), September 1976.

21. *New York Times,* 3 November 1976.

22. Sithole, "Dynamics of Foreign Interest in the Liberation of Zimbabwe," p. 16.

23. *Africa* (London), January 1976, p. 13.

24. "Message to Zimbabwe by ZPRA Commander Albert Nikita," *Zimbabwe Review* (Lusaka: ANC/ZAPU), February 1977, pp. 14, 15.

25. Mozambique Information Agency, "Zimbabwe People's Army (ZIPA): Interview with Dzinashe Machingura," *Journal of Southern African Affairs* (University of Maryland), October 1976, p. 16.

26. Factors and events connected with the assassination of Chitepo are highlighted in Republic of Zambia, *Report of the Special International Commission on the Assassination of Herbert Wiltshire Chitepo* (Lusaka: Government Printer, 1976). The commission, an eleven-nation OAU group set up at Zambian initiative, concluded that the Chitepo killing was the culmination of personality and ethnic feuds in ZANU's Supreme Council of Revolution then based in Lusaka.

27. See Ndabaningi Sithole, "Explanation to the OAU Heads of State on the True Nature of ZIPA which has been imposed on the People of Zimbabwe by the Frontline States," Dar es Salaam, mimeographed, 17 January 1977.

28. *Zimbabwe Review* (Lusaka), February 1977, p. 10.

29. Frantz Fanon, *The Wretched of the Earth* (New York: Grove Press, 1965).

30. Reference has already been made to the 1974 Zambian-South African inspired "ceasefire" in Zimbabwe with its deleterious effect on the ZANLA campaign in the northeastern theater. Further, the Zambian–South African "Pretoria Agreement" of 1975, paving the way for the abortive Victoria Falls conference on Zimbabwe in August 1975, barred "infiltration of terrorists" into Zimbabwe during the negotiations. See Colin Legum, *Vorster's Gamble for Africa* (London: Rex Collings, 1976), p. 127.

31. The original text of the Kissinger formula was never published. Ian Smith's statement concerning the formula was printed in full in many newspapers: for example, *The Rhodesia Herald* and the *New York Times,* both of 25 September 1976.

32. Ibid.

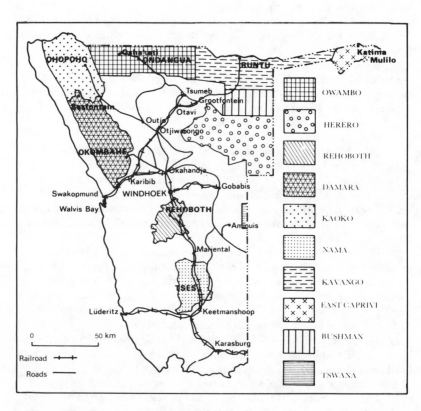

Map 3. South West Africa/Namibia: Ethnic-Based Regional Government Boundaries. Source: The Africa Institute of South Africa, from *Bulletin* 14, no. 4, 1976, p. 105.

5

South West Africa/Namibia: A Study in Polarization and Confrontation

Gerhard Tötemeyer
John Seiler

South West Africa/Namibia is not unique among African territories in its ethnic heterogeneity. But its ethnic diversity in combination with other elements make for an extraordinarily unstable and volatile political situation. First, there is a severe population imbalance between the Ovambos (who make up 47 percent of the population) and the whites (12 percent, but internally divided between Afrikaner, German, and English-speaking groups) on the one hand, and ten other ethnic groups (none of which has as much as 10 percent of the toal population of less than 900,000) on the other hand. White domination of political, economic, social, and administrative activities is another crucial factor. Finally, to complicate matters considerably, the territory's future has been a central concern of the United Nations since 1947 and has been increasingly intertwined with Black African–Western powers conflicts in the United Nations since 1960. Whether energetic U.S.-led diplomatic efforts directed at achieving Namibian independence by peaceful means will ultimately succeed remains very much in the balance despite acceptance of the July 1978 Security Council resolution endorsing a UN-supervised transition by both SWAPO (South West Africa People's Organization) and the government of South Africa.

The basic conflict over the future of an independent Namibia stems from the continued white domination of the society. This domination existed long before the Portuguese coup and, despite the flurry of political activity in the territory since then—including rhetorical white gestures about building a multiracial society—it has changed in no basic way.

A preliminary version of this chapter was presented at a workshop, "Southern Africa Since the Portuguese Coup," held at Rhodes University on 24 and 25 June 1976.

The white man remains the predominant administrator, employer, entrepreneur, banker, and farm owner. Urban blacks (and the small Coloured population of 37,000) live apart from the comfortable white centers, with poorer and usually inadequate social amenities and with severely limited access to those facilities available in the white centers—except for commercial shops. Apart from a véry few businessmen, mostly engaged in noneconomic shopkeeping, the tiny black and Coloured middle class is composed of professional and administrative people—doctors, attorneys, school principals, teachers, nurses, and lower-level civil servants (most serving in homeland areas).

Advancement opportunities for blacks have been even more severely limited than they have in South Africa. Unlike industry in the Republic, territorial industry is not large enough to provide a meaningful number of semiskilled or skilled jobs. Almost all of the blacks employed in the operating mines at Tsumeb and Rössing are unskilled, with only minimal provisions made or under consideration for their further training and upgrading. The substantial Ovambo and Kavango seasonal labor force brought to Walvis Bay to work in the large fishing fleets there remains essentially unskilled. In addition, there is little scope for employment of blacks in the South West Africa (SWA) administrative services (a situation unlike that in South Africa's administrative services). The so-called South West Africa Administration, although responsible for public works, communications, and other infrastructural activities for the entire territory, in fact provides education and social services only for the white population. All its senior and middle-level officials and most of its lower-level staff, except for laborers and clerical assistants, are white, and most are from South Africa. Until early 1978 education and social services for blacks and Coloureds were provided by departments based in Pretoria (Bantu Administration and Development and Coloured Relations, respectively). Operating under the strict logic of separate development, every effort was made to employ blacks and Coloureds at work in schools or other facilities for their specific ethnic groups. But even for the Ovambo, relatively few professional positions are open because these remain in the hands of whites. For the smaller ethnic groups, there are few facilities and very few jobs.

This profound frustration in employment and self-advancement may be the most significant outcome of the separate development policy that has been predicated since the Odendaal Commission's favorable report on that policy in 1964.[1] For the South African government, and for whites in the territory, the Odendaal report justified the strengthening of the status quo of white domination. For the blacks, who until 1964 had some hope that the UN interest in SWA might lead to rapid political change, the report marked entrenchment of white privilege. By the time of the Portuguese coup, most educated blacks in the territory were persuaded that the South African government would not acquiesce peaceably to the major changes required to achieve a more just society. The pattern for racial polarization was set and the prospect growing for violent confrontation.

Black Namibian Response to the Portuguese Coup

For Namibian blacks, the 1974 Portuguese coup with the accompanying changes in Angola marked an important upturn in their long-frustrated hopes for political betterment. For the first time, with an independent black nationalist regime at its northern border, effective military pressure could be brought to bear on the South African government. Before 1974 SWAPO guerrillas depended on Zambian sanctuaries (because of Portuguese cooperation with South Africa in denying camps or transit routes within Angola to the guerrillas), which meant that they could enter and leave SWA only through the narrow and relatively easily protected Caprivi strip area or through Botswana. Now they could move back and forth across the Angolan-SWA border (some 800 miles long). Immediately after the Portuguese coup the border was essentially unpatrolled and had no security fences and few border posts.

Before the coup black political activity had been fitful and largely limited to the tiny elite and to migrant Ovambo and Kavango workers who moved from the north to "southern" jobs—in the Tsumeb mine, the De Beers diamond mines at Oranjemund, and in the Walvis Bay fishing industry. In December 1971, for the first time, a major strike of Ovambo workers took place, but without any apparent next step in political organization.[2] SWAPO had had little success in building its organization within the territory. After initial SWAPO guerrilla attacks in August 1966, the South African government quickly squelched SWAPO's organizational efforts and placed most of its leaders in the territory on trial for treason.[3] The formal organization was permitted to continue, perhaps in deference to international opinion and because it made surveillance easier.

The Portuguese coup brought about an immediate and massive act of political defiance by Namibian blacks. Between June 1974 and early 1975, several thousand Ovambos (perhaps as many as 6,000)—teachers, nurses, clergymen, civil service clerks, students, and laborers—walked across the unprotected border into Angola. Most of them went on to Zambia, where they made contact with SWAPO.[4] Only after most of the movement had ended were plans made by the South African government to expand border security—more police posts were established and planning began for a system of border fences and nonaccess strips.

Black political activity remained episodic until 1978, when the imminence of independence stirred increasing interest and participation. Most of the existent political parties were very small—almost always limited to members from a single ethnic group—and too often the self-centered projections of individual ambitions. Given the official focus of political activity within ethnic frameworks and the parallel official preoccupation with the dangers of nonethnic black nationalism, there was little impetus for more broadly based political activity. Even now the influences that bear on black Namibians are extraordinarily hard to trace and predictions of future political success or failure by SWAPO, by moderate ethnic coalitions, or by traditional ethnic-based parties are hazardous.[5]

One clear, powerful influence is at work. The churches (in particular the Lutheran church and to a lesser extent the Episcopal and Catholic churches) provide a striking demonstration of alternative values and lifestyle in their missions and schools. White clerics and teachers work closely with black teachers (many of whom received their university degrees at Fort Hare College in South Africa before it was transformed into an ethnic-based university in 1959) and live in relatively open, even intimate, circumstances with their black students. In the SWA context, this has been an intrinsically revolutionary experience. To a considerable extent these white and black clerics and teachers share with their black students a view of Namibia's past and present that makes them a potentially powerful force in Namibian politics.

The two black Lutheran churches—the Evangelical Lutheran Church (whose president is Dr. Lukas de Vries) and the Evangelical Lutheran Ovambo-Kavango Church (ELOK, for its Afrikaans acronym, headed by Bishop Leonard Auala)—have a total membership of 450,000. Even before they joined formally in a federal structure in 1972, they acted together in growing support of black political frustration. Following the International Court of Justice (ICJ) 1971 advisory opinion "ending" the South African mandate over SWA, the two churches made representations to Prime Minister Vorster and, in an open letter, bitterly attacked apartheid and its social and spiritual implications. Vorster met with church leaders in August 1971, but without any effective reconciliation of views. Again, in November 1971, church leaders met with Jannie de Wet, commissioner-general of the indigenous peoples of SWA (a kind of governor general, to use an analogy from British colonial days). At that meeting Bishop Auala called attention to the contract labor system (in which most participants were Ovambo men), which he termed "forced slavery." De Wet replied that it was a voluntary system. Apparently in reaction to the communication failure of this meeting, Ovambo workers began their December 1971 strike.[6] Church newsletters conveyed to congregants information about police repression of the strike and about the growing frustration and foreboding felt by the leaders of the federated church, VELKSWA (the Afrikaans acronym for the

United Evangelical Lutheran Church of South West Africa). Again, in April 1973, VELKSWA leaders told de Wet of their dissatisfaction at continued police repression and the various restrictions being placed on the activities of both black and white clergy. Their request for the appointment of a judicial commission was rejected by Prime Minister Vorster.

Symbolic of the polarization between VELKSWA and the South African government was the destruction by bombs of the ELOK printing plant at Oniipa in Ovamboland in May 1973. The security police never apprehended the culprits, leaving the widespread suspicion among blacks that either BOSS (the Bureau for State Security) or the security police itself had committed the crime.[7]

Thus, by the time of the Portuguese coup, VELKSWA's political role in strong opposition to government policy was firmly established; the coup only consolidated the situation. At its July 1974 conference, VELKSWA stated its position unequivocally:

> For VELKSWA the Gospel has political consequences. It is thus difficult to preach the message of peace, reconciliation, and love, when the opposite is witnessed by society. The Kindgom of Christ has a responsibility towards the worldly kingdom. Therefore the Church should go to the Government and say: "So speaks God. These are the consequences that follow from the vertical relationship of the church with God."[8]

Later in 1974 VELKSWA played an instrumental, though informal, role in the formation of the Namibia National Council (NNC)—an unsuccessful effort to link SWAPO with various moderate black parties—through the activities of two church officials, Daniel Tjongarero (now a senior official of SWAPO's internal wing) and the Reverend Zephania Kameeta, who became NNC president in January 1976.[9]

Throughout 1975 and 1976 black churchmen grew increasingly bitter toward the South African administration, especially regarding the border areas of Ovamboland, Kavango, and Caprivi (and especially during the 1975 Ovambo election). These became de facto military operational areas at the time of the 1975 South African intervention into Angola. Despite a strong reluctance to give unequivocal endorsement to armed struggle because the use of violence conflicted with their views of Christianity, more and more black clergymen found SWAPO's argument for guerrilla activity irresistible. By September 1976 participants in a consultation on "the responsibility of the churches in the changing SWA/Namibian situation" could agree that "the Churches should denounce the legalized violence of the South African regime, commend disobedience to unjust laws as a Christian Action, and support genuine resistance movements which are working for a freer and more just Namibia."[10]

The principal of one of the few private black secondary schools in Namibia—J. J. Tjozongoro of the Martin Luther School at Okambahe—summarized the situation succinctly in March 1976 in a complaint published by *The Windhoek Advertiser* about security police interference with students and staff at the school:

> Such action should be detested. This action on the part of the Security Police is regarded by the school as a blatant violation of the democratic principle of freedom of speech and expression of opinions. The school has been at no stage a threat to State security, nor is it a political institution or a body associated with any political movement. Those regarding the Martin Luther High School as a SWAPO institution and consequently a communistic breeding ground, are either stupid or simply deliberate liars. Or do the authorities regard everybody who is critical about the unchristian apartheid system as SWAPO-inspired?
>
> It should be borne in mind that the continuing deteriorating conditions in South West Africa, tensions among the population groups, and the lack of confidence prevailing among inhabitants of the territory can be ascribed, without doubt, to the detestable action of the illegal South African Police in South West Africa, who are making use of bribery, assault, torture, and obstinate refusal to report the true state of affairs to [their] bosses.[11]

This pivotal role for VELKSWA in Namibian politics means that its theological efforts to define "Black Consciousness" and to come to grips with the church's proper stance vis-à-vis violence have a more immediate impact on black political attitudes than similar theological efforts among black clergymen in South Africa. Although VELKSWA has not yet defined its view of what independent Namibia should be, some black churchmen have already made it clear that integration will be no more acceptable for the future than separate development has been up to now, if true equality is to be achieved. Whether this preoccupation takes a radical or a conservative tone, or some mixture of both, remains to be seen.

South African Policy in Post-Coup South West Africa

South African official confidence was at a peak just before the 1974 Portuguese coup. During the previous fifteen years, every apparent threat to South African control of the territory had either proved illusory or had been quickly squelched. In 1963 the Carpio mission, representing the U.N. secretary-general, proved ineffective, partly because of the political equivocation of its chairman, and the South African government concluded rightly that the United Nations lacked the will to put serious pressure on its mandate. In 1966 the ICJ's technical ruling — that neither Liberia nor Ethiopia had standing to bring the SWA case before it — was taken by South Africa as a far broader political justification of its continued role in the territory. The quick repression of the first SWAPO raids in August that year enhanced South African confidence. As a result, implementation of the Odendaal Commission recommendations for separate development of ethnic home-lands (recommendations that had been deferred until the ICJ ruled on the mandate) was begun with considerable impetus in the economic boom of the late 1960s. At the same time, the future of SWA whites was linked with that of white South Africans by giving them six representatives in the South African House of Assembly.[12]

So confident was the South African government of its position that it invited both the UN secretary-general and later his representative to visit the territory in 1972 as an integral part of its "outward" policy intended to demonstrate South African bona fides to the world. The joint statement issued by Dr. Alfred M. Escher and the South African government after the second visit reflected the South African motivation and the part innocent–part calculating South African effort to identify its goals for the territory with those of the United Nations. The statement spoke of agreement on the goal of "self-determination for the people/peoples of South West Africa." (The South African official version used the plural form, in line with the South African emphasis on ethnic-based politics, while the UN version used the singular, with its emphasis on some kind of national referendum to determine the territory's political future.)[13]

In the South African contacts with UN Secretary-General Waldheim and Escher, no effort was made toward concessions in overall policy. In general, the South African attitude was that its separate development policy was the only one that made sense for the territory; it was pleased to have an opportunity to explain its motivation and to show its effectiveness. In short, before 1974 the South African government did not feel threatened in any way by the United Nations or by any other government, within or beyond Africa.

The first irony about the coup's impact is that the coup strengthened the South African commitment to separate development for SWA ethnic groups. Despite U.S. pressure between April and September 1974 — pressure intended to evoke South African concessions to UN resolution requirements — the South African government was not prepared to give way on its basic policy.

The evidence of this strengthened resolution remains circumstantial, but it is nonetheless persuasive. First, the South African government did respond to the tacit U.S. threat of holding back from a Security Council veto unless some progress was made toward territorial self-determination. A.H. du Plessis, leader of the National party (NP) in SWA and later minister of community development in the South African government, announced in September 1974 that the National party, as political representative of all whites in the territory, was prepared to talk with other ethnic groups about the territory's future. In du Plessis's words, "all options would be open"—there was no advance commitment to any specific political structure or to the terms of relationship with South Africa that might be optimal.[14] Admittedly, no commitment was made to independence, so one of the options might be a more thorough absorption into the Republic. But despite the apparent openness of the proposed consultations, the focus on ethnic discussions (precluding formal contacts with SWAPO, the NNC, or any other multiethnic black political parties) and the insistence that the NP's electoral victories meant it represented all whites (thus leaving out the United party [UP] and the sizable number of Germans who did not feel adequately represented by either the NP or the UP) suggested strongly that the South African government was firmly committed to separate development.

Jannie de Wet's initial reaction to the Ovambo exodus reinforced this assessment. He was concerned with halting any further emigration of Ovambos but, at the same time, he saw an opportunity to end the threat of Ovambo preponderance in the territory. A separate political status for Ovamboland and an accelerated evolution to independence, perhaps together with those Ovambo tribesmen living in Angola, would solve this problem. At the same time, every effort would be made to ensure good relations between the residual SWA, independent Ovamboland, and a friendly Angola, given their economic interdependence. The South African government seemed genuinely persuaded that such a solution would result in a residual SWA in which no one ethnic group, including the whites, would dominate. Commissioner-General de Wet conveyed these views to a South African reporter in October 1974.[15] Although he was scolded by Pretoria for his clear indication that some options were more attractive to the South African government than others, he was not replaced then and remained in his post until September 1977.

During 1975 and 1976 the South African administration continued its policy of devolving administrative and executive functions to the SWA ethnic homelands. Ovamboland provided the primary focus for this activity. Because a 1973 Ovambo assembly election had been effectively boycotted by SWAPO, Commissioner-General de Wet felt it necessary to hold another election in January 1975. In fact, few Ovambo at work outside of Ovamboland bothered to vote, reflecting a general sympathy for SWAPO and an antipathy toward Ovambo separatism. In Ovamboland itself voting began slowly, but by the end of the five-day voting period 76 percent of registered voters had voted. The discrepancy in voter turnout between Ovamboland and other parts of South West Africa was shaped partly by massive official intervention in Ovamboland, including the traditional threats of force by police and local chiefs, but the most potent lever was undoubtedly the threat to withdraw the permit necessary to enter the migrant labor force outside Ovamboland.[16]

The assassination of Chief Elifas, the Ovambo chief minister, in August 1975 intensified police activities. Because external SWAPO took credit for his death, a number of its internal leaders were detained and interrogated. Several were tried on charges of murder and conspiracy in Swakopmund, but their convictions were overturned on appeal in 1977. Just before Elifas's death, Prime Minister Vorster had announced South African willingness to accept Ovambo demands for further movement in political devolution.[17]

The military buildup just before and during the South African intervention in Angola, from mid-1975 into 1976, had a major impact on the ethnic homelands adjacent to the border—Ovamboland, Kavango, Caprivi, and Kaokoland. All four became military operations areas. Although the civilian administration under Jannie de Wet retained operating control, the South African Defense Force and security units of the South African Police became decisive forces. The border itself was closed, first with the extensive posts and patrols and then by a system of fences and plowed "open" zones. Within the four areas, police security units tried to watch closely all those suspected of political activity. The strain on police capacity was considerable and individual officers were assigned to border duty from permanent posts all over South Africa. SWAPO and other black Namibian leaders accused the police and the military of threats and occasional violence against innocent blacks.

The Constitutional Conference

The South African government entered into SWA constitutional talks with considerable reluctance. It did so only because first the U.S. government and then the U.K. and French governments made it clear that continued support in the UN Security Council against resolutions calling for international sanctions rested on continuing signs of South African initiative. The original September 1974 announcement of informal consultations was prompted by a U.S. diplomatic move. Subsequently, very little movement toward the start of formal discussions was discernible until the first months of 1975, when the U.S., U.K., and French governments reminded South Africa of a Security Council "deadline" of 30 May 1975, by which date some substantial progress had to be shown. The conference—usually called "the Turnhalle conference," after the refurbished Windhoek building in which it met—didn't begin until 1 September 1975.

SWAPO had been formally excluded from Turnhalle. In turn, it rejected talks based on ethnic groups as "a gathering of stooges and misguided peo-ple."[18] At the same time it expressed its willingness to talk with either the South African government or the SWA National party leaders, but only as long as it was understood that the South African government remained the party responsible for SWA developments.

This proviso was unacceptable to the South African government, which insisted from the beginning that the Turnhalle talks were entirely in the hands of white and black SWA residents. Pretoria would not interfere, although it would support whatever decision Turnhalle reached about the territory's future. In practice, of course, the South African government was intimately involved in shaping the direction taken by Turnhalle. Prime Minister Vorster kept in touch with developments through the conference secretary, Billy Marais, who had been the prime minister's personal represen-tative in SWA before his appointment to Turnhalle. In November 1975 Vorster decided to send A. H. du Plessis back to Windhoek to take the leadership of the white delegation from Dirk Mudge, who seemed to be tak-ing too conciliatory a line vis-à-vis the black delegates. Vorster intervened again toward the end of 1976 when frustrated black delegates asked to see him in Pretoria. After the delegates expressed their bitterness at the reluc-tance of the SWA white delegation to make any effective concessions to their moderate social and economic demands, he accused them of delaying the conference for trivial reasons at a time of great national urgency.[19]

Four sessions were held at Turnhalle between September 1975 and June 1976. All were short and mostly unproductive. The September 1975 session presented a Declaration of Intent, which emphasized the conference's pre-occupation with peaceful means to reach a constitutional agreement "as soon as appropriate and if possible within a period of three years." This statement implied political independence for the territory (without spelling out whether it would be unitary, confederal, or federal) shortly after 1978. In itself, the setting of an approximate date marked an enormous forward step. Although Vorster had suggested a ten-year plan to reach independence to both Escher and Waldheim during his 1972 talks with them, there had been nothing very precise about that timetable. The September session also ap-pointed a number of committees to inquire into problems of finance, educa-tion, economic development, employment practices, and various aspects of black-white social relations.

The second session, in November 1975, lasted only five days. It broke up over the return of A. H. du Plessis from Pretoria, a step that most black delegates took as a *verkrampte* ("hard-line" conservative) move by the South African government to ensure continued control of the talks.

The third session, in March 1976, lasted three weeks. Its preoccupation with consideration of committee reports foundered over repeated indications that the South African government was unwilling to forsake its separate development policies in any area of territorial administration. Even the prospect of a multiracial university was anathema to du Plessis and his *verkrampte* colleague, Eben van Zijl, although they finally conceded.

The fourth session, in June 1976, lasted only three days. It recommended the ending of apartheid practices in hotels, restaurants, and other public facilities. Although these were substantial advances, given traditional practices in the territory and the continued lack of progress in South Africa, the white delegation expressly reminded the black delegates that the recommendations had no weight until and if approved by the SWA executive committee, an all-white body.

Given this lack of productivity and faced with another Security Council "deadline" on 31 August 1976—and U.S.-U.K.-French pressure to demonstrate some progress before that date—in March 1976 the Turnhalle delegates appointed a smaller constitutional committee, with three members from each of the eleven participating groups, to draft a constitution. This committee met briefly in April and again at the end of May, held a three-week session in June, and reconvened in early August.

In its first sessions, du Plessis and van Zijl argued for retention of the existent apartheid structure, with only minimal powers to be held by the central government. Mudge, on the other hand, argued that more concessions were necessary. During its June session, apparently after intervention by Prime Minister Vorster and R. F. Botha (then South Africa's UN and U.S. ambassador and now its minister of foreign affairs), consensus was reached on some basic points. An announcement of these underlying principles was made on 19 August 1976:

1. Independence would be achieved on 31 December 1978.
2. There would be a political entity, the particular structure of which still had to be established, but in which protection for minority groups would be a pivotal concern.
3. Once Turnhalle reached agreement on the proposed constitution, an interim government would be set up to make plans for and to implement the transition to an independent state.

While it was not acknowledged then as a basic change in South African policy, the acceptance of independence for the entire territory as "a single political entity" finally put to rest the South African notion of giving Ovamboland separate independence. But when the Constitutional Committee continued its discussions in September 1976, it became obvious that the white delegation did not intend to budge from the basic pattern of apartheid. On 16 September, committee agreement was announced on the general concept of a "three-tier" government, which du Plessis and van Zijl saw as an ambiguous device to forestall effective political and economic change. Most black delegates and SWAPO recognized this underlying motivation. The black delegates, although deeply embittered by the turn of events, tried to wrest the bulk of power for the first tier—the multiracial central government, in which decisions were, somehow, to be made on a consensual basis among representatives of the eleven ethnic groups. The white delegation resisted with considerable success, keeping important powers in education, housing, and other social policies for the second and third tiers. The second tier was defined as the embryonic homelands (Ovamboland, Kavango, Caprivi, Rehoboth, etc.) and the "white" part of Namibia. The third tier was defined as distinct black and white local communities—for instance, white Windhoek and black Katutura township would be governed separately—despite bitter criticism from black delegates.

As 1977 began, black delegates (especially those from the "southern tier" outside Ovambo, Kavango, and Caprivi) felt general frustration at the outcome of Turnhalle. Throughout their participation, strong divergent pressures had worked on them. First, most of them had reservations about SWAPO and some degree of personal political ambition. They had a stake in a Turnhalle that would give blacks a greater role in Namibian government while simultaneously strengthening their own political positions. The idea of a multiracial central government was attractive for its promise of achieving both goals, but if the white political leadership insisted on keeping to itself the bulk of its existent political, economic, and social predominance, the black delegates' efforts to achieve stable government apart from SWAPO were doomed. If they themselves were frustrated, both their urban and rural supporters were equally so, and SWAPO could only gain support as a result.

The conference had been a strain on a more personal level. From the white delegation, and occasionally in a cruder form from the South African Police and the SWA administration, black delegates had received entreaties and even threats to elicit their support for white proposals. At a technical level, almost all the expert witnesses before the committees and almost all the legal advisors made available to black delegations were selected by the white delegation or by Pretoria.

Then, after several rounds of sustained diplomatic effort led by the United States (joined by the United Kingdom, France, Germany, and Canada) during the first months of 1977, Prime Minister Vorster announced policy changes in June 1977 that ended Turnhalle's constitution-making role and provided for transitional administration. An independent administrator-general would be appointed by the South African government, with the approval of the five governments involved and the United Nations; the steps leading to the general election of a constituent assembly would begin, with the United Nations taking an active role throughout the process; and the constituent assembly would lay the groundwork for an independent Namibia.[20] In July 1977 Justice Marthinus Steyn, a member of the Orange Free State Supreme Court (and grandson of the Free State's last president before Union in 1910) was appointed administrator-general.[21]

Steyn took office in September 1977, without waiting for UN authorization of his appointment. With a speed remarkable for SWA, he dismantled apartheid's administrative structure by ending the roles of the Bantu administration and the Coloured relations departments, while taking over from Pretoria most administrative functions previously centered there. But at the same time, although he eased legal constraints against political campaigning and gave an extra impetus to the effort already begun to break down apartheid in public facilities, he resisted any moves calculated to lessen the schism in the territory's economic and social-residential patterns.

Political activity accelerated toward the end of 1977 and slowly coalesced around three major poles. First, in white politics, a basic split took place in the dominant National party. Dirk Mudge, who had been Turnhalle chairman and was the only white participant trusted by black delegates, left the NP—along with almost half of the SWA party delegates—to form the Republic party (RP). Mudge intended to work cooperatively with moderate black leaders and parties, building on the basis of Turnhalle. The residual NP, led by A. H. du Plessis and Eben van Zjil, insisted that such cooperation would lead to the defeat of white interests. The residual NP regrouped as Aktur SWA. The Republic party liaison with various black parties, including the Herero-based National Unity Democratic Organization, was named the Democratic Turnhalle Alliance (DTA). At the same time white supporters of the United party opposition, led by Bryan O'Linn, and the liberal wing of the German community, represented by Frederick Dahlmann (the editor of *Allgemeine Zeitung*), established ties with SWANU (South West African National Union) and other black parties in the Namibian National Front (NNF). When Andreas Shipanga and other dissident SWAPO leaders were released from Tanzanian prisons in 1978, apparently in a move by Nyerere to expedite Namibian peace negotiations, they formed the SWAPO Democrats, which allied itself with the NNF.

Throughout 1978 and 1979, NNF and DTA activities reflected sometimes bitter personal animosities, a broad mutual lack of understanding between black and white political leaders, and the increasingly unsettled state of Namibian politics. The two parties continued to differ over ethnicity. Even though NNF constituent parties were based on ethnic ties, most were uncomfortable with that arrangement and some tried—with little success—to diversify their membership. The DTA, on the other hand, proclaimed the virtues of ethnicity. Both parties were averse to SWAPO rule, but from very different perspectives, since SWAPO Democrats and SWANU leaders came from a similar nationalist background and hoped to win support from the same base of urban and migrant workers.

SWAPO's own position was changing. In addition to the differences between Nujoma and Shipanga, there were other foci of potential conflict. One of the original SWAPO leaders, Herman Toivo y Toivo, who had been held on Robben Island by the South African government since 1968, represented a symbolic challenge to the authority of Sam Nujoma and at least a potential challenge to Nujoma's effective control of SWAPO.[22]

Then there were the policy and personality differences between external and internal SWAPO. External SWAPO was a militant revolutionary organization, while its internal wing had taken remarkably moderate positions about the future of an independent Namibia. The 1975 Constitution of Independent Namibia, developed in Windhoek, was a strikingly nonradical document, with its call for a unitary state with administrative devolution to protect minority group interests (an element that internal SWAPO rightly noted was far different from the involuntary devolution inherent in separate development). In 1976 internal SWAPO informally discussed a bicameral legislature also intended to protect minority groups. To some extent, the external-internal SWAPO differences reflect their very different political situations, but, whatever the explanation, it seems unlikely that the differences will disappear once the two wings are free to consolidate their political activities.[23]

The prolonged diplomatic efforts to bring SWAPO and the South African government to accept peace plans for Namibia apparently reached fruition in 1978. South Africa accepted the plan in April and SWAPO accepted it in July. The ambiguity inherent in their acceptance was manifested in the July 1978 Security Council debate, in which two resolutions were approved. The first resolution simply requested the secretary-general to appoint a representative to facilitate processes leading to independence. The second called on South Africa and independent Namibia to reach agreement on the disposition of Walvis Bay, the only deepwater port in the territory. This second resolution angered the South African government, which claimed it had no warning that the issue would be raised and then reiterated the traditional South African claim to Walvis Bay apart from the rest of the territory. Apparently, previous negotiations had suceeded only because the Western negotiators dealt ambiguously with the issue. While SWAPO was reassured that Walvis Bay would be part of independent Namibia, South Africa had been allowed to believe that the disposition of the bay would be decided through bilateral negotiation between Pretoria and the government of independent Namibia, taken up at South African convenience and without UN pressures or potential sanctions.

Apart from the issue of Walvis Bay, the plan itself contained a number of basic provisions that were ambiguous and subject to misinterpretation. The effective relationship between the Security Council's representative, Martti Ahtisaari of Finland (chairman of the UN Council on Namibia), and Judge Steyn was not at all clear. Growing out of that ambiguity was the broader ambiguity of the 1,000-man UN administrative force that was intended to assist in the preindependence transition. Finally, given the South African reluctance to reduce its military forces to 1,500 men and withdraw them to two designated base areas in the northern part of SWA until such time as guerrilla activity ceased and overall security was ensured, the possibility of differences and even armed clashes between the proposed 7,500-man UN force and the SADF seemed considerable.

Some of these differences seemed to have been resolved by Ahtisaari's January 1979 visit to the territory and to Cape Town, during which he talked with Judge Steyn and with P. W. Botha, the new South African prime minister, and other South African government members. Paradoxically though, that visit marked the start of a prolonged deadlock in the negotiation process, because the South African government was profoundly angered by a Waldheim-Ahtisaari decision to reject a draft security-transition timetable worked out in Cape Town by two senior generals of the South African Defense Force with the UN's senior military advisor.

Since then two issues have symbolized the stalled negotiations: whether the UN should monitor SWAPO bases in Angola and Zambia, and whether SWAPO should be entitled to military bases within SWA/Namibia after a cease-fire takes effect. The South African government insists that these issues were resolved at earlier stages of negotiation—positively and negatively, respectively. But the U.S government counters that they were not. For the South African government, the UN refusal to accept the negotiated security plan intensified long-held suspicion that UN and Western motives were not to bring about a balanced outcome but rather to optimize SWAPO's chances of success. This suspicion led directly to the South African decision to encourage the DTA in its desire to expand territorial self-government without the prerequisite of a UN-supervised election.

This DTA interest can be understood only in the context of the constituent assembly elections held in December 1978. The South African decision to hold those elections reflected frustration at Western willingness to modify the plan that South Africa had accepted in April 1978. The South African government insisted that this interim step did not rule out a subsequent UN-supervised election for a legislature. Although SWAPO and the NNF parties boycotted the election, the voter turnout was large. The DTA—its campaign heavily financed, probably by the South African government—felt triumphant. But in the first months of 1979, with negotiations stalled and independence receding once again, the DTA worried that it might lose black support unless it could do two things quickly: convince at least some of the parties that had boycotted the election to take an active role in the constituent assembly, and implement some of the antidiscriminatory legislation that had been promised in the DTA electoral campaign.

The DTA was hamstrung in meeting these goals. Its position as a constituent assembly did not permit it to make laws for the territory. Despite the massive powers given the administrator-general, legislative powers had been left to the SWA legislative assembly, a small all-white body dominated by Aktur SWA. Aktur SWA instinctively was resistant to antidiscrimination legislation and delighted in frustrating the DTA. In turn, Mudge pressed the South African government to expand the constituent assembly's role. Finally Pretoria agreed to do so in May 1979. The constituent assembly became a "national assembly." The DTA moved quickly to end discrimination in housing and employment, passing legislation with surprisingly stiff criminal penalties for violations.

Until this step was taken the DTA had been unsuccessful in attracting opposition black parties into the assembly. With the passage of antidiscriminatory legislation and the opportunity to work toward further legislative change, some black leaders found participation increasingly attractive, but eventually rejected it. They argued that such participation would only detract from the necessary UN-supervised election, which they believed would result in a crucial role for their parties after a likely SWAPO-DTA stalemate.

But even if all the other opposition parties did join the national assembly, it seems unlikely that SWAPO's internal wing would ever do so. SWAPO's external wing also remains unalterably opposed to the present political arrangements in the territory. Only a UN-supervised election might elicit the participation of all Namibian political parties, but given the growing mutual distrust and the unwillingness of both the DTA and SWAPO to accept electoral defeat, the prospects for peaceful transition to Namibian independence are dim. Even continued strong pressure from the five Western governments now appears unlikely to break the deadlock.

Despite the revival of Western diplomatic efforts, led by an official of the U.K. government, and the appointment of Professor Gerrit Viljoen, prestigious rector of Rand Afrikaans University and Broederbond chairman, to replace Judge Steyn as administrator-general (both events occurred in August 1979), the most likely prognosis for SWA/Namibia's immediate future is that the sole channel for acceptable political change will be the national assembly, with internal opposition to this framework either ignored or repressed. In reaction to the slow but continual expansion of SWAPO's guerrilla activities, the SADF and the South African Police will take an increasingly central role in the administration of the northern half of the territory.

Notes

1. For a general assessment of the territory's political situation, see Gerhard Tötemeyer, *South West Africa/Namibia: Facts, Attitudes, Assessments, and Prospects* (Randburg, South Africa: Fokus Suid Publishers, 1977). Also, on implementation of separate development after the Odendaal Commission report, see Anthony A. D'Amato, "The Bantustan Proposals for South West Africa," *Journal of Modern African Studies* 4, no. 2 (October 1966), pp. 177–192; and Richard Dale, "Ovamboland: Bantustan Without Tears," *Africa Report* 14, no. 2 (February 1969), pp. 16–23.

2. Peter Fraenkel, *The Namibians of South West Africa* (London: Minority Rights Group, Report no. 19, revised edition, July 1974), pp. 37–39.

3. Charles W. Petersen, "The Military Balance in Southern Africa," pp. 314, 315, in Christian P. Potholm and Richard Dale, eds., *Southern Africa in Perspective* (New York: The Free Press, 1972).

4. J.H.P. Serfontein, *Namibia?* (Randburg, South Africa: Fokus Suid Publishers, 1976), pp. 229–232; also Gerhad Tötemeyer, *Namibia Old and New: Traditional and Modern Leaders in Ovamboland* (London: C. Hurst & Company, 1977).

5. Gerhard Tötemeyer, "The Potential Role of Political Parties in the Political Development of South West Africa," *The South African Journal of African Affairs* 6, nos. 1 and 2 (1976), and his *South West Africa/Namibia: Facts, Attitudes, Assessments, and Prospects,* esp. pp. 57–178.

6. Serfontein, *Namibia?*, p. 204.

7. Ibid., pp. 206–208.

8. Ibid., p. 210.

9. Ibid.

10. "Resolution Unanimously Adopted at the End of a Consultation on the Responsibility of the Churches in the Changing SWA/Namibian Situation," Swakopmund, 4–6 September 1976, mimeod.

11. *The Windhoek Advertiser,* 15 March 1976.

12. C. W. De Kiewiet, "The World and Pretoria," *Africa Report* 14, no. 2 (February 1969), pp. 46–52.

13. For Hilgard Muller's optimistic assessment of the talks, see Republic of South Africa, *House of Assembly Debates,* no. 13, 9 May 1973, column 6090. For an analysis, see Clive Cowley, *The Star* (Johannesburg), 19 July 1973, p. 26.

14. Clive Cowley, *The Star,* 17 September 1974, p. 29; Hans Strydom, *Sunday Times* (Johannesburg), 22 September 1974, p. 3; and *To The Point* (Johannesburg), 4 October 1974, pp. 7, 8.

15. Caroline Clark, *Sunday Times,* 13 October 1974, p. 1; also *Financial Mail*

(Johannesburg), 4 October 1974, pp. 37, 38.

16. Serfontein, *Namibia?,* pp. 232–238; also Tötemeyer, *Namibia Old and New.*

17. John Patten, *The Star,* 7 August 1975.

18. *The Star,* 25 July 1975.

19. John Seiler, "Appraising South African Foreign Policy: The Limited Impact of the 1974 Portuguese Coup on Perspectives and Actions," paper given to the International Studies Association convention, St. Louis, 16–20 March 1977, p. 10; also, Clive Cowley, *The Star,* 26 November 1976, p. 1.

20. *The Star,* weekly airmail edition, 18 June 1977, pp. 8, 9.

21. Ibid., 9 July 1977, p. 1.

22. John F. Burns, "Key Namibian Leader Facing Opposition," *New York Times,* 1 August 1978, p. A5.

23. Tötemeyer, *South West Africa/Namibia: Facts, Attitudes, Assessments, and Prospects,* pp. 61–83, and pp. 301–303.

Part 4

South Africa in the Region

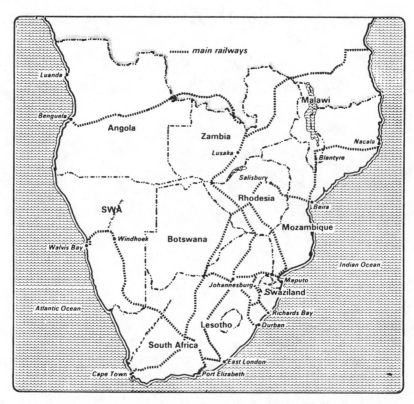

Map 4. Southern African Rail Links. Source: *Financial Mail* (Johannesburg), 10 December 1976, p. 973.

6

South Africa's Regional Role

John Seiler

Introduction and Summary

Until the April 1974 Portuguese coup that brought about the rapid end of Portuguese control in Mozambique and Angola, South Africa dominated the entire Southern African region. South Africa's informal military alliance with Portugal and Rhodesia contained nationalist insurgency throughout the region, with the partial exception of northern Mozambique. Its position as a major producer of minerals demanded by industrial nations gave South Africa both massive income and substantial influence in overseas banking and government circles. South Africa's own growing industrial production ensured its ability to sell many products more cheaply to its regional neighbors than overseas competitors could do, while its position athwart the major regional lines and harbors ensured control of most regional movement of exports and imports. Although very little progress was made in persuading its black neighbors of the virtues of South African domestic racial policies, those neighbors could bring no effective pressure to bear; so there seemed no reason to be concerned by this absence of formal political acceptance. Finally, despite continued international attention since the end of World War II, culminating in the first imposition of economic sanctions against Rhodesia at the end of 1965, international influence on regional events was, in fact, minuscule. Western governments effectively acquiesced in South African regional and domestic policies. The Soviet Union and other communist countries could find no productive way to gain control of the region's fragmented black nationalist movements.

The coup seemed at first to change this overall pattern. The independence of Mozambique and Angola, the bloody Angolan civil war, and the multi-sided intervention in that war caused immediate changes in the nature of regional politics. But, paradoxically, six years after the coup, the preexistent patterns seem more significant than the changes.

South African economic primacy has grown. Although its dependence on black workers from neighboring states has dropped, the dependence of those states on South African transport facilities has grown considerably. The South African Defense Force (SADF) is the strongest military force in the region. No single government in the region, nor all the regional governments combined, could challenge it effectively. Even the residual Cuban forces in Angola are unlikely to cope well with the SADF, unless they are given a massive infusion of Soviet aid. Because of its role in Angola, the SADF feels confident of its ability to deal with any foreseeable regional military challenge, except for direct Soviet military intervention. If that were to occur, the South African government still hopes forlornly for U.S. support. Finally, the South African government believes that pressures for change from the United States and other Western countries have about run their course. Despite the sustained Western effort directed toward change in South West Africa/Namibia, South Africa is now doing essentially what it prefers there, with only minimal acknowledgment of Western interests. Economic sanctions will not be applied against South Africa, and therefore that government is finally free to implement domestic and regional policies in its own best interests.

In short, South Africa dominates the Southern African region and expects to do so for the foreseeable future. Though in the past it seldom focused clearly on regional policy because it was preoccupied with domestic problems and broader international policies, in the present South Africa is disenchanted with the U.S. government and the West in general and is giving extraordinary attention to its role in the region and the manner of fulfilling that role. Despite the continued antipathy among its black neighbors to South African domestic policies, it hopes that practical concern for economic development and social stability will lead them to accept at least tacitly South African involvement in regional economic activities, which might, in time, lead to some sort of loosely structured confederal system for the entire region. This policy is partly naive, partly very clever, and it might succeed, if the pace of domestic change quickens and at the same time moderate black governments become more sensitive to the costs of continued regional unrest for economic development, social stability, and their own survival.

South Africa's Regional Role Before the Coup

It would be an exaggeration to talk of a South African regional policy before 1966, because in practice there was no coherent framework for South African relationships within the region. The South African government was preoccupied with squelching militant black nationalism within the Republic and was essentially defensive in its international posture. But South Africa did have active interests in the region. It was concerned about developments in the Congo and supported Tshombe's Katanga regime.[1] Similarly, it was concerned that the collapse of the Central African Federation (CAF) might lead to regional instability, and once Ian Smith declared UDI for Rhodesia in November 1965 South Africa ensured that petroleum supplies and financial support moved quickly to his new regime.[2] South Africa was also involved in a prolonged case before the International Court of Justice (ICJ) over its mandate in South West Africa, a case that it entered and continued because it believed in the credibility of its legal position.[3] Because of this confidence, South Africa was at first inclined to adopt in 1964 the recommendations for separate development in that territory proposed by the Odendaal Commission, but finally gave in to U.S. demands that implementation await the ICJ ruling.[4]

Before Rhodesian UDI, South Africa had relatively little trade with that territory and inconsequential amounts elsewhere in the region. The flow of black labor from Mozambique, Lesotho, Malawi, Botswana, and Swaziland to the South African mines matched by South African payments directly to the miners and remittances sent through their governments provided the primary regional economic linkage. Rhodesian and South African mineral exports moved through the Mozambican ports of Beira and Lourenco Marques, respectively.

After the ICJ disposed on technical grounds of the Liberian-Ethiopian case against South Africa, that government felt relatively confident and secure for the first time from both domestic and international pressures.[5] Calls for an "outward policy" came first from Piet Cillie, editor of *Die Burger,* and from D. P. de Villiers, head of South Africa's legal team before the ICJ. Both men argued that it was no longer necessary for South Africa to be defensive about domestic policies or its potential role in African development. They believed South Africa should make clear to black Africans its long-term domestic goals and, at the same time, its willingness to help with economic and technical aid for African development.[6]

This policy, sometimes called "dialogue," was tried throughout the regions and elsewhere in Black Africa between 1967 and 1974. While it had some success vis-à-vis the Black African states of the Ivory Coast, Senegal, Kenya, and Gabon—among others—Malawi was its only unequivocal success within the Southern African region. Prime Minister Vorster and President Banda exchanged state visits; South African aid went to build the new Malawian capital, Lilongwe, and an extension of the existent Beira rail link westward to the Zambian border; ambassadors were exchanged (Malawi remains the only Black state to have a resident ambassador in South Africa). Even in this relationship, aloofness and some racism on the part of South African officials detracted from the overall success of South African diplomacy.[7]

The South African government blamed the policy's general failure on political instability in Black Africa, pointing specifically to political coups in Ghana and Malagasy, but of course this interpretation could not explain the resistance of long-term leaders like Kaunda, Nyerere, and Seretse Khama. Initially these men were remarkably conciliatory in their concern for basic change within the Republic. Their attitude characterized the OAU's Lusaka Manifesto in 1969. Regrettably, a stance intended as conciliatory was seen by South Africa as intrusive. Despite this obtuse South African reaction, Kaunda continued to hold secret exchanges with South African representatives on the prospects for regional rapprochement. These contacts were broken off only in 1971 when Vorster angrily revealed their existence during a condemnation of Zambian support for South African and SWA black guerrillas.[8]

Similar secret contacts were made with a number of francophone African governments in 1969, with the help of the French government and Lesotho; but these fell through partly because the National party leadership was concerned that the splinter right-wing party, the HNP (Herstigte Nasionale party) might make an issue of such contacts during the 1970 general election and partly because Vorster seemed to have no great sense of urgency in pursuing them.[9]

South Africa's relations with its nearest black neighbors—Botswana, Lesotho, Swaziland (BLS)—reveal most vividly the limits of the outward policy. Although South Africans believed these relations were prototypes for wider regional economic ties, in fact they began on a bad footing with the initiation of a Southern African Customs Union in which the BLS governments were given disadvantageous terms.[10] The 1969 renegotiation of the customs agreement offset this bad start, but throughout this period South Africa intervened in a hamhanded way in the political and economic affairs of these governments. In reaction, as early as 1973 all three countries were making determined (although only marginally successful) efforts to move away from economic dependence on South Africa.[11]

Despite this basic political failure, South African economic preponderance grew. After UDI South Africa became the principal intermediary for Rhodesian exports and imports (although much traffic moved through Mozambique) and the principal source of Rhodesian investment capital and public financial aid. Because neither the United States nor the United Kingdom had compensated Zambia for the economic disruption caused it by its adherence to sanctions against Rhodesia, that country became increasingly dependent on South African transit routes for its imports and exports. In fact, until Rhodesia closed the Zambian border in January 1973, as a reprisal for guerrilla raids across the Zambesi, Zambian traffic moved through Rhodesia en route to and from South Africa. After that date it moved by ferry across the Zambesi onto a rough Botswana road that connected at Francistown, Botswana, with the Rhodesian-owned railway. To compound the ironic dependence, in the 1970s when the Botswana road was paved to facilitate Zambian traffic the equipment required was brought in from South African harbors, first on the South African railway and then on the Rhodesian-owned line in Botswana—with the approval of the UN committee overseeing Rhodesian sanctions![12]

Guerrilla challenges to South African forces were few and were met with success. In 1966 guerrillas entered Rhodesia, ostensibly en route to South Africa, and at about the same time SWAPO guerrillas entered South West Africa at the Caprivi strip. Almost all were caught, and in reaction South African Police (SAP) units were assigned to active duty at the Zambesi border between Rhodesia and Zambia beginning in 1967. When Zimbabwean guerrillas began infiltrating Rhodesia in force in late 1972, the SAP units were drawn into the campaign against them. In South West Africa, no more guerrilla attacks occurred until 1975. The only other substantial South African involvement was in Mozambique, where police (and possibly army) units were stationed in a defensive perimeter at the Cabora Bassa hydroelectric power project on the Zambesi river.

The Immediate Impact of the Coup

The South African government responded with remarkable confidence to the April 1974 Portuguese coup and its immediate aftermath. An early indication of this attitude came in September 1974 when Vorster, Defense Minister P. W. Botha, and Foreign Minister Hilgard Muller warned against any private South African support for right-wing whites in Mozambique. Botha said bluntly, "We do not believe it is in the interests of the Republic to interfere in the affairs of other countries, because we do not want other countries to poke their noses into our affairs."[13] Muller was more flowery: "[Frelimo's rise to power was] a challenge and not a disaster or a threat. It should rather be seen as an opportunity for us to prove further that we, as is the position in the case of our other neighboring states, are prepared to and can live and work together with these neighbors in peace and friendship, irrespective of who is in power."[14]

This "live and let live" atittude had often been expressed in South African political rhetoric, but it was nonetheless surprising to see it applied vis-à-vis a radical neighbor. In the case of Mozambique, the approach proved remarkably successful, essentially because mutual dependence outweighed longer-term ideological antipathies.[15]

South African confidence that the coup provided a compelling opportunity to achieve regional stability led to renewed secret consultations with the Zambian government. Although Rhodesian political progress was the explicit focus of these talks, Zambia was obviously also motivated to improve its awkward economic situation. At first the two parties achieved considerable agreement, and secret talks were capped by conciliatory speeches given by Kaunda and Vorster in October 1974.[16]

But neither government was capable of controlling the actions of its respective "client." South Africa, for example, was chagrined when Ian Smith returned Ndabaningi Sithole to detention. Zambia had no more success in getting Zimbabwean nationalist leaders to act in consort. However, on balance, South Africa put too much blame on the nationalists and too little on Smith for their joint failure to achieve a negotiated settlement.[17]

The SADF Angolan Intervention
and Its Immediate Aftermath

It is still not altogether clear what combination of entreaties and assurances led the South African government to intervene in Angola starting in August 1975, but enough evidence exists to sketch a plausible pattern.[18] First, South Africa was concerned about the physical survival and the utility of the massive Cunene River hydroelectric project (most of which was on the Angolan side of the border with South West Africa), which South Africa was underwriting in order to provide SWA with assured electric power and water for agricultural irrigation. South Africa's first venture across the border in early August was to protect the project against attack or unpremeditated damage. Then, in late August, a 1,000-man motorized column moved somewhat further into southeastern Angola, where it apparently stayed for some time. Only in mid-October did a motorized attack column, called "Zulu"—made up of Unita troops and some white Portuguese with at first only seven South African officers and enlisted men—begin to advance rapidly through south and central Angola. Artillery, air cover, and logistical support were gradually increased, but even at the end of the South African operation in late January, when the SADF pulled back to points just north of the SWA border, no more than 2,000 troops were in Angola.

What prompted this SADF commitment? Why did it take the erratic course that it did? What led to the precipitous withdrawal, at a time when SADF units were at least holding their own against reinforced MPLA and Cuban troops?

Two very different kinds of encouragement prompted involvement. First, both Zambia and Zaire asked the South African government to intervene against the MPLA. While Zambian and Zairian concern over a radical Angolan government controlling access to the Benguela railway and serving as a base for attacks on their own territory was understandable, there are not yet any signs that they thought through carefully either the basic strategy of intervention or its probable political consequences. At about the same time, the U.S. government, long committed to the FNLA, increased its covert FNLA support and then, in July 1975, decided to support Unita as well. It was logical at that point to elicit South African involvement. How this was done and with what degree of authority remain unknown, but the postintervention bitterness on the part of the South African government strongly suggests that the U.S. invitation was portrayed as authoritative and was taken as such by the South Africans.[19]

Despite its deeply held convictions about communist aims for domination of Southern Africa, and its genuine concern about the Soviet-Cuban presence in Angola, the South African government would not have entered Angola without these two demonstrations of interest and apparent support.

The resultant political failure came not so much from the original limited intervention, nor even from the first modest expansion into southeastern Angola, but from the conspicuous role the SADF took in the subsequent sweep north to the outskirts of Luanda. At first it seemed that the South African goal was to secure southern Angola for Unita. Once Unita achieved political/administrative control there, it could return to interparty negotiations from a stronger base. After independence in November 1975, when it became apparent that the Portuguese departure left the MPLA with effective legitimacy through its control of Luanda, South African strategy changed. Luanda became the primary target. Even if the dual attack on Luanda had succeeded, with the FNLA entering the city from the north and the SADF-Unita column from the south, it is not clear what the SADF proposed to do if the by-then massively reinforced MPLA-Cuban troops had counterattacked. South African supply lines were impracticably overextended and its artillery and air force were not ready for such a pitched battle.[20]

The December 1975 U.S. Senate decision to halt further covert aid to the FNLA and Unita marked the turning point for the South African intervention. Although the SADF retrospectively argued that a total victory in Angola would have been achieved very quickly if the U.S. "betrayal" had not occurred,[21] the U.S. decision is more reasonably viewed as a saving one for the SADF and the South African government.

In strategic terms alone, South Africa emerged from Angola with considerable gains. The MPLA did not gain a total victory. Four years later the Benguela railway remained closed to general traffic because of continuing Unita harassment, and it seems likely that the MPLA has a tenuous hold over southern Angola—outside the major towns. The SADF soundly defeated Cuban forces in their few direct encounters, and left Angola reassured of the competence of its citizen soldiers and ready to make changes in operations, logistics, equipment, and training to improve SADF performance.[22] Its residual role in northern SWA was expanded and made more effective, so that after Angola it was more difficult for SWAPO to enter that territory than it had been before the SADF intervention.

In political terms, the intervention seemed a total calamity, but even that judgment now looks overstated. The 22–22 split vote on the South African intervention at the January 1976 OAU meeting made clear that half the membership deplored other extra-African intervention at least as much. Zambia and Zaire were profoundly embarrassed by press reports of their request for South African intervention, and to assuage their embarrassment and restore their lost standing have made no further public efforts at political accommodation with South Africa. Despite this, both maintain contact with South Africa and have taken steps to ease their economic problems through greater use of South African facilities.

From the South African point of view, the central political lesson was a constructive one: the U.S. government in particular, and the West in general, could no longer be trusted to take South African interests into account. Henceforth, the South African government would calculate its own best interests in all policy situations, whether within the Republic, in Southern Africa, or elsewhere in the world, without worrying overmuch about Western views and possible reactions.

The Present Pattern of South Africa's Regional Relations and Policy

The Economic Dimension

There is an ironic aspect to the present economic relationship between South Africa and its regional neighbors. While South Africa has become markedly less dependent on them for unskilled mine labor—for many their most valuable export to South Africa—they have become more dependent on South African harbors and railways for both imports and exports. This shift has taken place in the context of a prolonged international recession, coupled with inflationary price increases for petroleum products, which has reduced the ability of non-African governments to give additional aid to black regional governments either bilaterally or through UN agencies.

The overall increase in dependence on South Africa is made apparent when the two issues—labor utilization and use of South African transit facilities—are examined, because it becomes clear that each issue has an adverse effect on a different set of regional black governments. The reduction in South African use of foreign black labor especially affects Malawi, Mozambique, Lesotho, and Botswana, while the major regional producers of minerals—Zaire, Zambia, and Zimbabwe Rhodesia—all make increasing use of South African harbors and railways. Only Angola is essentially unaffected.

South Africa's reduced use of regional black labor came about accidentally, although it is now occasionally rationalized as a logical step in the modernization of South African mining.[23] In fact, it began with Malawi's abrupt decision to withdraw all its laborers after 74 men were killed in a plane crash near Francistown in 1974. In 1973 Malawi had contributed 130,000 of the 400,000 regional workers imported into South Africa. That number fell off sharply for the next few years, although it rose again in 1978 to a level of 15,000 to 20,000.[24] After Mozambican independence, that country's contribution to the labor force in South African mines fell from more than 140,000 to 38,000 in April 1977. The number dropped even further in 1978.[25] At the same time, pay in the gold mines was sharply increased. As a result, black South Africans, especially from rural homelands, found mining employment as attractive as industrial work. The foreign workers were easily replaced by the available South Africans, and the proportion of foreign workers in South African mines fell from 81 percent in October 1973 to 48 percent in April 1977.[26]

The economic impact on Malawi, Mozambique, and Lesotho was somewhat cushioned by the higher wages, which resulted in higher remittances per worker. For Malawi, at least, it appears that many of the men formerly employed in South African mines were absorbed into productive agricultural work.[27] It remains more difficult to generate such alternative employment in Lesotho. Mozambique's situation was further complicated by an additional loss of jobs and revenue from transit when it closed its border with Rhodesia in March 1976, and it was hurt severely when South Africa decided unilaterally after 1977 to revalue the gold that it gave Mozambique in lieu of miners' deferred wages at the current market price, rather than at the official price of $46 per ounce.[28]

For the mineral-producing countries, dependence takes a different form. Because the Benguela railway remains unusable and the Tanzara railway cannot handle the copper tonnage produced by Zaire and Zambia, those two countries have no choice but to ship their exports via Zimbabwe Rhodesia and South Africa. Kenneth Kaunda openly conceded this necessity in October 1978, when he announced that Zambia would use the Rhodesian rail system but only to export copper and import urgently needed fertilizer.[29] Zaire, on the other hand, while pursuing a similar course, refuses to publicly acknowledge that it is doing so.[30] Zimbabwe Rhodesia has a more complex relationship with South Africa. At various points in 1975 and 1976, the Smith government was threatened with a cut-off of access to South African harbors and railways if the government failed to take sufficient political initiative in ongoing negotiations. While a resumption of that threat is unlikely now that South Africa stands apart from U.S. and U.K. regional policies, it is conceivable that the Republic might be tempted to forge greater ties with the Thatcher government in the United Kingdom or with a Republican president in the United States at the cost of pressing Muzorewa to make political changes both those Western governments find necessary.

An entirely different kind of relationship exists between South Africa and Mozambique involving a more balanced mutual dependence. Mozambique receives a large income from the transit of South African mineral exports. That income is practically irreplaceable. South Africa could ship Transvaal-mined raw materials from Natal or Eastern Cape ports (Richards Bay, Durban, East London, or Port Elizabeth), but the distances are greater and the costs higher. For South Africa, the working relationship between the South African railway system and the Mozambican rail and harbor authority is an exact model of relationships it would like throughout the region. South Africa extends considerable technical aid, equipment, and some economic aid to the Mozambicans. The relationship is amicable. In an agreement re-negotiated in early 1979 both governments aim to double the volume of South African freight traffic on the Mozambican system.[31] The Mozambican authority is so pleased by the arrangement that it has repeatedly taken ads in South African financial journals encouraging use of its facilities.[32]

The emphasis here on continuing economic dependence is not intended to obscure the fact that the longer-term aim of all regional black governments is to reduce dependence on South Africa as much as possible. The problem remains that alternatives to dependence cost money and the amount required can be enormous. The construction of new rail lines, harbors, and international airports is very expensive. Development aid from international agencies and non-African governments helps reduce dependence, but most often cannot match the sums available from mine workers' wages, South African tourists' payments (especially for gambling), and private investment by South African corporations. Lesotho is a case in point. Despite receiving the most aid per capita of any country in Africa, it cannot relinquish the income available to it from its mine workers, South African visitors, or South African investors. For example, the De Beers Consolidated Mines diamond mine at Letseng-la-Terai represents a two million rand investment providing employment for seven hundred Basothos. Under-standably, the Lesotho government seeks to reduce dependence by focusing efforts on adding alternative income sources—rather than cutting off the South African ones—and on such symbolic steps as the recent establishment of its own currency and its possible departure from the rand monetary system.[33]

The Military Dimension

Intervention in Angola was a crucial experience for the South African Defense Force. Except for the involvement of some air force units in the UN

Korean force, it was the SADF's first fighting experience since World War II. Admittedly, the nature of the intervention was atypical of SADF planning. Most of the men were young national servicemen who happened to be on active duty at the time, whose utilization could be managed with minimal risk of public attention to the high-security operation. The total manpower involved was very small. Little artillery or air support was provided. Nonetheless, the SADF learned a good deal about the readiness of national servicemen (who, in any case, make up the bulk of available manpower); about the variety of logistical problems associated with launching a preemptive strike force deep in an unfriendly neighboring state; and about the limited competence of the MPLA and even of the Cubans to react to this force. The Angolan intervention represented the first test of the SADF's central commitment to landward defense. Although the SADF was generally pleased with its performance, it has since moved to make a number of improvements.[34]

Since Angola, manpower and training have become basic preoccupations. Historically, the SADF has had a very small permanent force (PF), which now numbers less than five percent of the total SADF manpower on active duty at any given time. While it might want to expand that proportion, in practice the SADF finds it difficult to keep the permanent force staff it now has. The average term of service in the PF is only six to seven years. Apparently, servicemen and officers with technical and managerial skills are attracted by higher industrial pay. The SADF has yet to devise a scheme of pay, professional development, and pension attractive enough to retain a larger portion of the PF for a longer time.[35]

The small size of the PF means that short-term national servicemen (serving two years active duty, of which the first year or so is taken up with training) must fill many important staff positions. It also means that the SADF lacks the capability to put together an effective strike force, of a high standard of competence, that would be used to deal with preemptive and reactive raids in the regions—the central task of the SADF for the foreseeable future, until such time as guerrillas are able to raise and sustain conventional attacks on either South West Africa/Namibia or the Republic. Because the SADF has said nothing about such a strike force, it would be risky to make any assumptions about its prospects. The SADF may feel that its national servicemen were so effective in Angola that a professional strike force is not required. On the other hand, it is possible that recent pay and benefit improvements for the permanent force augur the early development of a strike force.[36]

Considerable attention has been paid to training Coloureds, Indians, and Africans for the SADF. They serve in distinct, segregated units, almost always with white officers (although there are a number of black noncommissioned officers who presumably in time will be promoted), but do get the same pay and in operational situations share the same facilities with white units. Within South West Africa/Namibia, the black units now on active duty are intended to serve as the nucleus of a postindependence army, modeled on the SADF and with continued ties to the SADF.[37]

During 1978 and 1979 important changes were made in SADF equipment, reflecting lessons learned in Angola. The army will have a new lightweight rifle and a highly mobile, longer-range 155mm artillery piece, although it still has no modern tanks.[38] After the French broke their contract to build frigates and two submarines for the South African navy, a swift reassessment of naval strategy led to the conclusion that South Africa should not try to defend the Cape sea route for Western shipping but should confine its naval role to protection of its own harbors and coastline. In response to this change in strategy, patrol craft are now being produced in South Africa and marines will be assigned to harbor protection duties.[39] On the landward side, the defensive perimeter already established along the border with Mozambique (double fences, plowed intervals) has been extended to include the entire border with Zimbabwe Rhodesia and a large portion of the border with Botswana. In addition, fortified keeps are being set up, exservicemen encouraged to farm on the border, and a military communication network expanded to include farmers.[40]

All these developments make South Africa remarkably capable of withstanding any forseeable military challenges emanating from within the region for the indefinite future. In this context, whether or not the South African government has nuclear weapons is almost irrelevant. Given the preponderance of military power in its favor and the paucity of regional targets suitable for even small nuclear weapons, the possibility of possession (and the ambiguity surrounding it) may serve as sufficient deterrent against regional military attacks.[41]

Although circumstances may change, the key to the SADF role in the region is its unswerving loyalty to Afrikaner nationalism. The SADF is especially close to the present government because P. W. Botha served twelve years as minister of defense, but it is likely to serve any nationalist prime minister with equal loyalty. There are no divisions in the SADF like the class or rank divisions that have led to coups by other armies, nor is there the self-image of holding a special constitutional responsibility. That role lies with the National party, and so long as the government manages to hold that party together reasonably well, there is little chance of the SADF's acting independently of its political masters.

The Political Dimension

As an indirect outgrowth of the Angolan intervention, the P.W. Botha government has committed itself to a series of structural changes intended to facilitate overall policymaking—not just for defense and security matters. It approaches this task firmly convinced that South Africa faces a total onslaught alone and that its very survival rests on more effective governance.[42] Its domestic policies, especially those dealing with black labor and with urban blacks generally, reflect this concern. Some of the policy changes, however modest, may expand black support within South Africa.[43] In turn, such increased support might make it easier for regional neighbors to accept a South African political system moving ultimately toward some sort of confederation or even federation.

For the region itself, the present South African government has not yet worked out any substantial policies, but its rhetoric has taken on a new tone. Added to the traditional talk of the important South African contribution to the development of the region, if only ideological differences could be put aside, is a new emphasis both on South African self-reliance and on regional cooperation in the face of a threatening world.[44] It is hard to see regional black governments sharing this political assessment, but what seems sure is that the P. W. Botha government, unlike the Vorster government before it, is determined to work out the implications of its regional perspective.

Notes

1. Newell M. Stultz, "The Politics of Security: South Africa under Verwoerd, 1961-1966," *Journal of Modern African Studies* (hereafter *JMAS*) 7, no. 1 (April 1969), pp. 3-20; and James Barber, *South Africa's Foreign Policy, 1945-1970* (London: Oxford University Press, 1973), p. 162.

2. Robert C. Good, *UDI: The International Politics of the Rhodesian Rebellion* (Princeton, N.J.: Princeton University Press, 1973), esp. pp. 126-132.

3. John Dugard, *The South West Africa/Namibia Dispute* (Berkeley and Los Angeles: University of California Press, 1973).

4. Anthony A. D'Amato, "The Bantustan Proposals for South West Africa," *JMAS* 4, no. 2 (October 1966), pp. 177-192; and Richard Dale, "Ovamboland: Bantustan without Tears," *Africa Report* (hereafter *AR*) 14, no. 2 (February 1969), pp. 16-23.

5. C. W. de Kiewiet, "The World and Pretoria," *AR* 14, no. 2 (February 1969), pp. 46-52; and John Seiler, "South African Perspectives and Responses to External Pressures," *JMAS* 13, no. 3 (September 1975), pp. 447-468.

6. John Barratt, "South Africa's Outward Policy: From Isolation to Dialogue," in Nic Rhoodie, ed., *South African Dialogue* (Johannesburg: Macmillan, 1972), pp. 543-561; John Barratt, "South Africa's Outward Movement," *Modern Age* (Chicago) 14, no. 2 (Spring 1970), pp. 129-139; and Edmond A. Marco, "Dialogue in Africa," *Optima* (Johannesburg) 21, no. 3 (September 1971), pp. 106-117.

7. Edwin S. Munger, "New White Politics in South Africa," in William A. Hance,

ed., *Southern Africa and the United States* (New York: Columbia University Press, 1968), pp. 66, 67; also Edwin S. Munger "Die Afrikaner Soos Gesien in Die Buiteland"[Foreign views of the Afrikaner]. Centre for Intergroup Studies, University of Cape Town, March 1974; and Jim Hoagland, *Washington Post,* 21 August 1971.

8. John Barratt, "South Africa's Outward Policy," pp. 558, 559.

9. Confidential interviews, Johannesburg and Pretoria, 1972–1976.

10. P. M. Landell-Mills, "The 1969 Southern African Customs Union Agreement," *JMAS* 9, no. 2 (August 1971), pp. 263–281.

11. Seiler, "South African Perspectives and Responses to External Pressures," p. 457; D. J. Geldenhuys, "Lesotho en Suid Afrika—'n studie in waagpolitiek" [Lesotho and South Africa: a study in political brinkmanship], *Politikon* (Pretoria) 1, no. 1 (June 1974), pp. 28–43; and "Southern Africa: Weakening Links," *Financial Mail* (Johannesburg), 22 June 1973, pp. 1109, 1110.

12. Confidential interview, 1974.

13. Republic of South Africa, *House of Assembly Debates,* no. 6, 9 September 1974, column 2537.

14. Ibid., 10 September 1974, col. 2590.

15. See Keith Middlemas, Chap. 13 in this book.

16. Seiler, "South African Perspectives and Responses to External Pressures," pp. 462–465; and Colin Legum, *Southern Africa: The Secret Diplomacy of Detente* (London: Rex Collings, 1975).

17. See C.M.B. Utete, Chap. 4 in this book.

18. The most rewarding analysis is Robin Hallett, "The South African Intervention in Angola, 1975–1976," *African Affairs* (London) 77, no. 308 (July 1978), pp. 347–386.

19. John Stockwell, *In Search of Enemies: A CIA Story* (New York: W. W. Norton & Company, 1978); confidential interviews, Cape Town and Pretoria, January–April 1979.

20. Hallett, "The South African Intervention in Angola"; Willem Steenkamp, *Adeus Angola* (Cape Town: Howard Timmins, 1976); "South Africa's Lightning War in Angola," *Rand Daily Mail* (Johannesburg), 4 February 1977; Republic of South Africa, Department of Defence, *White Paper on Defence 1977;* confidential interviews, Pretoria, 1979.

21. "South Africa's Lightning War in Angola."

22. *White Paper on Defence 1977.*

23. W. J. de Villiers, "Interdependence in Mining and Labour," paper to ninth international economics congress of the International Association of Economics and Commerce Students, Pretoria, p. 6.

24. Siegfried Hannig, "The Changing Face of South African Mine Labor," *The Bulletin* (Africa Institute of South Africa), no. 5 (1975), p. 185. The 1978 figure is an estimate drawn from the total of deferred payments and remittances for Malawian miners during that year— 10,600,374 rand. (*South African Digest* [Pretoria: South African Information Service], 15 June 1979, p. 18.—quoting *December Report,* Chamber of Mines review for 1978.)

25. A similar estimation based on 1978 payment of 24,374,364 rand; also see *Financial Mail,* 10 June 1977, p. 871.

26. *South African Digest,* 23 February 1979, p. 17 — quoting *Standard Bank Review;* and G.M.E. Leistner, "Economic Interdependence in Southern Africa," *The Bulletin* (Africa Institute of South Africa), nos. 9 and 10 (1978), pp. 311–317.

27. "Malawi: Model of Development," *The Bulletin,* no. 1 (1979), pp. 5–16.

28. *Sunday Times* (Johannesburg), 20 February 1977; also Chap. 13 by Keith Middlemas in this book.

29. For the decision to reopen the rail link, see *Financial Mail* — 27 October 1978, p. 309; 3 November 1978, p. 407; 1 December 1978, p. 803; and 22 December 1978, p. 1033. For Zambian interest in reopening road ties, see *Financial Mail* — 1 June 1979, pp. 760, 762; 8 June 1979, p. 863; 22 June 1979, pp. 1060, 1061; and 29 June 1979, p. 1148.

30. A public address by the Zairian foreign minister, Center for Strategic and International Studies, Georgetown University, Washington, D.C., October 1978.

31. *South African Digest,* 2 March 1979, p. 7; *The Star,* international airmail weekly edition, 3 March 1979, p. 3.

32. *The Star,* weekly edition, 12 May 1979, p. 17; *Financial Mail* — 18 May 1979, p. 571; 8 June 1979, p. 851; 29 June 1979, p. 1139.

33. *Financial Mail,* 11 May 1979, pp. 478, 479.

34. *White Paper on Defence 1977.*

35. *Financial Mail,* 1 June 1979, pp. 758, 759.

36. Ibid.

37. *The Star,* weekly edition, 12 May 1979, p. 9; and Harvey Tyson, *The Star,* weekly edition, 2 June 1979, p. 11.

38. *The Star,* weekly edition, 28 April 1979, p. 7, and 12 May 1979, p. 9.

39. *The Star,* weekly edition, 28 April 1979, p. 7.

40. Republic of South Africa, *House of Assembly Debates,* no. 8, 29 March 1978, col. 3462; *Sunday Times,* 21 January 1979, p. 4; *Rand Daily Mail,* 3 March 1979, p. 5; *Financial Mail,* 11 May 1979, pp. 493, 496; confidential interviews, Pretoria and Johannesburg, March 1979.

41. *Financial Mail,* 10 November 1978, pp. 500, 501.

42. *The Star,* weekly edition, 12 May 1979, p. 4; also John Seiler, "South Africa: One Government Against the World," *Africa Report* 24, no. 5 (September-October 1979), pp. 9–15.

43. For the evolution of South African domestic policy under the P. W. Botha government, see *Financial Mail* — 24 November 1978, p. 703; 13 April 1979, pp. 117, 118; 4 May 1979, pp. 389–391; 11 May 1979, pp. 475–477; 18 May 1979, pp. 567, 568; and 25 May 1979, p. 674.

44. Republic of South Africa, Department of Defence, *White Paper on Defence and Armaments Supply 1979;* also *The Star,* weekly edition, 10 March 1979, p. 3; and *Financial Mail,* 13 April 1979, pp. 123, 124; 20 April 1979, p. 197; and 4 May 1979, pp. 394, 397.

Part 5

The Widening Conflict Within South Africa

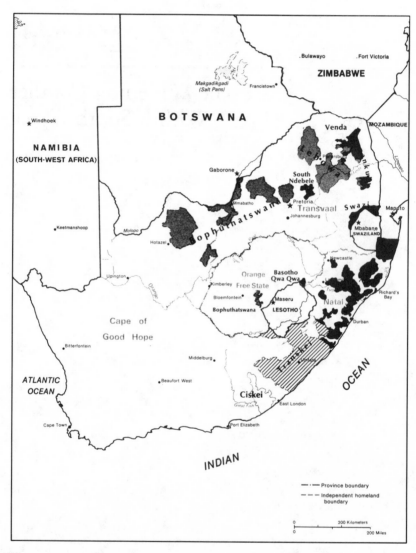

Map 5. South Africa with Homelands. Source: The Africa Institute of South Africa, from *Bulletin* 19, no. 5, 1979, pp. 4 and 5.

7

Afrikaner Nationalist Perspectives About Change in South African Domestic Policies

Mary Simons

The 1974 Portugese coup presented a stark challenge to the maintenance of the present policies of apartheid practiced by the South African government and to the continued political-economic domination of the society by Afrikaner Nationalists. The South African government understood this challenge. Its foreign policy responses, under the general rubric of "détente," are sketched out in other chapters in this book. This chapter examines the underlying motivation for that foreign policy response and the extent to which immediate domestic policies and longer-term goals for South African society were modified by the awareness of enlarged external pressure.

The 24 April 1974 general election (held one day before the Portuguese coup) was fought by the National party (NP) on the basis of white identity and white unity. Reconciliation between Afrikaner and English was seen as a prerequisite to the implementation of the next stage in white-black relations—"the emergence of a meaningful partnership with the black man."[1] This reconciliation could be achieved only by voter acceptance of the National party policy of separate development: "A vote for the National Party is no vote for an Afrikaner ideology, but for the only realistic policy in Africa. This National Party formula of separate development is much aligned to the English values of democracy, freedom, justice, and equality, as well as their living patterns."[2]

The overwhelming NP electoral victory, coupled with the Portuguese

Ms. Simons was placed under a five-year banning order by the South African government in November 1976. That order forbade, among other things, her publishing or contributing to a publication, whether within or outside South Africa. She had already completed a revised version of this chapter when the banning order took effect. The editor made some minor changes and takes full responsibility for all references to events occurring after November 1976.

coup, led the Afrikaans-language press to plead for acceleration of a two-prong policy: defense against guerrilla attack and full implementation of separate development, with the rapid removal of "bottlenecks" that caused group conflict and were unnecessary to policy implementation. Otherwise, the imminent presence of black governments in Angola and Mozambique "could have a particular effect on the Coloured and black people of this country who would naturally be inclined to identify themselves with those who achieved power in the Portuguese territories."[3]

Most whites believed that South Africa's "détente" policy would in itself ensure the continuation of their "traditional" way of life with at most only minor adjustments. Prime Minister John Vorster echoed this complacency in May 1975, assessing with satisfaction the results of "détente" to that date:

> I do not know what the future holds but I do know that today, six months after I put my political career at stake, the world accepts that we are as much part of Africa as any other people in Africa. . . . It is accepted that we have as much right to be in Africa as any other nation in Africa; that this is our land of birth and where our graves will be marked.[4]

The Afrikaans press ironically led white opinion with repeated demands for substantial changes within the framework of separate development. But from the very beginning of the debate among Afrikaner Nationalists, there was confusion and even open conflict (still a rarity in Afrikaner discussion of policy issues) about the implications of the general goal. For instance, did the 1974 renewal of strikes by Durban's black textile workers argue for the desirability of legal recognition for black trade unions? Did the Johannesburg City Council (then dominated by the opposition United party with a strong Progressive party element) remove a "bottleneck" in race relations by ending segregated library, park, and other public facilities (not including swimming pools, public toilets, or schools), or was the initiative a step toward integration and therefore an effort to reverse the proper course of separate development? In general, which changes were constructive, which changes were at least acceptable, and which were destructive of the underlying policy?

What Is Meant by Change?

However academic it might seem on the surface, we should define what is meant by change. Here, three variant definitions used in the analysis of South African society require delineation. First, as suggested by the Afrikaner Nationalist press, change may be directed at a fuller implementation of the existent policy of separate development. Second, change may involve the goal of an open society achieved peaceably, a society in which the private economic sector would have a decisive role and in which individuals could compete for jobs, social status, and political influence without confinement to racially defined groups. Proponents of this view hope for an ameliorative incremental impact on present social structures coming especially from economic forces — especially those typified by major corporations engaged in consumer-based industrial activities.[5] The third definition of change argues that such amelioration (or liberalization) is not feasible (some argue not desirable) in South Africa, because of the near-universal white (English-speaking as well as Afrikaner) resistance to any change that diminishes their dominant economic and political status. Proponents of this view demand radical transformation of all social structures and institutions, especially the economic ones.[6]

While the liberal analysts agree with the radicals that South African economic growth has so far only strengthened white supremacy, they see signs of change, including: (a) a shift of resources to blacks; (b) an increase in black political-economic bargaining power; and (c) desirable changes in the attitudes and norms of whites toward blacks and hence in the status of blacks.[7] Both liberals and radicals agree that any meaningful change would require the incorporation of blacks into the country's decision-making processes and the redistribution of economic resources. Since these goals cannot be met without a drastic reshaping of the present policy and structure of separate development, the crucial question is how committed are the South African government and Afrikaner Nationalists generally to that policy and to the preservation of an exclusive white identity (in which Afrikaners would lead and, to a considerable extent, dominate English speakers)? Are the constraints on basic change imposed by racialism, by the Afrikaner Nationalist ideology, by the economic structure and economic imperatives, or by some intricate interaction of all three?

The liberal analysts argue that continued industrialization is basically incompatible with separate development. Industrialists will demand an efficient use of labor resources, without regard to racial constraints, and a profitable access to the largest possible market, including the black one. English-speaking industrialists could be dismissed as naive about, or even as enemies of, Afrikaner survival when they criticized government policy, but when well-placed Afrikaner Nationalist industrialists begin to do so, it is a very different matter. In its effort to respond to such internal critics, the National party is already adjusting its definition of separate development. In time, the NP will concede that the pressures are too strong to contain within the confines of a political party based essentially on preservation of Afrikaner identity: "These cleavages within white South Africa may well form the basis for new alliances across the color line, which could still ensure a relatively evolutionary and peaceful change in place of the often predicted confrontation."[8]

Liberals argue further that racialism (mainifested in discriminatory practices and legislation) has outlived its utility for whites. Having achieved their dominant position in society, whites may now securely make political concessions to blacks—incorporate them into the overall political structure—without risking the loss of white economic dominance. The more naive liberals even see some chance of nonracism being accepted by whites.[9]

But few whites want to do more than remove the most obvious kinds of public injustices, which have minimal effect on their own underlying political-economic dominance and social distance from blacks. Opening the Johannesburg Public Library reference room to black students and the Nico Malan theater in Cape Town to a few affluent blacks and Coloureds may represent the outer limit of white desire for ending racially determined practices. And, in any case, the government has made altogether clear since it came to power in 1948 that it will not tolerate any efforts to carry on nonracial practices, however trivial their impact on the structure of separate development may seem.

While it is practically impossible to disassemble the elements of racial superiority, economic and political self-interest, and genuine religious-ideological commitment that together make up the driving force of Afrikaner Nationalism in power, it is constructive to examine the two somewhat divergent directions between which Afrikaner Nationalism has always vacillated—segregation and separation. To some extent, which of the two an Afrikaner chooses reflects a greater weight either for racism and self-interest in some combination (segregation) or for a religious-ideological impulse (separation).[10]

The National party, on coming to power in 1948, codified longstanding segregation practices and introduced the first elements of separation in its domestic policies. This involved a measure of social and cultural separation between Afrikaners and English-speaking whites, but the tendency toward full separation involving autonomous institutions never overcame the desire to control. Thus, dual school systems were set up (making functional bilingualism more difficult), but an Afrikaner-dominated bureaucracy kept administrative control of both systems.

The separationist impulse vis-à-vis blacks was always stronger, undoubtedly because blacks posed a greater challenge to Afrikaner domination than did English-speaking whites. A separationist ideology was first articulated after Union in 1910 by groups within the South African Labor party. It was formulated as a policy in the 1940s by the Rasserverhoudingsbond Vir Rassestudie and was subsequently adopted by its lineal descendant, the South African Bureau for Racial Affairs (SABRA—not to be con-

·fused with the liberal South African Institute of Race Relations).[11] In May 1974 Dr. C. J. Jooste, then SABRA chairman, called for effective separation of the races to ensure that Afrikaners kept exclusive control of their country. Echoing long-held government reservations about separation, W. A. de Klerk, the influential editor of *Die Transvaler*, rejected this "extremist view" and stated that "separate yet connected is the complete concept. . . . We have established separation and it is accepted by all. We must now establish association and this must be done without diluting or endangering separateness. The pair—separation and association—is the only acceptable and practicable answer in principle."[12]

By the end of 1976, the concern of the Afrikaans press and Afrikaner intellectuals about the prospects of unchanged government policy for ensuring a peaceful, stable future had increased. Demands for separation—usually called partition—received more attention. For example, the 1976 SABRA conference called for the consolidation of the nine existent fragmented homelands into four coherent political entities and the parallel establishment of a black city-state centered on Soweto. The Afrikaans press gave this proposal some support:

> [It] would amount to the partitioning of South Africa—a drastic step—but one that could become necessary for white survival, bearing in mind population projections, the proportions of which are less and less favorable. However, the consolidation plan will not only entail unknown sacrifice, land transfers, and the moving of people, but in our opinion would not be politically feasible. Consolidation could be intensified, but we want to predict that it should rather be done according to a pattern of incorporating white towns and communities in greater homelands, with the necessary guarantees to whites as the West is prepared to offer white Rhodesians—a plan endorsed by South Africa.[13]

In passing, it is ironic that the Afrikaans press should be so concerned about the impact of partition on whites when it had almost never shown similar concern about the known and visible sacrifices of millions of blacks moved under the terms of the Group Areas Act (no. 41 of 1950 and no. 77 of 1957 as amended) to implement homelands policy and the removal of "black spots" of black settlement in "white" parts of South Africa.

During 1977, discussion of possible partition plans continued in the Afrikaans press and among Afrikaner academicians and was even referred to obliquely by a cabinet member, Dr. Piet Koornhof, minister of national education and of sport and recreation.[14] Official policy remained wedded to an ambiguous combination of separation and "association," which was slowly being elaborated, while official rhetoric had moved far more drastically from the "apartheid" of the 1950s to the "separate development" of the

1960s to "plural democracy" in the 1970s: "South Africa's policy is aimed at plural democracy. The government believes in separate identities. It also understands separate nationalisms and is granting separate parliaments to other race groups so that they can determine their own destinies, but it will not allow other races to share power in the white parliament."[15]

Assessing Elements of Change in Post-Coup
Government Domestic Policies

A closer examination of six related areas of South African domestic policy should help clarify for each area the direction and degree of change envisioned by Afrikaner Nationalist sources and the responses of the government to these pressures from within its own *volk* (ethnic community). The areas are industrial development, homeland development, the position of urban blacks, the position of Coloureds, the officially accepted definition of racial discrimination, and the prospects for power-sharing in any form at the level of central government.

Industrial Development

Statements and demands made by various business organizations indicate a shared concern among capitalists — regardless of their ethnic background or color — over the state of the economy, the extent of unemployment, and the growing difficulty in raising foreign loans for capital projects. They also share a common desire to abolish job reservation, create a black middle class, improve black housing, recognize urban blacks as permanent residents, establish training institutions to provide industry with skilled labor, improve influx controls, and implement changes in the migrant labor system in order to increase labor productivity. However, none press for the legal recognition of black trade unions, except for three employers who have given de facto recognition to black unions. On the whole, capitalist demands reflect industry's need for the skilled labor and increased consumer market that a black middle class would provide. The Afrikaans press is entirely correct in its conclusion that all these changes could take place within the framework of the separate development policy and therefore pose no fundamental challenge to National party principles.

Nonetheless, the government holds back on some steps, in large part from fear of the political repercussion among white unionists. In particular, white workers in mining and in the iron and steel industry demand the retention of job reservation and resist employer efforts to place blacks in skilled occupations. At the same time, other white workers within the Trade Union Council of South Africa (TUCSA) acknowledge the need for black unions and are debating whether they should be separate or integrated with white unions. Ironically, within TUCSA two unions representing Coloured and Indian workers have withdrawn in protest against the prospect of black workers sharing union benefits and competing for jobs with their own members. In the longer run, the preponderance of black workers compared with all other groups will lead to a growth in their political significance.

The government has shrewdly coped with increased needs for skilled black labor in government services — especially railways and harbors. More blacks have been employed, but with different titles and lower wages, and never in situations where whites do the same work in close proximity. On the other hand, until 1974 no training of black artisans for jobs outside the homelands was permitted. Since then, in response to urgent labor needs, four training centers have been established. In 1977, as the continuing recession engendered unemployment among white artisans, several of these centers were closed. The government took a somewhat different line in the western Cape, an area that since the 1950s had been designated for Coloured priority over blacks in industrial employment. Because some industrialists expressed a preference for black workers, despite a high Coloured unemployment rate, the government approved the establishment of a training center for black workers at Guguletu, near Cape Town.

Homeland Development

The first major change in homeland policy after the 1974 coup was the prime minister's announcement in October 1974 that white South Africans would be permitted to invest in the homelands. Later, foreign investment was similarly encouraged. Both had been previously banned by the strongly separationist homeland policy evolved under Prime Minister Verwoerd, in which great stress had been put on the need for black self-reliance and the risk of continued domination of blacks by whites if white economic activity were allowed to continue (this argument was not couched in Marxist terms, needless to say, but in terms of innate white superiority). The Afrikaans press saw the moves as inevitable deviations from previous policy, because the government could not by itself provide sufficient development aid to make eventual political independence meaningful.[16]

The next major step involved further consolidation. In May 1975, M. C. Botha, minister of Bantu administration and development, announced plans to reduce the homelands from over one hundred fragments to twenty-four by the purchase of white-owned farms and the removal of blacks from "black spots." Although this step met with general approval, some Afrikaans papers pressed for the granting of additional land to the homelands.[17]

Afrikaner optimism about consolidation was clouded in October 1975 by Botha's announcement that scheduled land purchases would have to be deferred because of the deteriorating economic situation in South Africa.[18] The Afrikaans press saw this step as a major setback to the implementation of separate development: "The speedy consolidation of the black homelands is extremely important. Only in this way can tangible expression be given to the policy of separate freedoms."[19]

Given the continuing economic recession, homeland consolidation remains stalled and the more ambitious schemes involving even more land purchases and radical partitions receive no hearing from a government inclined to caution in economic commitments. At the same time, the Afrikaner argument for accelerated homeland consolidation remains compelling:

> The implementation of the policy cannot be merely measured in terms of money. The greatest eventual asset will be the existence of independent homelands, where the inhabitants will be able to progress to the highest level of sovereignty. People who have misgivings should not be blinded by the hugeness of the sums of money involved in the development of the homelands. They should rather pose themselves the question what the position would have been in South Africa today if this hope of eventual autonomy did not exist for the black man. They need look no further than Angola, Mozambique, and now also Rhodesia for an answer.[20]

Segregationist Afrikaner Nationalist analysis responds to this eloquent plea by reiterating the economic impracticality of the plan and by suggesting that compulsory homeland citizenship reduces somewhat the human strain on homeland resources, while ensuring a continuing supply of required labor for white South Africa without threatening the political survival of Afrikaners.

> To participate in a series of defined and valuable privileges in the Republic blacks must identify themselves with their own nation and must through the acceptance of citizenship of their own fatherland acknowledge that they will find their political and national fulfillment there and not compete with the whites in the latter's part of South Africa.[21]

> Equally simplistic is the view that political partnership for the urbanized and westernized blacks is the magic formula to resolve the present situation. Advocates of this idea, among whom are some of our most eminent academics and commentators, must realize that the white voters have time and again, and to an increasing extent, rejected the idea of sharing power at the ballot box, and that any movement in that direction will come up against a wall of white opposition. . . . [22]

Verligte ("enlightened") Afrikaner columnists take a subtly different line:

> It is fairly generally accepted in thinking circles that eventually we shall have to accommodate politically a certain number of black people within our own national frontiers. The question is: how many and how should we do it without committing political suicide? The government's problem is that from its side such an acknowledgment cannot, at this stage, be risked. Obviously most black people outside the homelands would, for economic reasons, prefer South African citizenship. By opening that door now, the homelands policy could virtually be destroyed.[23]

Thus, it is apparent that *verligte* Afrikaner Nationalists share the commitment to segregation of *verkrampte* ("inward-turning") Afrikaners, but they nurture the optimistic belief that the government, if given sufficient time to consolidate the homelands and to persuade the majority of homeland leaders to accept independence, will somehow be able to create a multiracial democratic society in the residual "white" areas of South Africa.

In another intended policy change, M. C. Botha announced in October 1975 (in response to homeland leaders' demands at the summit meetings held with Prime Minister Vorster in 1974 and again in 1975) that irritating and frustrating aspects of influx control would be eliminated wherever possible. Presumably, the government intended also to placate industrialists and the Afrikaans press, both of which had been especially critical of the implementation of influx laws.

In practice, influx control has been made harsher rather than more humane. During 1976, in the Johannesburg area, prosecutions increased by 50 percent over 1975, although convictions actually dropped from 98 percent in 1975 to 39 percent in 1976. But it appears that some numbers of those arrested were sent away from the Johannesburg area to their place of origin if they were unemployed or did not have proper papers. In addition, the Bantu Laws Amendment Bill introduced in the House of Assembly during 1977 calls for harsher penalties for pass offenders and generally increases the stringency of influx control measures. It is quite clear that influx controls will be used to reduce the large numbers of unemployed blacks, estimated at between one and two million, now in urban areas. This use of influx controls was made clear by M. C. Botha in October 1976:

> We are living now in a position where about half of all blacks are in the white areas and half in the homelands. And we are working daily to shift more and more into the homelands. . . . It will depend on how many blacks will go back to the homelands should their countries become independent. . . not only because their countries have become independent but also because of develop-

ment. . . . The position isn't static. It is fluid—with a big tendency from our side to help the drift [to the homelands].[24]

Throughout the world, industrialization has resulted in a steady drift from rural areas to urban centers. In South Africa, coercive measures are used to impede this movement among blacks. Nonaccess to land, economic development of the homelands, and the limits on the political rights of non-homeland residents merely underline the basic issue of the exclusion of blacks from South African economic wealth by means of the policy of separate development.

Urban Blacks

Two issues involving urban blacks were taken up by the Afrikaans press immediately after the Portuguese coup: black rights to own property in the "white" area, and the broader question of political rights for blacks. In addition, industrialists argued that the economic development of black townships was crucial and requested that the government examine the possibilities of allowing white businesses to operate in black urban areas (using the analogy of their entrance into the homelands).

Punt Janson, the deputy minister of Bantu administration, announced to the House of Assembly in early 1975 that legislation that would "improve matters" for urban blacks would be introduced during that session. In May 1975 M. C. Botha presented a bill granting blacks the right to sell or bequeath their houses although the land would remain the property of the local authority. In addition, doctors and other professional people could own their consulting rooms in black urban areas. Perhaps most important, black businessmen were granted a number of concessions, the effect of which was to permit them (for the first time) to make use of their profits to expand their business in both urban and homeland areas.

The right of home ownership was at first reserved to those blacks willing to take out homeland citizenship. After considerable criticism from the press and from blacks, this decision was reversed in August 1976. At the same time, the period of ownership was changed from thirty years to an "indefinite" period, which the government insisted was meant to be a longer period, barring unforeseen developments. The underlying motive of this apparent concession became clear with the granting of independence to Transkei in October 1976. All blacks of Transkeian origin automatically lost their South African citizenship and were assumed to become Transkeian citizens. For them, and presumably for "citizens" of homelands subsequently to get independence, this provision meant no incentive to take up homeland citizenship was any longer necessary. In fact, the number of blacks who have been granted the right to buy their homes remains considerably smaller than the number of applicants, partly because of administrative delays.

Nonetheless, the right of black home ownership was an important concession to urban blacks, especially insofar as it ran directly against the long-held principle that all blacks held status in "white" areas only as long as they provided necessary labor for the white community. Clearly, the pragmatic argument emanating from industrialists, among others, that the development of an effective and stable black middle class was indispensable to stability had taken precedence over ideological imperatives.

The question remained whether these socioeconomic steps would in any way accommodate the growing interest of urban blacks in some form of political participation outside the homeland framework. W. A. de Klerk, editor of *Die Transvaler,* argued they would not.

> The old long-term theory of evolutionary development of the black and Coloured man towards political maturity has got stuck. . . . The attitude of no power-sharing is unacceptable to both black and Coloured. . . . Discrimination is too interwoven in our policy that moving away [from discrimination] can hardly be accomplished according to the old model of the policy.[25]

> In three years the situation right here on our borders has changed almost beyond recognition. Are there really people who believe that we will be able to persist in perpetuity with blueprints drawn up twenty, thirty years ago — without even looking at them again, without even considering changes to them? Nationalists could again reflect seriously on what the true principles of their policy are and what are mere fringes that could safely be cut off. They might be surprised to see how much better the robe looks without those fringes.[26]

In a voice of total complacency, just one week before the start of the Soweto riots, at a time when signs of potential unrest were evident, *Die Volksblad* criticized such questioning of the existent structure of separate development:

> The peace in the country and, at least, the resigned acceptance by the black man of Transkei's approaching new status, which is only a prototype of other homelands, belies the prophecies of doom in and outside the House of Assembly. "Powerful confrontation, explosive situation through grievous deprivation of rights" sounds rather thin when nobody is making the least preparation for anything like it — so different to the fifties and early sixties with their riots and demonstrations when matters such as changes of rights were also at stake. The point is that since that time whites and blacks have been thoroughly preparing themselves for the change now being brought about, so that most blacks no longer believe the opposition when it says that an independent homeland is an artificial creation by the whites in their own interests. . . . The plans on the National Party drawing boards are too dynamic to allow

something like this [increase in the number of blacks in the "white" areas]. Independent homelands are in many respects the great starting point of internal
development and of grouping manpower for convenient linking up with the
new black fatherlands. The prophets of doom do not, or do not want to
realize, even after so many years, how much ingenuity and drive are inherent
in a nation wanting to hold its own, and other nations who are not begrudged
the right to realize themselves.[27]

This apparent political calm was shattered after 16 June 1976, with the
outbreak of violence first in Soweto and then in urban and rural areas
throughout South Africa. What began as peaceful demonstrations against
the use of Afrikaans as a medium of instruction in black schools ended in
violent confrontations between blacks and white authority. The government's policy of separating black and white residential areas enabled the
police and army to contain the resistance within the black areas, but it did
not totally prevent some impact on the city centers of Johannesburg and
Cape Town and on those white suburbs adjacent to black townships. The
violence of police action against the schoolchildren and students united (to a
large extent) parents and workers in support of the scholars. The destruction
of the outward symbols of separate development—beer halls (major sources
of revenue for the Bantu Administration Boards), Bantu Affairs buildings,
schools, white-owned vehicles, factories—forcefully demonstrated black opposition to government policy and to the position given blacks in South
African society. For the next three months, and intermittently since, white
South Africans have been confronted increasingly by black resentment and
growing indications of black unity.

Commerce and industry called for immediate action by government in
the area of social reform—improved housing, educational facilities, and
social amenities. They stressed also the need for better communication between government departments and the black community, but they failed
to acknowledge a similar need on their part.

Government's first response was the establishment of a cabinet committee
to investigate alternatives to the parliamentary system of government. Then
the government decided that black school boards should choose the medium
of instruction and that Bantu Administration Boards should confer "real
powers of local government" on the Urban Bantu Councils. In addition,
blacks would be represented on all statutory bodies that affected their lives
and welfare (such as the Roads Safety Council).

The Afrikaans press was divided in its reaction to Soweto. Some editors
called for a show of force by the government:

By this time they [blacks in Soweto] should know that an overwhelming majority of whites in this country will not allow violence and threats of more

violence to divert them from the course taken constitutionally for blacks. If the blacks despise their homelands they should not come and nag the white man in his homeland. The minority of blacks—and they will remain a minority— who prefer violence, will get back more of it than is good for them. . . . If blacks want goodwill, they must accept the choice of black political realization elsewhere then in the white republic outside the homelands.[28]

But the majority of editors felt Soweto was a warning that could not be ignored:

The investigation of adjustments can, and dare, no longer be postponed so that peaceful and benevolent blacks are not outdone by militant hostile people who can be persuaded and who desire an explosion.[29]

There is one aspect which is not always understood, frequently the least by champions of change and adjustment. It is that times of profound changes such as those needed in South Africa, evidently go hand in hand with tension and unrest. Important social changes do not mean an easy and smooth movement away from the tensions and confrontations inherent in a rigid status quo to a euphoric new state of equilibrium, order, and calm. The transition, which could be lengthy, involves formidable possibilities of turbulence and unrest. It is when change is really in the air, when expectations rise, that people demonstrate and become receptive to the message that blackmail and violence are legitimate political instruments. The unavoidable and dangerous tensions of change must not be allowed to get out of hand.[30]

The most significant change in government policy toward urban blacks in 1976 was the abandonment of the principle that blacks must finance the bulk of their own services and amenities through revenues from beer sales and taxes. After the widespread destruction in the riots, and with severe competition for use of government funds during the continuing recession, it was understandable that the government should be more responsive to corporate offers to provide funds for housing development and electrification on a large scale (despite official reservations about the motives of people like Harry Oppenheimer, chairman of the Anglo American Corporation and a central figure in the founding of the opposition Progressive Federal party, now the Progressive Reform party).

The Position of Coloureds and Indians

The Portuguese coup brought to the surface an "integrationist" element in Afrikaner Nationalist thinking that had repeatedly called for the progressive integration of the Afrikaans-speaking Coloureds (most of whom were members of the same church denomination as Afrikaners). The Afrikaans press generally shared this view, which was focused on the pending report of the Theron Commission of Inquiry (established by the government in 1973 to examine the role of the Coloureds). The commission presented its findings in June 1976. An interim White Paper released by the government at the same time made clear that the government, while accepting the bulk of the recommendations, would not accept the central ones concerning a shared political future between Afrikaner and Coloured. Without exception, and partly because the English-language press was attacking the government, the Afrikaans press reversed its previous preference and rallied to the government's support.

> Now they [the opposition] demand that the government must include Coloureds in parliament without further ado, in the obvious hope that it would strengthen them. But it is precisely the danger that through frustrated white politicians, Coloureds would be involved in a power struggle between the white political parties—with disastrous results for the relations between white and Coloured—that makes it necessary that another way be sought.[31]

> Would it not be clearer to state that the further study be guided by three principles? No sharing of power in the sense that the right of self-determination and decision-making competence of white and Coloured be affected. The right of self-determination of both groups should not be impeded. The fields of the participation and the structures for it must be enlarged, with the retention of the aforementioned two principles.[32]

After Coloureds took part in the 1976 riots, especially in the Cape Town area, the Afrikaans press became more explicit in its objections to political integration between Afrikaners and Coloureds. First, accepting Coloureds into parliament would lead inevitably to accepting Indians and this, in turn, would lead to accepting urban blacks.

> [This] would mean a black majority. This would place Coloureds, with the whites and Indians, in the position of a helpless minority group, unable to protect their interests.[33]

> Participation is given to the Coloureds and the Indians through representation on the Cabinet Council, where their leaders take decisions together with the white leaders. The only problem is that these leaders would not be responsible to three similar parliaments. Without territorial separation the ideal of absolute equality and effective participation in rights is unattainable. Without further development of the political structures, the parliament of the whites must remain the decision-maker. But . . . the eventual say can be placed with another body. It could be a States-General, in which the blacks are also represented.[34]

In the above editorial there is a hint of separationist doctrine: both Coloureds and Indians should somehow be given territorial homelands. But this view finds no support from segregationists who, without being willing to share political power, recognize the utility of the Coloureds and the Indians as reluctant and powerless allies against blacks. This vision has been badly tarnished in two ways. First, after the Coloured Labor party under Sonny Leon was elected as the majority in the Coloured Persons Representative Council (CPRC), the party refused to carry out decisions made by the House of Assembly or by the minister of Coloured relations as a protest against its political impotence. The CPRC has since operated under a chairman appointed by the government. While Coloured support for the CPRC (as manifested in voting turnouts) had already been dropping progressively, support is at a low ebb since the Labor party boycott. In addition, since Soweto there is a strong revulsion among young Coloureds against any cooperation with the government and its separate development institutions.

Despite this reaction, the government moves blithely ahead. The Cabinet Council, with cabinet members plus participants from the CPRC and the Indian Representative Council, met for the first time in September 1976. The CPRC executive, led by Leon, refused to attend until urban blacks were permitted to take part. The elaborately formal discussions of Coloured and Indian problems in the Cabinet Council provided minimal satisfaction for Coloured and Indian leaders, since the shaping of programs and budgets remained in the hands of the white government. Nothing less than full participation in government and full equality with whites seems likely to be accepted.

"Ending" Racial Discrimination

Few substantial changes have occurred since South Africa's UN ambassador R. F. (Pik) Botha told the UN General Assembly in 1974 that South Africa would move quickly to end unnecessary racial discrimination. City councils in Johannesburg and Durban took initiatives within the narrow range of initiative legally available to them. After the first South African multi-racial games were held in Pretoria in 1974, a few public parks that had been specially opened to black participants remained open. The government-operated postal service began a gradual program of removing apartheid signs from major post offices (but very slowly from *platteland,* or country, offices), but by habit most blacks continued to use the "black" counter, tacitly guided there by the continuing segregation of black and white postal clerks on the opposite side.

The opening to all races of the Nico Malan Theater in Cape Town and some twenty major hotels (mostly in the larger cities) was justified by the government as a short-term necessity in the absence of equal facilities for blacks, Coloureds, and Indians. It was not intended to lead to any wider social liberalization. At the same time that this handful of hotels was given "international" status (a governmental reference to their access to more than one ethnic group), laws that sharply limited the availability of liquor in hotels to blacks were modified. In brief, any registered guest in an "international" hotel may use any of its facilities—restaurant, bar, swimming pool.

The government has made much of the improvements in its sports policy. Admittedly, however slowly, better facilities for training and competitive opportunities are now open to black athletes. They do compete with whites, even in such physical contact sports as boxing and rugby. Nonetheless, the government's justification for these changes must be understood. Once again, the changes have been approved only because they appear to fit in the framework of separate development. Blacks competing with whites represent their ethnic groups; therefore, these are multinational or "international" events. Blacks are forbidden by policy to play on the same team (rugby, cricket, soccer) as whites, at least at club level; but an erratic movement is underway to permit "mixed" provincial and South African teams, again on the grounds that a multiplicity of ethnic groups is being represented.

In the more substantial area of higher education, despite the recommendations of the Snyman Commission in February 1976 (investigating student riots at the black University of the North—Turfloop) that all South African universities be open to postgraduate students without regard to race, it seems likely that the government will maintain its present policy, under which each individual application by a black (or Coloured or Indian) to study at a "white" university must be approved by the government department responsible for his ethnic university and by the minister of national education, who is responsible for the "white" universities.

In addition, Afrikaner universities (with the sole exception of Stellenbosch) remain unwilling to take the initiative necessary to encourage black applicants and ensure consideration of their applications by the appropriate government departments.

The government and the Afrikaans press agree that the abolition of racial discrimination must not go to the point that it threatens white identity or the right of whites to self-determination. Partly because they lack any insight into the effect of discriminatory laws and practices on blacks, Coloureds, and Indians (despite being constantly told by leaders of these groups what the impact amounts to), they tend to make minimal effort to change discriminatory patterns and (to exacerbate already bad race relations) then trumpet endlessly the enormous advances involved.

"Power Sharing"

Because Afrikaner Nationalists remain unalterably opposed to any institutional change that they believe involves the sharing of power with blacks, Coloureds, or Indians (indeed, in a more muted fashion, even with English-speaking whites), it is this issue that more than any other exposes the fallacy of separate development's stated goal of political equality for all people within what is presently South Africa. The central problem remains how to share power with blacks without dividing and diminishing white power. White privilege requires continued white domination and the economic exploitation of blacks.

This dilemma is recognizable in all the consultative and advisory bodies set up by the government ostensibly to provide blacks with some voice in the governance of their own affairs. Whether or not entirely by design, participation in these bodies removes blacks even further from those points in South African national government at which the crucial decisions affecting their well-being are made.

The segregationists have no solution to this problem, unless they make a commitment to total separation or to the abandonment of segregation—the establishment of a nonracial society with white dominance ended. They will do neither. Even the separationists override the continued frustrations of urban blacks in their preoccupation with the dangers posed by sharing power:

> The unrest, even violence, that may accompany the implementation of separate development in South Africa, is insignificant compared with the race and tribal murders, destruction and general bloodshed that would inevitably occur if separate states were not created and South Africa continued to exist as a unitary state.[35]

> Whoever rules this white nation does after all remain free. Should it be endeavored, however, to get all South Africans to vote for one government, the Afrikaners would become a subordinate minority section of a color-mixed South African nation that does not even remotely exist yet—perhaps never could exist. In the interim it would mean domination of the white nation (with its Afrikaner core) by other nations. It means the sacrifice of liberty. It means a fight to the death, as it could not be any other way for the Afrikaner.[36]

Debate will continue among Afrikaner Nationalists about the dilemma of sharing political power. Separationists who argue for partition will have to convince the white electorate that a smaller, more self-reliant, and poorer white South Africa is acceptable. Segregationists may find themselves attracted increasingly to various kinds of confederal or even federal schemes that protect Afrikaner political autonomy while simultaneously maintaining effective economic domination of a number of states that have formal political independence. In addition, external and domestic security pressures will result in increased repression of political opposition and a larger defense force, thus effectively strengthening the Afrikaner tendency to continue their present political and economic domination of black South Africans, whatever form political institutions may take.

Conclusion

Although events in Southern Africa following the Portuguese coup affected South African foreign policy and the style of National party politics and rhetoric, the underlying ideology of Afrikaner supremacy has not been changed. The expanded debate among Afrikaner Nationalists is limited to improvements or modifications in the separate development policy and does not consider scrapping or radical revision of that policy. The larger implications of white supremacy are supported tacitly by the growing acceptance of homelands among the white opposition parties, with most English-speaking whites now apparently content that their concerns about social justice be met within these frameworks, thus minimizing any challenge to their own security or status.

Neither government policy nor white attitudes since the Portuguese coup support the liberal analysts' contention that peaceful change leading to expanded democracy can occur in South Africa. On the contrary, the post-coup period has been marked by increasing repression of black dissidents and the growing militarization of the South African state, dominated by the Afrikaner Nationalist vision of threat and survival. This motivation will dominate even more in the coming years:

> The prophets of doom do not, or do not want to realize, even after so many years, how much ingenuity and drive are inherent in a nation wanting to hold its own.[37]

Notes

1. *Die Transvaler* (Johannesburg), 4 April 1974.
2. Ibid.
3. *Die Burger* (Cape Town), 29 July 1974.
4. *Cape Times* (Cape Town), 6 May 1975.
5. For two examples of this approach, both in Adrian Leftwich, ed., *South Africa: Economic Growth and Political Change* (London: Alison & Busby, 1974): See Norman Bromberger, "Economic Growth and Political Change in South Africa," pp. 61–123; and Michael O'Dowd, "South Africa in the Light of the Stages of Economic

Growth," pp. 29–43.

6. For examples of this approach, see Frederick A. Johnstone, "White Prosperity and White Supremacy in South Africa Today," *African Affairs,* April 1970, pp. 124–140; Martin Legassick, "Legislation, Ideology, and Economy in Post–1948 South Africa," *Journal of Southern African Studies* 1, no. 1 (1974), pp. 5–35; and Howard Wolpe, "Capitalism and Cheap Labour Power in South Africa: From Segregation to Apartheid," *Economy and Society* 1, no. 1 (1972).

7. Merle Lipton, "South Africa: Authoritarian Reform?", *The World Today* (June 1974), p. 247.

8. Heribert Adam, "Ideologies of Dedication versus Blueprints of Expedience," *Social Dynamics* 2, no. 2 (1976), p. 91.

9. H. Dickie-Clark, "The Study of Conflict in South Africa and Northern Ireland," *Social Dynamics* 2, no. 1 (1976), pp. 53–59.

10. Andre du Toit, "Ideological Change, Afrikaner Nationalism, and Pragmatic Racial Domination in South Africa," in Leonard Thompson and Jeffrey Butler, eds., *Change in Contemporary South Africa* (Berkeley and Los Angeles: University of California Press, 1975), pp. 19–50.

11. Geoff Cronje, *'n Tuiste vir die Nageslag* (Johannesburg), 1945; Cronje, W. Nicol, and E. Groenewald, *Regverdige Rasseapartheid* (Stellenbosch), 1947.

12. *Rapport* (Johannesburg), 12 May 1974.

13. *Beeld* (Johannesburg), 1 October 1976.

14. *The Star* (Johannesburg), weekly airmail edition, 28 May 1977.

15. C. P. ("Connie") Mulder, minister of information and of the interior, quoted in *Oggendblad* (Pretoria), 15 September 1976.

16. *Die Transvaler,* 4 October 1974.

17. *Rapport,* 18 May 1975.

18. *The Argus* (Cape Town), 16 October 1975.

19. *Rapport,* 19 October 1975.

20. *Hoofstad* (Pretoria), 10 March 1976.

21. *Die Volksblad* (Bloemfontein), 29 April 1976.

22. *Hoofblad,* 25 June 1976.

23. *Die Vaderland* (Johannesburg), 8 June 1976.

24. *Rand Daily Mail* (Johannesburg), 4 October 1976.

25. *Rapport,* 4 April 1976.

26. *Rapport,* 11 April 1976.

27. *Die Volksblad,* 9 June 1976.

28. *Die Volksblad,* 1 July 1976.

29. *Die Transvaler,* 1 July 1976.

30. *Die Burger,* 5 August 1976.

31. *Die Burger,* 21 June 1976.

32. *Die Transvaler,* 21 June 1976.

33. *Die Volksblad,* 7 July 1976.

34. *Oosterlig* (Port Elizabeth), 15 September 1976.

35. *Die Volksblad,* 28 July 1976.

36. *Oosterlig,* 1 April 1976.

37. *Die Volksblad,* 9 June 1976.

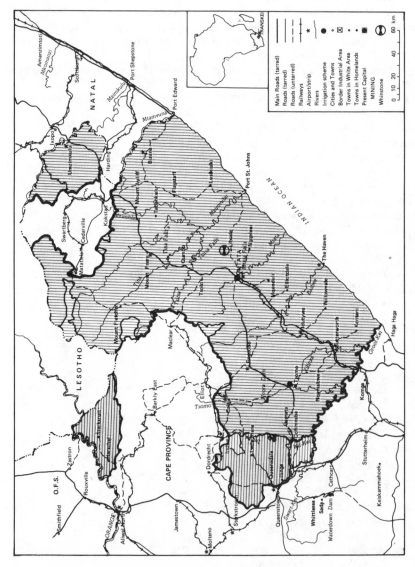

Map 6.   Transkei.   Source: The Africa Institute of South Africa, from *Bulletin* 14, nos. 7 and 8, 1976, p. 237.

8

Independence for the Transkei: Mystification and Diversion in the Model Bantustan

Roger J. Southall

The Portuguese coup of 25 April 1974 and the subsequent decolonization of Angola and Mozambique resulted in the acceleration of an "independence" process of a very different kind — the granting by South Africa of formal political autonomy to the Transkei, its model Bantustan, on 26 October 1976. Although the separate development policy has been the South African government's main domestic strategy since its assumption of power in 1948, there were many (including National party members themselves) who doubted whether the government had either the political will or the inclination to actually set about the fragmentation of the Republic.

But in March 1974 the Transkeian Legislative Assembly approved a motion proposed by Chief Minister Kaiser Matanzima that the South African government be asked to grant full independence to the territory within the next five years.[1] Talks between the Transkeian and Republic governments were then held in May and August 1974, following Prime Minister John Vorster's oral confirmation in April that independence would indeed be granted within the five-year period requested.[2] The surprising result of the subsequent negotiations (centered about the deliberations of a cabinet committee composed of members of both governments that focused on the legal, constitutional, fiscal, and related implications)[3] was that independence was moved forward by three years to 1976. Although there were forces within the ruling Transkei National Independence party (TNIP) — including Kaiser Matanzima himself — that pressed for earlier independence, it was not

A preliminary version of this chapter was presented at a workshop, "Southern Africa Since the Portuguese Coup," held at Rhodes University on 24 and 25 June 1976. In this chapter, the preindependent territory is referred to as *the* Transkei, the postindependent territory as Transkei.

these forces but the radically changed situation within the former Portuguese territories that persuaded the South African government to accept the earlier date for independence.

South Africa's overall policy response to regional change — the policy of "détente" — is discussed in a number of chapters in this book. Here it is enough to make clear that the advancement of Transkeian independence to October 1976 was a conscious part of this policy. In order to defuse external pressure, the Vorster government saw Transkeian independence as a demonstration to the world that South African determination to grant freedom to the separate "peoples" under its control was genuine and directly comparable to the decolonization process experienced elsewhere in Africa. Transkei, it was argued, was no different from other former colonies — notably the former High Commission territories of Botswana, Lesotho, and Swaziland — and if South Africa as the colonial power chose to grant Transkei its independence, the world should not object to its receiving full international recognition.[4] If recognition were granted by at least a number of significant states, then the policy of separate development would achieve respectability and the security of whites in the South African heartland would be considerably strengthened.

Despite the fact that the OAU and the United Nations both repeatedly warned that they would refuse membership to Transkei, South Africa continues to hope that some countries may extend recognition. For reasons of economic self-interest, the Ivory Coast, Malawi, and the Central African Empire are all possible candidates. In addition, a number of Western states — the United States, France, and Germany, in particular — and their client-states — such as Israel and Taiwan — may wish to do so in the hope of promoting stability for their South African investments.[5] Finally, the situation of Botswana, Lesotho, and Swaziland remains precarious. Reluctant though they be to endanger their own international standing by extending any form of recognition, South Africa will undoubtedly bring pressure upon them to engage in de facto cooperation within the framework of the Southern African Customs Union.

The question of international recognition for Transkei is of fundamental importance insofar as it affects the rights of black South African citizens deemed to be Transkeians after independence under South African law. The land division upon which the Bantustan policy is based springs from the Native Trust and Land Act of 1936, whereby 87 percent of the land was reserved for the white population. Acceptance of independence by the incumbent Transkeian government thus constitutes a denial of a future claim by all those designated as Transkeian citizens to a fair share of South African resources and accumulated wealth when liberation for the black majority within South Africa is ultimately achieved. Accordingly, recognition of

Transkei might well institutionalize this denial. It is this factor that raises two questions of fundamental importance. First, how meaningful will Transkei's independence be and what are the implications for its citizens? Second, what potential for change within South Africa comes from Transkeian independence?

Transkei as the Model Bantustan

According to apartheid theory, South Africa is composed of a multiplicity of national groups, each of which aspires to maintain its own separate political and cultural identity. Apartheid logic argues that this desire for national self-expression can ideally be achieved by the partition of the country into distinct national areas. To this end, groups such as the Xhosa, Zulu, and Tswana have been allocated "homelands" in which they are free to exercise full political and economic rights. In order to protect one national group from being dominated by another, apartheid also demands that non-nationals be denied political rights outside their homelands.

Competent critics have pointed to the inability of apartheid theory to conform to reality. First, while the black homelands constitute only 13 percent of the total land area of South Africa, blacks make up 71 percent of the total population. Second, the land allocated to the homelands constitutes some of the poorest in the entire Republic, and a basis for economic development apart from the industrialized areas of South Africa hardly exists. Third, the homelands are hopelessly fragmented and cannot become meaningful countries. Although the government recently announced plans to "consolidate" the various territories, they will remain conglomerations of disconnected lands. For example, KwaZulu, which had 188 pieces in 1973, will be reduced to no fewer than 10.[6] Fourth, the theory is based on an artificial concept of nationality and overlooks the extent to which the black population is inextricably intermixed and shares many similar political objectives.[7]

The Bantustan concept, then, comprises what Heribert Adam labels the "Utopian aspect of apartheid," which attempts to replace crude racial domination of black by white (*baaskaap*) with a modernized form of oppression.[8] The policy is utopian, because there is a vast gap between promise and reality that could only be bridged by undermining white supremacy and white living standards—the maintenance of which is the basis of the policy. However, the Bantustan policy serves to fulfill the function of deflecting black political aspirations away from the centralized state to areas in which they pose no danger to white rule. It seeks to conceal continued white control over dependent quasi-states through economic, political, and (ultimately) military domination.

From the introduction of the Bantu Authorities System in 1951 the Transkei was regarded as the most advanced, or "model," Bantustan because it conformed most in outward appearance to apartheid theory. One of the two homelands for the Xhosa-speaking people, Transkei is not unduly fragmented, made up of only three pieces, the largest of which is bordered not only by white areas but also by Lesotho and the Indian Ocean. The Transkei was incorporated into the Bantustan system in 1955, when the United Transkeian Territories General Council (which originated in 1895, included a number of elected members, and enjoyed a relatively high degree of debate and popular support) was replaced with the Transkeian Territorial Assembly (TTA), largely composed of chiefs. In 1961 the TTA requested "self-government." The ensuing negotiations with the South African government resulted in the promulgation of the Transkei Constitution Act of 1963, which replaced the TTA with a legislative assembly and allowed for various other constitutional reforms, including the introduction of direct elections for 45 of 109 assembly seats. The act also allowed for the election by the assembly of a chief minister and a cabinet of six other ministers.[9] The Transkei was the first homeland to attain "self-governing" status and pioneered the route since followed by other homelands. More recent constitutional provisions have given the chief minister increased power and increased the size of the cabinet.[10]

Finally, it should be noted that Matanzima has consistently supported separate development and was the first homeland leader to opt for independence.[11] Given his willingness to fall in with the official scheme, Pretoria reciprocated by concentrating a proportionately higher degree of attention and resources on the Transkei than on other homelands in order to boost the international credibility of the Transkei at independence.[12]

The creation of new governmental structures for the Transkei, although apparently devolving increased responsibilities to black ministers and heralding a march to freedom and independence for the Transkeian population, in fact marked a new era in the subordination and domination of the black population of South Africa. To justify this assertion, it is necessary to examine the role that independent Transkei plays in the economy of South Africa as a whole. Only then is it possible to gauge the significance of the political structures that have emerged and the social forces that they represent.

The Role of Transkei in
South African Political Economy

South African official rhetoric argues that Transkei is an economically backward area that — in order to develop — needs capital investment, external aid, and technological advance in both industry and agriculture. But officials in Pretoria have no intention that Transkei should become economically autonomous or even free itself from subordination to the South African economy. Rather, the South African policy is that the Transkeian dependence on South Africa should be rationalized. This means expanding the local economy to the extent that it provides opportunities for educated and skilled Transkeian blacks who might otherwise become radicalized by the lack of middle-level and upper-level openings in the white-dominated South African economy. And, at the same time, such an expansion is expected to draw off "surplus" population from the growing black proletariat in "white" urban areas without endangering an adequate supply of migrant workers to South African industries. In addition, Transkeian industrial expansion must be noncompetitive with the overall development of the South African economy. Analyses that fail to treat Transkei as playing an integral part in the South African political economy and instead treat the local economy as if it were capable of autonomous development serve the function of "mystification and diversion" — creating illusory hopes for black advancement and diverting attention from exploitation of blacks in the central economy.

Bundy and others argue that the structural underdevelopment of the areas that now constitute the Bantustans was a necessary component of the process of South African capitalist development.[13] Precolonial contact between the pastoral cultivators and the white settler economy resulted in the emergence of a black peasantry in response to the opportunities provided by a cash crop economy. However, various forces worked to undermine the peasant mode of production and to transform black agricultural areas into underdeveloped labor reservoirs for the white-dominated central economy. The growing demands of white farmers for cheap labor and their fear of effective black competition in produce markets resulted in political authorities' levying taxes and enacting laws the purpose of which was to extrude black peasants from the land into wage employment. But the critical factor influencing the nature of black participation in the economy was the discovery of minerals in the nineteenth century. Although the expansion of the economy provoked by new capital investment initially offered greater opportunities for peasant production, demand by mining companies and white farmers for increasing supplies of cheap labor led to the increasing use of political means to ensure an adequate flow. "The early twentieth century saw a substantial rise in the social cost of peasant participation in the produce market, and a correlatively increasing reliance by peasants upon migrant labor for a cash income,"[14] so much so that by the 1920s black rural areas had been underdeveloped into *sub*-subsistence agricultural labor reserves whose population was, to a great extent, dependent for continued survival on wage remittances from the white-dominated economy. Limitation of land available to blacks via demarcations in 1913 and 1936, combined with expansion of the black population (through natural increase and forced resettlement into the reserves), continued until recently to debilitate black agriculture and to maintain Bantustan dependence on the South African economy.

Independent Transkei's primary economic function remains to serve as a supplier of cheap labor and effectively to subsidize the white economy of South Africa. In 1974 Transkei exported 256,971 migrant workers to the Republic.[15] Although these migrant workers remit a portion of their earnings to Transkei (so that superficially it might appear that the white economy subsidizes the local economy), their dependence on family subsistence agricultural production and their own restricted trade union rights effectively depresses total income.[16] Like neighboring Lesotho, the greater portion of Transkeian cash remittances is used to purchase food and consumer goods produced in South Africa, thereby creating an adverse "balance of payments" between the local and the central economy and giving a fresh twist to the cycle of dependency.[17]

The prospects of overcoming Transkeian underdevelopment appear remote. One economist offers the following analysis. Transkei has no absolute advantage over South Africa in anything but the production of cheap labor. However, the general lack of facilities for industry in Transkei means that if a strategy of capitalist development is to be pursued, positive incentives will have to be offered to outside capital in order to attract investment. Indeed, political uncertainties might require making conditions more favorable than in the Republic. In addition, given the low level of effective demand for consumer goods in Transkei (because of the general poverty of its people) industrial expansion would have to be oriented toward "export" to the South African economy. The only way to make Transkeian industry competitive with South African industry would be to rely on various forms of government subsidy—either fiscal advantages created by the government or the deliberate holding down of wages to lower production costs.[18]

In addition, the territory's continuing reliance on migrant labor earnings for financial viability offers little prospect for agricultural development. Absence of male labor for long periods has a deleterious effect on productivity, holds back the acceptance of agricultural innovation (such as new techniques of animal management), and reduces agricultural investment and attention to soil conservation and rehabilitation.[19]

The economic strategy being pursued in Transkei suffers from all these deficiencies, and its effect will be to augment the territory's dependence on South Africa. Insofar as industrial expansion takes place in Transkei, interlocking of the local economy with the central South African economy will assume a new dimension. The provision of capital and the supply of essential resources (such as electricity and oil) will continue to come from South

Africa. Even when investment comes from overseas, the bulk of it will be oriented toward access in the South African market. In addition, Transkei will continue to be financially dependent on Pretoria. Not only will it be bound by the constraints of belonging to the rand currency area, but it will be reliant on transfer payments from the Republic to support its budget, whether these take the form of a straightforward financial subsidy or come under the cover of a Customs Union agreement.[20]

The major political function of new economic developments in Transkei will be to lessen what South Africa considers to be the "oversupply" of black labor to "white" areas in the Republic. Homeland development is in part designed to bring about a significant reduction in the number of blacks permanently resident in the major urban areas of South Africa. This is the purpose of the industrial decentralization policy (which encourages white capital to create employment on the borders of homelands) and the promotion of industrial growth within homelands themselves.[21] However, given Transkei's relative economic isolation, the expansion of border industries has been minimal. Instead emphasis has been laid on the creation of employment inside the territory, notably in the urban areas of Umtata and Butterworth.

The major funnel for investment capital into Transkei is the Transkei (formerly Xhosa) Development Corporation (TDC). Since 1968 white capital (previously restricted to the border areas) has been permitted inside the homelands on an agency basis, with the intention that white management (and, in theory, white ownership as well) will in the course of time be replaced by black. Hence, the TDC builds factories and leases them over varying periods to white industrialists. Given the incentives offered outside capital,[22] the policy has had some success. Nearly 32 million rand was committed by white investors by 31 March 1975 and there were hopes of a further 16 million rand investment.[23] These amounts included capital investments from West Germany and Italy, with the prospect of additional investment from the United Kingdom, France, Holland, and the United States. Such foreign capital is explicitly courted,[24] with Transkei held up as a paragon of stability in comparison to Angola and Mozambique.[25] It is also implied that foreign investors in Transkei (which has no legal racial segregation, although little mixing takes place) will be spared the overseas criticism focused on investors in South Africa.

In addition to attracting outside capital, the TDC trains Transkeian entrepreneurs to run their own businesses. The number of Transkeian-owned businesses in the territory increased from 597 in 1964 to 2,162 in 1972. The TDC gave loans of 6.5 million rand to such undertakings by the end of 1974–1975. Of the 653 white trading stations in Transkei in 1964, 541 were taken over by the TDC as of December 1975. Up to the 1973–1974 period,

377 businesses had been handed over to black Transkeian owners.[26] The majority of these businesses were in the service sector — notably retailing, hotel management, garage ownership, and passenger transport — and local entrepreneurial activity in productive enterprise is as yet extremely limited.[27] The TDC activities have created relatively few jobs in Transkei: in the period 1974–1977, an estimated 4,488 employment opportunities were created for Xhosa males; while in the same period more than 17,150 additional males per year entered the labor market.[28]

The strategy of economic and political devolution outlined above has involved the creation of relatively privileged social strata in Transkei. These strata have a different relation to the system of South African domination than do the rest of the Transkeian population. Primarily composed of politicians, chiefs, civil servants, managers, and traders, these strata together can be characterized as a petit bourgeois, bureaucratic class the main function of which is to stabilize a form of Transkeian neocolonialism. The apartheid strategy assumes that giving such opportunities for the acquisition of wealth and the exercise of a degree of power to a dependent black class denies their potential radical leadership to the masses of urban and rural black workers and removes a threat to the continued white control of the Republic's economy and polity.

Transkeian independence provided this bureaucratic class with greater control over the Bantustan state apparatus, allowing increased appropriation of economic surplus in the form of higher salaries, promotions, and favorable access to public appointments and to trade licenses, and giving greater prestige to the position of class members. These rewards can be rationalized ideologically in terms of enhanced black dignity or possibly Xhosa nationalism.

The bureaucratic class occupies an economically privileged position achieved by access to political power. This is illustrated most strikingly by an examination of the parliamentary component of this class, for membership in Transkeian political institutions offers an income not easily available to blacks in the rest of the Republic. The parliamentary component totals 150 members — 75 elected and 75 appointed chiefs.[29] Matanzima himself earns 14,600 rand per year, while his ministers receive 12,100 rand. Other members of the parliament receive 3,000 rand, plus a daily allowance of 8 rand for attendance during legislative sessions.[30] There are also other benefits. Recently, for instance, white farms purchased by the South African government and handed over to Transkei under consolidation plans were appropriated by Kaiser Matanzima, his brother George, who is minister of justice, and other chiefs.[31] Finally, it should be remembered that chiefs and headmen who sit in parliament also receive payment for performance of administrative functions in their home areas.

The largest part of the Transkeian bureaucratic class is composed of nearly 7,000 civil servants, many of whom receive salaries (and, increasingly, benefits such as housing and educational training) comparable to those received by parliamentarians.[32] Although there is no available evidence of their attitudes about Transkeian independence, they are recruited from a section of more educated Xhosa ideologically predisposed to acceptance of the homeland concept. Although a 1969 survey of students at Fort Hare (the ethnic university for Xhosa) showed only one-third of those interviewed prepared to work in the Ciskei or Transkei,[33] it seems likely that the proportion has increased since the setting of the date for Transkeian independence. In any case, personal conversations with bureaucrats in Umtata suggest that they do favor Transkeian independence. There can be little doubt that they appreciate the increased material opportunities offered them by the future expansion of the Transkei administration and economy.

But the benefits of Transkeian independence will not be equally distributed. For a start, Matanzima has stated explicitly that he intends to "create a well-behaved, prosperous, middle-class society"[34] in which men will receive differential rewards for varying displays of initiative and industry. This, he claims, is consonant with the "capitalist nature" of the Transkeian people and will be linked to the high value they place on personal property, whereas a socialistic orientation would fly in the face of man's instinctual acquisitiveness and would only serve to downgrade the elite's standard to that of the masses.

Although Matanzima subscribes to a strategy of "capitalism with a conscience,"[35] he has been steadfast in his refusal to allow the formation of trade unions, which "with all their potential for disruption," he considers to be "undesirable and even harmful in a developing country such as the Transkei, where continuing peak productivity is essential."[36] "Unrealistic" and militant wage demands serve only to dissuade foreign industrialists from investing, and the best guarantee of future prosperity lies in "harder and better work."[37] Matanzima has been as good as his word. He has kept wages at an "attractively" low level. The minimum wages payable in South Africa do not apply in the homelands, and the Transkeian government has rejected the opportunity to introduce similar legislation.[38] Taken together with a battery of security measures that can be utilized to repress opposition, it seems unlikely that the Transkeian proletariat will gain substantial benefit from independence. Those employed permanently in local industrial centers will be called upon to accept lower wages than elsewhere in order to subsidize white capital that otherwise would leave the territory.[39] At the same time, the majority of the population faces the prospect of continued migrant labor in South Africa, where they will be treated as Transkeian citizens, devoid of all political rights.

Potential for Change

Two questions were posed earlier that were deemed to be of fundamental importance: How meaningful will Transkeian independence be and what are the implications for its citizens? What are the potential changes within South Africa caused by Transkeian independence? Given the preceding analysis of the Transkeian political economy, a third, related question should be added: Does Transkeian independence offer any possibility of progress toward the genuine liberation of South Africa's black majority, as opposed to the mere provision of better material opportunities for the black bureaucratic class?[40]

From a broader South African perspective, the prospects of Transkeian independence bringing about significant political change seem extremely slim. Indeed, not only does the whole strategy of granting independence—of creating a neocolony—have the conservative objective of preserving the dominating position of South Africa vis-à-vis Transkei, but it is also intended to (in Adam's now time-honored phrase) "modernize racial domination."

This latter aspect is best illustrated by reference to the citizenship issue. The Transkeian Independence Constitution, as codified in South African law, provided that all persons defined as Transkeians before independence and all persons born to Transkeian citizens *outside* the homeland became Transkeian citizens at independence. In addition, predominantly Xhosa- or Sotho-speaking blacks descended from or associated with residents of Transkei also became Transkeian citizens.[41] The effect of these provisions was to automatically deprive some 1.5 million blacks permanently resident in South Africa of South African citizenship. The move's political-legal utility lies in relieving the South African government of residual responsibility for the housing, employment, welfare, and pensions of these people. Such services would fall away, unless the Transkeian government took them over. As a result, urban Transkeians are now regarded by the South African government as "foreign migrants" (in the land of their birth) with no claim to political rights within the Republic. Eventually, if all the homelands become independent, almost all blacks will become foreigners and the present white minority will become a numerical majority of citizens in the core area. Transkeian citizenship thus increases the insecurity of urban blacks, especially those blacks of little utility to the white economy—the young, many women, the old, and the infirm. Finally, the citizenship clause allows a refinement of the apparatus for repression. "Agitators" of Transkeian citizenship could now be "sent back" to their homeland, where the burden of imprisonment, restriction, and other political limitation falls on a black government. To be fair, the Transkeian government has repeatedly denied that it is bound by this inclusive definition of Transkeian citizenship, so it remains uncertain whether such "deportees" from South Africa will be accepted into Transkei.[42]

This wholesale conversion of black South Africans into Transkeian citizens involves what Sachs terms *symbolical* change. Symbolical laws, such as various petty apartheid laws and the Immorality Act, emphasize race distinction in itself. By enforcing this transfer of citizenship, the relationship of oppression of blacks by a white government will be obscured. Transkeians will be urged to seek redress from "their own" government, while in the Republic race relations will superficially be replaced by "international" relations. But this symbolical mystification will in no way change *instrumental* laws—those that directly serve the economy and maintain security. Thus, while symbolical laws may be allowed to lose their vigor—to defuse potential conflict—no changes will be made in the instrumental relations that constitute the repressive elements in the economy and polity.[43]

In the same vein, the postindependent Transkeian government can be expected to engage in a great deal of antiapartheid and anti–South African rhetoric. This will earn, if not the blessing, at least the stiff-lipped tolerance of the South African government, for such apparently radical posturing will serve the function of demonstrating the "reality" of Transkeian political independence from South Africa, thereby increasing the chances of international recognition.

This process of "rhetorical radicalism" began even before independence. For instance, in March and April 1976 the world was treated to the spectacle of Matanzima negotiating with the Vorster government for the release of ANC detainees—including Nelson Mandela, Walter Sisulu, and Govan Mbeki—who are Xhosas. The negotiations were based on the premise that the detainees, if released, would live in Transkei and openly acknowledge its independence. Even if the detainees were willing to accept such terms, which they were not, it is highly unlikely that Matanzima would have permitted them much political freedom, since even their physical presence in Transkei would constitute a threat to his authority.[44]

Matanzima's attack after the June 1976 Soweto riots on the South African government for "aggravating the deteriorating racial situation in South Africa" and for permitting the police to use guns on a "peaceful demonstration of schoolchildren" may be viewed in the same light.[45] Although the genuine nature of Matanzima's anger at the Soweto killings is not in question, his very statement served symbolically as witness to his goverment's apparent autonomy, when—to the contrary—its existence and survival depend on the repressive apparatus of instrumental law against which the Soweto riots were directed.

Notwithstanding the purpose and immediate effect of the Bantustan policy in its reiteration of the status quo of white domination, there may be a dynamic process at work in independent Transkei to transmute symbolical change into instrumental change. In the first place, conflicts may exist within the bureaucratic class that weaken Matanzima's (and the TNIP's) position, thereby exposing the contradictions of "separate development." The ultimate loyalty of Transkeian civil servants to Matanzima personally and to the chiefly factions he represents is as yet an unknown quality. It seems likely (although no data are available to the writer) that civil servants come from a better educated, more urbanized, and more non-chiefly background than that of the most influential members of the TNIP. Therefore, it is quite conceivable that there may be conflict between the bureaucratic and chiefly strata concerning the distribution of state resources in the form of trading licenses, land, and loans. In addition, it is possible that civil servants may push for policies that though not in any way radical, run contrary to the interests of the rural, traditional elite.[46]

To the extent that bureaucrats push for more "modern" and egalitarian policies, they may in the future claim to oppose apartheid from within its own framework.[47] Even then, the ideological utility of a position that justifies continued participation in a Bantustan bureaucracy would need close scrutiny.[48] Since the bureaucrats' material interests lie firmly within homeland systems, their potential for bringing about any significant change is extremely limited. Of course, as the movement aimed at liberating South Africa grows stronger, bureaucratic conflict with the chiefs could become more open and civil servants might try to negotiate a working relationship with representatives of the broader black nationalism.

It is also conceivable that conflict between the TNIP and groups represented by the opposition Democratic and New Democratic parties, both of which opposed independence, might prove a source of change. The National Democratic party (NDP) is of fairly recent origin, founded in January 1976 by Knowledge Guzana after he had been toppled from leadership of the Democratic party (DP) at a party congress.[49] Guzana had led the DP since the 1966 resignation of its founder-leader, Chief Victor Poto, due to illness; but Guzana had come under increasing pressure from party members dissatisfied with his moderate, old-fashioned opposition to Matanzima, based as it was on parliamentary eloquence and belief in a qualified franchise (resting on educational attainment) throughout South Africa. Since the 1976 election in which Guzana lost his seat and the NDP's representation was reduced to three, the NDP seems unlikely to be anything more than an ineffective opposition whose primary function will be to give Transkei a facade of parliamentary democracy. It may keep alive the awareness of alternative policies—in particular its own preference for the reintegration of Transkei into South Africa as a separate province or as a constituent unit in a new federation.[50]

It is the reformed Democratic party, presently led by H. B. Ncogazi, that Matanzima has singled out as his main opponent. The arrest of the entire DP executive during the 1976 election campaign testifies to this antipathy. The DP appears to draw support primarily from teachers, students, and the Transkeian younger generation. Its opposition to "separate development" is far more militant than the NDP's. Its leadership established, or at least has tried to establish, links with the Black Peoples' Convention and the South African Students' Organization. Certain incidents of arson (the burning of George Matanzima's car and a school dormitory and the attempted arson of a secondary school) at the time of the 1976 election and the Soweto riots were probably the reaction of DP supporters to the detention of their leaders.[51]

Given the increasing militance of the DP since Ncogazi assumed leadership in January 1976, perhaps the party is properly viewed as part of the larger black resistance to white rule in South Africa. As such, it is likely that relatively soon it will be banned completely. Chief Minister (now President) Matanzima has always been lavish with accusations that the Ncogazi group espouses communism and revolutionary ideals. He warned DP members as early as March 1975 that they might be detained after independence,[52] but such repressive action will not extinguish the forces of opposition represented by the party. If harassed in this way, the DP probably will resort to sporadic acts of violence, especially when inspired by acts of black resistance within the Republic.

Radical action like that of the DP led by teachers and students is likely to receive increasing support from proletarianized elements among the Transkeian migrant labor force. First, if the security of large numbers of urban workers in the Republic is endangered by their involuntary adherence to Transkeian citizenship, resentment will be directed at both South African and Transkeian authorities. This will be especially true if, as presently planned, a portion of their wages is paid directly to the Transkeian government, for taxation and subsequent retransmittal.[53]

Second, low wages paid in Transkei may lead to a greater willingness in the homeland labor force to strike illegally. Such militancy was foreshadowed by strikes in October 1974 (of 700 workers in three concerns at Butterworth) and January 1975 (at a Butterworth textile factory by 500 workers).[54] In both cases, the management conceded slightly higher wages (which might be taken by the workers as a demonstration of the effectiveness of the strike weapon). However, at the time of the South African riots in July 1976, Pep stores chose to fire 1,000 striking workers in Transkei who were, according to the TDC general manager, the victims of agitators from the Transvaal.[55] If the manager was correct, then it is an excellent illustration of the authorities' inability to insulate Transkei from political disturbances taking place in South African industrial centers.

Dissatisfaction in Transkei urban centers may be linked to grievances in rural Transkei. The natural increase in population is already leading to a land shortage—a situation to be aggravated if Transkeian citizens are "endorsed out" of the Republic. Although factional conflict between present landholders may result, the increased pressure could also produce a radical revolt against the rural authority structure.[56]

It should be remembered that the Pondoland revolt of 1960 had its origin in a land shortage, the consolidation of chiefly political and economic power under the Bantu authorities system, increased taxation, and agricultural reform and rehabilitation.[57] A similar constellation of factors could easily spark off a new revolt. The newly created Transkeian Army—trained in counterinsurgency techniques—would be used to put down the revolt. If this step failed, Matanzima might be forced to ask the South African government for either police or military assistance. This humiliating step would expose in its most naked form the nature of his collaborationist alliance with the white supremacist regime.[58] However, neither urban militancy nor rural revolt in Transkei will be sufficient to bring significant change in South Africa itself, unless these spontaneous forces can be harnessed, along with others throughout the Republic, into organized opposition. Given the repressive nature of the political system, this remains highly unlikely in the foreseeable future.

Conclusion

Independence for the Transkei constitutes a further stage in the modernization and refinement of the repressive apparatus of the South African political economy. The apparent decolonization process, intended to divert international criticism from South African treatment of urban blacks, is in fact a process of neocolonization. A new form of dependency between South Africa and Transkei was grafted onto the preexisting relationship of labor absorption and supply. The development of a Transkeian bureaucratic class is intended as a conservative bulwark against radical action by the growing black proletariat.

Various sources of potential mobilization among the Transkeian proletariat have been identified, but the possibility of revolutionary change being achieved entirely through proletariat efforts remains minimal. But migrant workers returning from their labors will be the transmitters of discontent from the Republic's industrial centers; students and teachers will continue to absorb the radical ideas of Black Consciousness; and Matanzima's domestic repression, extending into the rural areas through the rule of the chiefs, may provoke a rural resistance he will not be wholly able to contain.

Transkei cannot be isolated from events in South Africa. Changes within the homeland are likely to occur mainly in response to South African incidents. In turn, political opposition within Transkei to the Bantustan regime will complement other liberation forces at work throughout South Africa, whether in guerrilla activity at the borders or in political and industrial resistance in the cities and towns.

Transkeian independence, undesired by the majority of those now designated Transkeian, is likely to benefit only a small group of chiefs, bureaucrats, and traders. It seeks to deprive black South Africans of legal claim to the land and wealth of the Republic. The separate "freedom" of the Xhosa people in their ethnic state constitutes a symbolic exercise, designed to mystify external critics of South Africa's repressive policies and to divert radical challenge from the South African political system.

Notes

1. Muriel Horrell, Dudley Horner, and Jane Hudson, *A Survey of Race Relations in South Africa* (Johannesburg: South African Institute of Race Relations, 1975), p. 190.

2. *The Star* (Johannesburg), 2 April 1974.

3. Horrell, Horner, and Hudson, *A Survey of Race Relations*, p. 191.

4. "But for [that] accident of history, the Transkei would be preparing to receive independence from the British," claims Matanzima. (*Rand Daily Mail* [Johannesburg], 1 November 1975) The argument has a superficial attraction, and certain liberal-minded observers tend to swallow it uncritically. (See the editorial, *The Guardian Weekly*, 25 April 1975.)

5. Note Ambassador Andrew Young's article written in May 1976 in which he outlines a scenario in which South Africa increases its pressure on Ian Smith enough to achieve majority rule in Rhodesia, produces a convincing timetable for Namibian independence, and abolishes the cruder realities of apartheid, in return for which the United States might respond by lifting its arms embargo, adopting more favorable monetary policies toward the Republic, and possibly recognizing Transkei. (*Washington Post,* 17 May 1976)

6. Muriel Horrell, *The African Homelands of South Africa* (Johannesburg: South African Institute of Race Relations, 1975), pp. 19–28.

7. Merle Lipton, "Independent Bantustans," *International Affairs* 48, no. 1 (January 1972), pp. 1–19.

8. Heribert Adam, *Modernizing Racial Domination: The Dynamics of South African Politics* (Berkeley and Los Angeles: University of California Press, 1971), pp. 67–73.

9. Gwendolen M. Carter, Thomas Karis, and Newell M. Stultz, *South Africa's*

Transkei: The Politics of Domestic Colonialism (Evanston, Ill.: Northwestern University Press, 1967), pp. 46–69.

10. The main changes were introduced by: the Transkei Constitution Amendment Act, 1971—enabled the chief minister to choose his ministers instead of the assembly electing them by secret ballot; the Bantu Laws Amendment Act, 1972—gave the Transkei government increased powers over road transport, hospital, and health matters (in addition, the South African government undertook to transfer control of the prisons and the police to the Transkeian Ministry of Justice); the Bantu Laws Amendment Act, 1973—empowered the Transkei government to make public loans and established a Transkei Reserve Fund; the Independence Constitution—in terms of South African law, imparted all sovereign powers to the Transkei government.

11. Lucas Mangope, chief minister of Bophuthatswana, has since requested independence; and Chief Minister Dr. Cedric Phatudi of Lebowa recently asked the Lebowa legislative assembly "to review their long-standing objection to sovereign independence for the territory." (*Rand Daily Mail,* 6 April 1976)

12. For instance, of resources going to the two Xhosa homelands—Ciskei (population 510,000) and Transkei (population 1.75 million)—from the Xhosa Development Corporation up to 31 March 1974, nearly 45 million rand of a total of 49 million rand went to the Transkei. (*Business South Africa,* October/November 1975)

13. Colin Bundy, "The Emergence and Decline of a South African Peasantry," *African Affairs* 71, no. 285 (October 1972); Ralph Horwitz, *The Political Economy of South Africa* (London: Weidenfeld and Nicolson, 1967); and William Beinart, "Peasant Production, Underdevelopment and Stratification: Pondoland circa 1880–1930," paper given to African seminar at University of Cape Town, October 1974.

14. Bundy, "South African Peasantry."

15. *Transkei Annual 1976* (Natal: Visa Publications, 1975), p. 61.

16. See John C. Williams, "Lesotho: Economic Implications of Migrant Labor," *South African Journal of Economics* 39, no. 2 (1971); nearly 100,000 Transkeians work in South African mines.

17. The situation is similar to that outlined by Colin Leys, *Underdevelopment in Kenya: The Political Economy of Neo-Colonialism* (London: Heinemann, 1975).

18. G.C.K. Folscher, "The Economic and Fiscal Relationships of the Transkei vis-à-vis the Rest of the Republic as Determinants of its Economic Development," *South African Journal of Economics* 35, no. 3 (1967).

19. Williams, "Lesotho: Economic Implications of Migrant Labor."

20. In 1975–1976, 62.9 million rand of the Transkeian government's total income of 87.8 million rand came from the South African government. Only 15.8 million rand came from domestic sources. The balance came from an accrued budget surplus in 1974–1975. (*Transkei Annual, 1976*; also the budget speech by the chief minister, Debates of the Transkei Legislative Assembly, Third Session, 5 March 1975)

21. The decentralization of industry policy has significantly *reduced* the South African rate of industrial growth and the number of jobs that would have been available to black workers if comparable investment had been made in urban areas. (Horrell, Horner, and Hudson, *A Survey of Race Relations,* pp. 180, 181)

22. The TDC includes these lures to white capital: loan capital up to 50 percent on

plant and equipment at an interest rate of 3 percent for ten years; factories built to specifications, for leasing at annual rent equal to 6 percent of construction cost, for ten years; housing rentals for white staff at 2.5 percent of the construction cost; 40 percent railage rebate on goods sent from the Transkei; 50 percent rebate on harbor dues on goods shipped through East London; partial reimbursement to industrialists moving from the Witwatersrand and Durban areas; and tax rebates for seven years calculated on black employment and value of equipment. (*Business South Africa*, October/November 1975)

23. *Transkei Annual 1976*, pp. 39–43.

24. For instance, in July 1974 the Bantu Investment Corporation launched a campaign to attract British and German homeland investment. (Horrell, Horner, and Hudson, *A Survey of Race Relations*) In June 1976 George Matanzima made a trip to Europe for the same purpose.

25. "You will certainly not find the disruption of Angola. Violence is not a prerequisite for independence." (Keith Faure, secretary to the chief minister, reported in "Transkei: The Birth of a Nation," *To The Point* [Johannesburg], 17 October 1975)

26. *Transkei Annual, 1976*, pp. 39–43.

27. Ibid.

28. *Rand Daily Mail,* 22 October 1975.

29. For more background on how the TNIP parliamentary majority came into being, see Roger J. Southall, "The Beneficiaries of Transkeian 'Independence,'" *Journal of Modern African Studies* 15, no. 1 (March 1977), pp. 1–23.

30. Debates of the Transkei Legislative Assembly, 3rd Session, Third Assembly, 5 March 1975.

31. See the government-sponsored motion in the Legislative Assembly that proposed that, in order to protect their economic value, white farms given to the Transkei should be allotted to paramount chiefs and farmers "who had rendered faithful service in the development of the Transkei." (*Rand Daily Mail*, 13 April 1976)

32. *Transkei Annual, 1976.*

33. W. Becker, "Employment Opportunities for Graduates Offered by the Transkei," in W. Becker, ed., *The Economic Development of the Transkei* (Lovedale: The Lovedale Press, 1969).

34. *Daily Dispatch* (East London), 21 February 1975.

35. *Natal Witness* (Durban), 4 July 1975.

36. *The Times* (London), 17 April 1973.

37. *Natal Mercury*, 23 April 1975.

38. Debates of the Transkei Legislative Assembly, Third Session, 11 March 1975.

39. Data on wage payments in the private sector are scarce, but available sources indicate that the return to labor is kept at a very low level. For instance, in 1973 the largest Transkeian construction company reportedly paid its laborers a monthly minimum wage equal to only one-third of the poverty datum line established for the Durban area. (*Daily News* [Durban], 12 March 1973)

40. A minimum definition of liberation would entail "majority rule" plus a more equal distribution of economic resources throughout the population.

41. Republic of Transkei Constitution Bill, 1976, Sections 57 and 58.

42. This issue remains crucial to any international recognition of Transkei that

might seem to endorse this nonvoluntary change in citizenship. See Patrick Laurence, *The Transkei: South Africa's Politics of Partition* (Johannesburg: Ravan Press, 1976), pp. 114–123.

43. Albie Sachs, "The Instruments of Domination in South Africa," pp. 223–249, in Leonard Thompson and Jeffrey Butler, eds., *Change in Contemporary South Africa* (Berkeley and Los Angeles: University of California Press, 1975).

44. *Rand Daily Mail*, March and April 1976.

45. *Eastern Province Herald* (Port Elizabeth), 26 May 1976.

46. G. L. Kakana, the first black secretary to a minister, was fired for "insubordination" after only two months' service. (*Natal Daily News*, 2 October 1975; and *Rand Daily Mail*, 13 December 1975)

47. For a sympathetic discussion of Gatsha Buthelezi's efforts to work within the homeland system, see Lawrence Schlemmer and Tim J. Muil, "Social and Political Change in the African Areas: A Case Study of KwaZulu," pp. 107-137, in Thompson and Butler, eds., *Change in Contemporary South Africa.*

48. No criticism of individuals is intended, for the majority of Transkeian civil servants are ordinary people with ordinary needs.

49. *Rand Daily Mail*, 5 January 1976.

50. Interview with Knowledge Guzana, 3 August 1976. Just after independence, Cromwell Diko of the TNIP left to form a new opposition party, the Transkei People's Freedom party. Joined by several others, he was then designated leader of the opposition. This was no revolt against TNIP leadership, for Umtata rumor had it that Diko took the step at Matanzima's instigation, in order to foster Transkei's image as a functioning multiparty democracy. Certainly, Diko has done nothing and said nothing to hint of genuine opposition and remains fully in support of Transkeian independence.

51. *Rand Daily Mail*, 10 August 1976 and 10 September 1976.

52. *The Friend* (Bloemfontein), 25 March 1975.

53. *Sunday Times* (Johannesburg), 22 February 1976.

54. *Rand Daily Mail*, 8 October 1974; *Natal Mercury*, 9 October 1974 and 30 January 1975.

55. *Daily Dispatch*, 6 August 1976; *Rand Daily Mail*, 18 August 1976.

56. See Buthelezi's statement: "Thousands of evicted Zulus are wandering homeless through northern Natal and Zululand." (Muriel Horrell, *The African Homelands of South Africa*, p. 17)

57. J. A. Copelyn, "The Mpondo Revolt," B.A. honors thesis, University of the Witwatersrand, 1974.

58. For details on the Transkei Army, see *Rand Daily Mail*, 11 and 12 April 1975.

9

Retreat from Challenge: White Reactions to Regional Events Since 1974

Donald G. Baker

Regional events since the Portuguese coup of April 1974 have created a heightened sense of threat among whites in Rhodesia and South Africa, but the reactions of the two governments have been sharply different. Despite the massive electoral support that both the Rhodesian Front and the National party received from white voters in 1977 general elections, it would be wrong to conclude that similar appeals were made to similar electorates. In fact, the appeals were polar. In Rhodesia, Ian Smith asked whites to accept the inevitability of early black rule. In South Africa, John Vorster presented the National party as the sole guarantor of continued white political hegemony over the black majority. In each instance, substantial political differences existed among whites about the best course of action, but these real cleavages were submerged in overwhelming support for the governing party.

How can the massive support of two white communities for starkly different political futures be best explained? This chapter focuses on this question, with the hope that some insight may be provided into future political actions by whites in these two countries.

Perhaps nowhere more than in the instances of Rhodesia and South Africa do the particular values of observers shape their perceptions and prognoses of political events. Of course, it is generally true that an analyst's intellectual paradigm determines the "facts" that the analyst isolates, and even where several observers may agree on the "facts," their different paradigms may lead them to contrasting interpretations.[1] The implications of this problem for analysis of political change in Southern Africa are best seen in a close examination of work by Heribert Adam and work by R. W. Johnson, each focused particularly (but not exclusively) on South Africa, but each leading to sharply contrasting interpretations of the present scene and of future trends.[2]

Simply stated, Johnson argues that increased pressure on South Africa, be it external and/or internal in origin, will push whites in both attitude and action to the right. The *verkrampte*, not the *verligte*, will accede to power, paralleling the reaction of white settlers in colonial African societies to nationalist demands before the eventual nationalist assumption of power. Adam, to the contrary, reaffirms a thesis he posed originally in *Modernizing Racial Domination:* circumstances, including increased economic development and pressures, will prompt the South African regime (which he considers a pragmatic oligarchy) into basic concessions.[3] These concessions will include the political and economic incorporation of some blacks and a transition from a racially defined to a class-defined society.[4] Juxtaposing Johnson and Adam, the fundamental question must be: will increased pressure prompt the elimination of racial discrimination or will it lead to increased repression of racially subordinate groups? Which course of action will be taken depends largely upon the attitudes and motivations of the white political elites (and whites generally) in Rhodesia and South Africa.

The Johnson and Adam analyses provide a necessary starting point for an appraisal of white motivations, attitudes, and actions. From his study of South African developments, Johnson concludes of the future: "Anything other than white supremacy is unthinkable."[5] While the government may make minor modifications in apartheid policies (including black incorporation into the national economy at relatively low levels) to placate opposition and to adapt to new circumstances, apartheid and economic development "go hand in hand."[6] Black South Africans (be they homeland, rural, urban, or urban unemployed) have insignificant power resources, which precludes any effective pressure by them for major change.[7] If internal opposition (as well as external opposition) increased, the government with overwhelming white support would adopt "a sufficiently ruthless and brutal policy at home," discard both Rhodesia and Namibia, and thereby become "secure enough well into the 1990s."[8]

In Johnson's analysis, the analogy with earlier white settler societies is important. Black demands for power sharing initially prompt white "reform" responses, but the black nationalists reject the offered concessions. That rejection precipitates a white reaction, from which emerges a monolithic white bloc whose political leaders institute repressive measures. Rhodesian developments since the late 1950s illustrate this pattern, and Johnson argues that South Africa is following a somewhat similar path.[9]

Johnson recognizes the importance of differences between South Africa and Rhodesia, on the one hand, and earlier white settler societies on the other. The latter were dependent upon a metropole for military support. When the metropole acceded to nationalist pressures and withdrew support from colonial whites, the colonial whites were forced to yield; and the nationalists took power. Southern Rhodesia as a self-governing colony was different, for the United Kingdom had little effective control over it.[10] South Africa is altogether different, for the Afrikaners have no European home to which they could return.

It is this absence of an alternative homeland that supports Johnson's view that Afrikaners see themselves as under a growing siege. In reaction, they will use ruthlessly whatever power necessary to secure their position. "History, in a word," he suggests, "is again on the side of the *verkramptes.*"[11]

A recent analysis by the South African social scientist Lawrence Schlemmer supports Johnson's interpretation. While agreeing with Adam's view that "there occurred an increasing rationalization and 'modernization' of white control over the period until 1974," Schlemmer suggests that more-recent events "must have produced a pervasive sense of heightened threat to the established order in white-ruled Southern Africa."[12] This comes despite the continuation of general physical security for whites and general social stability. Nonetheless, because the regime perceives itself threatened, it has become less adaptable and less flexible: there is emerging an "apparent incapacity of the South African system to undergo progressive, even if gradual, mutation."[13] The result has been increasing "resistance to the extension of relatively marginal privileges to blacks," rather than "the sort of adjustments which would have been a rational response."[14]

Unlike Johnson, whose analysis fits in a comparative framework, Adam is concerned exclusively with South Africa. His central conclusion is that political power in that country rests with a pragmatic oligarchy within the ruling National party, which will—under pressure from confrontations and changing circumstances—discard some of its racial policies.[15] Over a longer period of time, the "outdated racial hierarchy . . . will be gradually undermined by an evolving class structure" in which "a small elite of the subordinate strata increasingly participates in the economic rewards and political status of the system."[16] The result will be "de-ideologized and increasingly de-racialized power conflict" in which the pragmatic oligarchy accommodates its policies to economic and political necessities.[17] Put differently, Adam argues that without a racial ideology as motivation for the ruling group "entrenched racial domination becomes negotiable" and that increasing pressures (whether external and/or internal) will *not* lead to stress, repression, or "dogmatic, rigid, and intolerant forms of behavior" but to concessions and changes that will "form the basis for new alliances across the color line, which could still ensure a relatively evolutionary and peaceful change in South Africa."[18]

A central weakness in Adam's analysis lies in his wavering about the importance (or even the existence) of racial ideology as a basic motivating force for Afrikaner Nationalists. Relying on Shils's definition of ideology, which he restates as "a program of action to remedy present ills in a future utopia" that "explicitly legitimizes a status quo or specific behavior both for the actors as well as the recipients of actions," he concludes that "in South Africa white rule is no longer efficiently legitimized with an ideology of Afrikaner identity or racist notions, but with bureaucratic notions of law and order."[19] He contradicts this conclusion in the very next paragraph by saying that "this state of affairs also constitutes a latent ideology," but shortly thereafter Adam reverts to his original position that race is negotiable, because of an "ideological lack" and "the relative absence of direct indoctrination of an official belief system."[20]

Adam seems to be arguing that any modification in an ideology means it is no longer an ideology.[21] Both Schlemmer and du Toit disagree. Schlemmer concludes that Afrikaners are a "corporate group" held together firmly by "a powerful mobilizing group-centered ideology."[22] And even though du Toit insists that the historical beliefs held by Afrikaners before 1948 did not constitute an ideology, he believes that since the assumption of power a "specific political ideology, that of apartheid" has emerged and that "there is a profound inner connection between the content of the ideology of apartheid and Afrikaner political supremacy."[23]

Adam also contends that racial beliefs are more negotiable than religious beliefs. This questionable argument rests on the work of Dickie-Clark, who has himself acknowledged that race as well as religion has "at times taken on a non-bargaining quality."[24] Neither author provides convincing evidence that racial beliefs are negotiable, being content to dismiss racial beliefs as rationalizations for privilege and exploitation. Because of their own biases, they ignore the possible reality of racial beliefs as a motivating force. In fact, racial beliefs may be as deeply imbedded as religious beliefs, and neither may be susceptible to rational argument or explanation. More basically, race and culture as motivating forces may be as fundamental as are power, privilege, and status.[25] Schlemmer's studies, for instance, indicate clearly that racial beliefs may shape both perception and behavior.[26]

Adam supports his argument for the absence of racial ideology by pointing to the shift in Afrikaner Nationalist thinking from white supremacy to cultural pluralism, but a contrary interpretation of this change can be made. Although racial ideology remains unchanged—and with it the belief that whites should remain a distinct and hegemonial group—the shifted emphasis to cultural differences fragments black groups from an integrative nationalism, limits their acquisition of modern skills and technology, and denies them a political voice within "white" South Africa. From this perspective, the emphasis on cultural pluralism involves not a changed ideology but a shift in tactics in order to preserve Afrikaner group identity that is based on racial ideology.

Adam's point about a pragmatic response to pressure is also arguable. He offers little evidence to substantiate his claim, and the evidence provided actually lends greater credence to the opposite interpretation. Certainly both psychological studies and South African events suggest that stress and threat seriously affect thought processes, perceptions, and responses of individuals and groups, resulting in rigid attitudes and dogmatic behavior.[27] Johnson's examples from white settler regimes support this view. He notes that the cycle of black nationalist demands, rebuffed white concessions, and renewed nationalist demands "led to a white reaction so fierce that the would-be [white] reformers not only lost their mandate but saw progressively more and more hard-line politicians (and generals) succeed them."[28]

By far the major weakness of Adam's analysis is his concentration on the 1960s. From that limited period he draws generalizations about National party flexibility that he then attempts to apply to other periods and situations. His analysis in *Modernizing Racial Domination* may be correct for the 1960s and the conditions that prevailed then. At that time the South African government wielded tight political and police control and was not threatened by either internal opposition or international pressure. It could afford to relax somewhat, particularly because it had recognized that limited incorporation of blacks at low and even middle levels of the economy would enhance overall development.[29] Hence Adam's analysis is situational, and his generalizations really apply only to that period; what Adam sees as a pragmatic principle was not more than a situational response to specific conditions. The basic situation changed markedly with the 1973 Durban strikes and with the events following the Portuguese coup, but Adam's rigid adherence to his notion about Afrikaner nationalist pragmatic flexibility limits his ability to explain these more recent events.

The 1975 South African intervention in Angola provides the most obvious of a number of examples in which Adam's analysis fails. If the South African government were rational and pragmatic, it would have weighed the consequences of failure before acting. Had it been rational, it would not have intervened—as Adam himself admits, "This illusionary assessment of reality provided the context in which, from the white point of interest, one of the greatest blunders was committed, namely to initially interfere militarily in Angola."[30] Although, given his perspective, Adam cannot perceive that increased stress led to a dogmatic and irrational action, his analysis implies this conclusion contrary to his own thesis: "the consequences of South Africa's involvement could be anticipated by any rational, pragmatically calculating analyst."[31]

The evidence of official reaction to black dissidence also refutes his thesis. Despite the increasing number of racial confrontations between 1973 and late 1976, the reaction was at first limited: "The police retaliation, though severe, was not massive in scale."[32] However, by October 1977 the cumulative impact of black unrest (beginning with the June 1976 Soweto riots) triggered mounting white fear and brought about expanded government repression, including the banning of most moderate urban black leaders and the closing of the influential black newspaper, *The World.* Steve Biko's death while he was in detention exacerbated black resentment and anger but simultaneously made little impact on most whites. The National party's campaign before the November 1977 election portrayed the country as under mounting siege. That rhetoric was a reflection of both the growing fear among whites and the government's increasing inflexibility, rigidity, and dogmatism in reaction to stress.

Recent events in Rhodesia suggest that another factor must be considered: racial beliefs, whether or not negotiable, may fall to secondary importance when a regime is confronted by a *force majeure.* Of course, not all individuals or groups give way even then, preferring instead to hold out stubbornly to the end, seeing themselves as martyrs to their cause. In the end, blunt power may be the most significant determinant of group conflict, whether it be racial, religious, or otherwise impelled. Thus, both race and power must be considered in an assessment of white motivations, attitudes, and actions in Rhodesia and South Africa since 1974.

The Centrality of Belief Systems

For all groups, but to an extraordinary extent for Afrikaners, an underlying system of beliefs binds group members together, shapes group perceptions, and serves as a determinant of behavior.[33] The Afrikaner belief system provides "an almost universal basic group-centered orientation" toward the world.[34] It determines how Afrikaners perceive and interpret the world, while fulfilling two basic group needs: "the need for a cognitive framework to know or understand [the world] and the need to ward off threatening aspects of reality."[35] In short, belief systems (including the Afrikaner one) need not be logical or rational; indeed, studies indicate that numerous components of a belief system that appear illogical or irrational to the observer have an inner logic for the holder.[36] Hence the observer who rashly discounts racial beliefs as less significant than religious or other beliefs mistakenly applies his own value judgments. In so doing, he ignores what may be reality.[37]

In general, belief systems become more dogmatic as the group's perception of threat increases: "To the extent that the cognitive need to know is predominant and the need to ward off threat absent, open systems should result. . . . But as the need to ward off threat becomes stronger, the cognitive need to know should become weaker, resulting in more closed belief systems."[38]

Although increased dogmatism is the usual reaction to increased threat, a recognition of limited power vis-à-vis its enemies may compel a threatened group to respond in an extraordinary manner.[39] The group will make concessions in order to avoid possible destruction. But if its perception of the "power factor" is distorted or illusory, it may act illogically and irrationally. Adam himself recognizes this condition among Afrikaners but does not appreciate that it is indicative of a high degree of anxiety, threat, and stress.[40]

The Range of White Attitudes Toward Blacks

Having stressed the importance of belief systems as a unifying force among Afrikaners, English-speaking South African whites, and white Rhodesians, it is equally important to recognize that these groups are far from monolithic. One very important impetus for differentiation among them — at least as important as differing economic interests — is the variety of ways in which they perceive blacks.

There are three distinguishable aspects to white attitudes about blacks: basic white beliefs and attitudes about blacks; white beliefs about the incorporation of blacks within the system, which means giving them some share of power; and white receptivity or resistance to political change.[41] Although these dimensions overlap, they can be discussed separately for the purpose of assessing white attitudes, motivations, and behavior.

White beliefs concerning blacks range from the view that blacks are inferior (and should therefore be kept completely subordinate) to the view that blacks are equal and should be fully incorporated. Four important intermediate beliefs should be noted. There are whites whose motivation for the maintenance of white dominance is their preoccupation with the power and privilege they hold. Other whites uphold the system and black subordination not because of any specific beliefs about blacks but because they are conformists to prevailing social norms. Still others are politically indifferent, virtually unaware of the prevalent exploitation and oppression of blacks, but indirectly support the system's perpetuation by their presence and behavior. Finally, there are some who believe blacks are equal but who maintain that only "civilized" blacks (those clearly westernized in belief and behavior) merit incorporation into the social system at the same level and pay as whites.

White beliefs about the incorporation of blacks and about sharing power can conveniently be viewed on an informal graph:

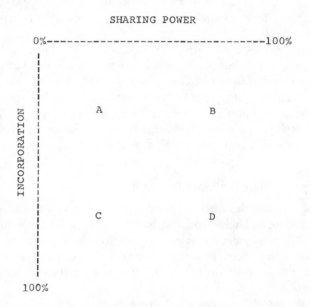

A represents black reserves in South Africa and Rhodesian tribal trust lands in which blacks are kept out of the white social structures, while at the same time their own structures are under direct or indirect white control. B represents the situation of South African homelands in which blacks are given increasing amounts of power over their own lives (although the South African regime retains ultimate control), but at the high price of losing even potential political rights in the white system. C fits both Rhodesia and South Africa. For Rhodesia, C reflects the limited structural incorporation of blacks into both political and economic realms during the Central African Federation (1953–1963) and, in somewhat different forms, under the Rhodesian Front government of Ian Smith. For South Africa, C reflects the very limited incorporation of blacks into the economic (but not the political) sector because whites believe doing so can contribute to South African development and hence to social stability. D involves full black incorporation and full sharing of power. Practically it means black control, an end opposed vehemently by most whites (English as well as Afrikaner) in South Africa and most Rhodesian whites.

White receptivity or resistance to political change also covers a wide range and includes a few prototypical points of view. At one extreme, there are those who reject change under any circumstances, even when resistance to

change means certain death—a position of complete rigidity and dogmatism. Then, there are those who, despite their opposition to change and
steadfast allegiance to core beliefs, accept change in some peripheral beliefs
and behavior, in an accommodation intended to preserve their control or
domination (this is Adam's "modernizing racial domination"). Others hold
steadfast to their beliefs, but under the pressure of *force majeure* accept
change, acquiescing in fear of their destruction. Finally, there are those few
who accept change because their belief system is more flexible, because they
fear the consequences of a refusal to change, or because changes in their
belief system lead them to accept the legitimacy of the change.

Changing White Attitudes Toward Blacks

In both Rhodesia and South Africa, events since 1974 have sharpened
white anxiety and fear and led to the growth of siege cultures. For Rhodesia,
the August 1977 elections reflected the general patterns of white attitudes.
Though a right-wing breakaway Rhodesian Front faction called for greater
racial separation and some small groups of liberals argued for an immediate
multiracial society, most whites supported Ian Smith in his paradoxical acceptance of black rule, because they believed (or at least hoped) that he
might be able to ensure some stable future for Rhodesian whites.[42]

Together with this basic change in attitude, there still persisted an atmosphere of self-delusion like that which Adam observed in South Africa.
Some white Rhodesians, and even the government, held the belief that the
"internal" settlement that resulted in the semblance of joint black-white executive control by April 1978 would be acceptable to Western governments.
On balance, only imminent *force majeure* produced a basic change in
Rhodesian official policy, and even this brought only partial and reluctant
change in the attitudes of most whites.

Much the same reaction occurred among South African whites after the
1974 Portuguese coup, although one basic difference in the situations facing
the two communities during the mid-1960s and into the 1970s is very important. While Rhodesian whites felt increasingly threatened and under
siege starting with UDI in 1965, South African whites felt increasingly self-
confident about their situation after the effectively favorable ICJ ruling on
South West Africa in 1966. Thus, regional and domestic events since 1974
marked a more abrupt and a more rapid shift in white attitudes in South
Africa than in Rhodesia.

Following the 1973 Durban strikes and the regional changes ensuing from
the Portuguese coup, a precipitous change took place in South African white
beliefs and behavior, reflecting growing stress and anxiety. At a personal
level, gun purchases rose markedly and willingness to give money to

charities helping blacks dropped significantly. At the political level, the government reacted to black dissidence with a heavy hand beginning in 1976 and continuing through 1977. Electoral support for the National party rose to a new high in the November 1977 election, and throughout 1977 and 1978 the National party increasingly stressed South Africa's isolation from international allies and the mounting threats with which it was confronted, both at home and abroad. Whites saw themselves as under siege. Prime Minister Vorster campaigned on the issue of whether white South Africans wanted to be "dictated to" by the United States and other Western governments. Were U.S. pressures for one man, one vote to succeed, Vorster warned, the end result for South Africa "would be exactly the same as if it were subverted by marxists."[43] The South African foreign minister stridently proclaimed that white South Africans "will fight like cornered animals" to prevent black rule.[44]

It now appears that the South African government, in reaction to increased black opposition and Western pressure, will become more rigid and inflexible insofar as it perceives challenges to the preservation of Afrikaner (and white) power. As long as blacks constitute a numerical majority within "white" South Africa and they continue to press for the sharing of political power (rather than its separate acquisition in homelands or in autonomous townships), the government will pursue strategies and policies aimed at restricting or even destroying black power resources. Whatever concessions might be made, however they modify components of ideology, the present dominance of blacks by whites will not be voluntarily altered. Until such time as South Africa is confronted by a *force majeure*, like that which forced white Rhodesians to reluctantly accede to black majority rule, few meaningful changes can be expected. In short, Johnson's analysis appears far more persuasive and predictive than Adam's.

Notes

1. For the general analysis of the relationship between values and the choice of intellectual framework, see Thomas Kuhn, *The Structure of Scientific Revolutions* (Chicago: University of Chicago Press, 1962); Gunnar Myrdal, *Objectivity in Social Research* (New York: Pantheon Books, 1969), Chaps. 9–13; Robert Brown, *Explanation in Social Science* (Chicago: Aldine Publishers, 1963); Eugene Meehan, *Explanation in Social Science: A System Paradigm* (Homewood, Ill.: Dorsey Press, 1968); and his *Value Judgment and Social Science* (Homewood, Ill.: Dorsey Press, 1969). For the particular problem in analyses of South African politics, see Leonard Thompson and Jeffrey Butler, eds., *Change in Contemporary South Africa* (Berkeley and Ios Angeles: University of California Press, 1975), pp. ix–xv, Introduction (by Thompson); Harrison Wright, *The Burden of the Present: Liberal-Radical Controversy over*

South African History (Cape Town: David Philip, 1977); and T.R.W. Davenport, *South Africa* (London: Macmillan, 1977), Chap. 20.

2. R. W. Johnson, *How Long Will South Africa Survive?* (London: Macmillan, 1977); and Heribert Adam, *Modernizing Racial Domination: The Dynamics of South African Politics* (Berkeley and Los Angeles: University of California Press, 1971); and Adam's more recent articles—"Internal Constellations and Potentials for Change," in Thompson and Butler, eds., *Change in Contemporary South Africa,* pp. 303–326; "Conflict and Change in South Africa," in Donald G. Baker, ed., *Politics of Race: Comparative Studies* (Lexington, Mass.: Lexington Books, 1975); and "Ideologies of Dedication vs. Blueprints of Expedience," *Social Dynamics* 2 (December 1976).

3. Adam, *Modernizing Racial Domination,* Chap. 6, and Adam, "Internal Constellations and Potentials for Change," p. 326.

4. Adam, "Ideologies of Dedication vs. Blueprints of Expedience," p. 90; and Adam, "Internal Constellations and Potentials for Change," p. 326.

5. Johnson, *How Long Will South Africa Survive?* p. 290.

6. Ibid. This basic question of the impact of industrialization was raised early by Herbert Blumer, "Industrialization and Race Relations," in Guy Hunter, ed., *Industrialization and Race Relations* (London: Oxford University Press, 1965). Both the Wright and Davenport books cited in Note 1 review the controversy, and it is renewed in articles by Adam Potholm, Gervasi, and Nolutshungu in Thompson and Butler, eds., *Change in Contemporary South Africa.*

7. On this point, see Donald G. Baker, "Race and Power: Comparative Approaches to the Analysis of Race Relations," *Ethnic and Racial Studies* no. 1 (July 1978); also, Johnson, *How Long Will Africa Survive?* pp. 295–301.

8. Johnson, *How Long Will Africa Survive?* p. 314.

9. Ibid., p. 304.

10. Larry W. Bowman, *Politics in Rhodesia* (Cambridge, Mass.: Harvard University Press, 1973).

11. Johnson, *How Long Will Africa Survive?* p. 303.

12. Lawrence Schlemmer, "Theories of the Plural Society and Change in South Africa," *Social Dynamics* 3 (June 1977), pp. 8, 9.

13. Ibid., p. 3.

14. Ibid., p. 10. Schlemmer acknowledges some flexibility, but he suggests that the reforms offered are "relatively superficial" and "inadequate palliatives or imperfect attempts at elite co-optation."

15. Adam, *Modernizing Racial Domination,* pp. 169–183.

16. Adam, "Internal Constellations and Potentials for Change," p. 326.

17. Adam, "Ideologies of Dedication vs. Blueprints of Expedience," p. 87.

18. Ibid., pp. 84, 89, and 91. Adam does not argue that the concessions will end racial domination. They will simply modify and thus "modernize" it. His concern here is to rebut the opposite thesis proposed by Donald G. Baker in "Race, Power, and White Siege Cultures," *Social Dynamics* 1 (December 1975).

19. Adam, "Ideologies of Dedication vs. Blueprints of Expedience," p. 83.

20. Ibid., pp. 83, 87.

21. Adam's rigidity here is reminiscent of that of fundamentalist religious sects

that demand a literal interpretation of the Bible. His static conception of ideology is far removed from the dynamic view outlined by Carl Friedrich in his *Man and His Government* (New York: McGraw-Hill, 1963), p. 89.

22. Schlemmer, "Theories of the Plural Society and Change in South Africa," p. 7.

23. Andre du Toit, "Ideological Change, Afrikaner Nationalism, and Pragmatic Racial Domination in South Africa," in Thompson and Butler, eds., *Change in Contemporary South Africa*, pp. 28, 29.

24. Hamish Dickie-Clark, "The Study of Conflict in South Africa and Northern Ireland," *Social Dynamics* 2 (June 1976), p. 55.

25. Norman Bromberger, "Economic Growth and Political Change in South Africa," in Adrian Leftwich, ed., *South Africa: Economic Growth and Political Change* (London: Allison and Busby, 1974); Davenport, *South Africa*, p. 375; and Schlemmer, "Theories of the Plural Society and Change in South Africa," p. 6.

26. Schlemmer, "Theories of the Plural Society and Change in South Africa," and his earlier monograph, *Privilege, Prejudice, and Parties* (Johannesburg: South African Institute of Race Relations, 1973).

27. Milton Rokeach, *The Open and Closed Mind* (New York: Basic Books, 1960), Chaps. 17–21; and Irving Janis, *Victims of Groupthink: A Psychological Study* (Boston: Houghton Mifflin, 1972).

28. Johnson, *How Long Will South Africa Survive?* p. 303.

29. Ibid., Chaps. 1 and 2; also Adam, *Modernizing Racial Domination*.

30. Adam, "Ideologies of Dedication vs. Blueprints of Expedience," p. 89.

31. Ibid., pp. 89, 90.

32. Schlemmer, "Theories of the Plural Society and Change in South Africa," p. 9.

33. Dickie-Clark, "The Study of Conflict in South Africa and Northern Ireland," pp. 54, 55.

34. Schlemmer, "Theories of the Plural Society and Change in South Africa," p. 13.

35. Rokeach, *The Open and Closed Mind*, p. 67.

36. Ibid., pp. 33–35; also Milton Rokeach, "The Nature and Meaning of Dogmatism," *Psychological Review*, no. 61 (May 1954).

37. See Dickie-Clark, "The Study of Conflict in South Africa and Northern Ireland," p. 58, where he claims that because "racist claims are open to rational and empirical refutation," they are not as deeply imbedded "as the claims made by sectarian religion."

38. Rokeach, *The Open and Closed Mind*, pp. 67, 68.

39. Baker, "Race and Power: Comparative Approaches to the Analysis of Race Relations."

40. Adam, "Ideologies of Dedication vs. Blueprints of Expedience," p. 89; also Janis, *Victims of Groupthink*, p. 204.

41. The variability in white views toward blacks, Indians, and Coloureds is discussed in Donald G. Baker, "Dominance Patterns in Anglo Fragment Societies," *International Review of Modern Sociology*, no. 4 (Augumn 1974).

42. In the absence of public opinion polls of white attitudes, this assessment is

based on the author's observations and discussions while in Rhodesia from May through September 1977, but also reflects his earlier stays during all of 1975 and part of 1976.

43. *The Star* (Johannesburg), international weekly edition, 8 October 1977, p. 13.

44. *The Star* (Johannesburg), international weekly edition, 15 October 1977, p. 2.

10
The Baptism of Fire: South Africa's Black Majority After the Portuguese Coup

Noel C. Manganyi

The remnants of the Portuguese colonial empire crumbled in 1974. This important event in the history of imperialism and colonial racism in Southern Africa must still be studied as contemporary history. The human drama of which the Portuguese coup was the historical denouement is currently accessible to us only in vague outline. Perhaps nothing else in recent history dramatizes so well the elements of contingency and ambiguity in the historical process—the emergence on the historical scene of the unexpected.

With regard to the probable impact of the Portuguese coup and the subsequent decolonization process on Southern Africa and its peoples, it seems prudent to assert with Merleau-Ponty that nobody has any science of the future.[1] The future, unlike the past, is always probable—but not in the reassuring statistical sense of that word. Given the problem suggested by Merleau-Ponty's statement, the social sciences use what is current and known (however dimly) to understand and delineate emerging and probable historical developments. This social science of the probable means walking on quicksand and losing ground all the time. Nonetheless, in full conviction and conscious awareness, it remains possible to project into the dimness of the future some plausible directions that phenomena such as political loyalties and self-identities may assume in the arena of group and race conflict.

These considerations constitute a baseline for the examination of the

A preliminary version of this chapter was presented at a workshop, "Southern Africa Since the Portuguese Coup," held at Rhodes University on 24 and 25 June 1976.

Because this chapter by a black South African academic seemed especially significant for a South African audience, the editor agreed to its publication in that country in advance of its appearance in this volume. See Noel C. Manganyi, *Mashungu's Reverie and Other Essays* (Johannesburg: Ravan Press, 1977).

following topics: some methodological issues in the study of subordinacy and superordinancy; multiple siege cultures—the South African case; prophets, academics, and the "dustbin" revolt; the future of the race supremacist ethos; and the "eclipse of reason."

Issues in the Study of
Subordinacy and Superordinacy

Contemporary societies under stress often turn to social science scholarship for direction and guidance. Although this distress signal is often muted, its existence in a society is easily detected in the restlessness of social scientists. Southern Africa after the Portuguese coup is not exceptional in this regard. More than any other professional group, sociologists in Southern Africa show notable restlessness. A note of urgency creeps into the themes they examine. In addition to the exploration of methodological problems in the study of attitudes,[2] themes range from a reexamination of sociological perspectives for the study of race[3] to consideration of research opportunities and problems for social science research in divided societies.[4]

Several statements must be made about this research on subordinacy and superordinacy. First, social science research about race relations requires the active participation of researchers who are themselves members of subordinate groups.[5] Second, because of the unsophisticated level of theory in the study of attitudes and the methodological problems encountered in its use, a full-dress assessment of the several important South African studies of attitudes is difficult to give.[6]

Nonetheless, there are two basic orientations that may be adopted in the study of situations of asymmetrical power relationships that lead to a superordinate-subordinate social structure. One orientation relates to objective social conditions: group cleavages, problems, and conflict over power and resource allocation in the economic, political, and military spheres. The other orientation points toward more elusive subjective conditions—experiences, cognitions, value orientations, perceptions of self and others—that exist as equivalents of the objective structural arrangements within a society. Sometimes a half-hearted attempt is made to capture reality at both levels, but not often enough and not satisfactorily either.[7]

In South African society, with its clearly demarcated domains of permissible experience, whites (members of superordinate groups) studying blacks (subordinates) find themselves face to face with an experiential hiatus of such magnitude as to denude their personal experience as a resource for both hypothesis formation and the meaningful interpretation of data. The implication of this point was summed up cogently by another psychologist in a different, but related, context: "The task of the psychologist is to understand people by making explicit what people can communicate to him concerning their experience and behavior. In order to make meaningful explications he will continually draw on his own experience which will have been built up out of his own dialogue with the world and fellow man."[8]

In studies of attitudes and perceptions of self and others (the main concern here), as well as potential behavior growing from these attitudes and perceptions, the researcher must (in the face of these unfavorable conditions) paradoxically undertake more than is usually required. In the study of the social psychology of superordinacy and subordinacy, facing several intermediate (and often unknown) variables between the existence of an attitude and its expression in language and behavior, the researcher must conceive that his scholarly responsibility is to make explicit the unconscious, or preconscious.

Thus a plea for an interdisciplinary approach to the problems of race is as refreshing as it is challenging.[9] For it must be remembered that white researchers may find in their studies of black reactions and adaptions to racial subordination a *false consciousness*.[10] It seems unlikely that social science in South Africa will unmask it. The task might be easier if a literature of the oppressed were actively encouraged or at least allowed to survive.[11] Such literature could help social science, because the creative impulse derives its momentum from various levels and dimensions of human consciousness, including the innermost core — the realm of the collective unconscious. In any case, social science would contribute much, if it did no more than introduce a rational ethos into the discourse about social reality in historically extreme situations like South Africa.

Multiple Siege Cultures:
The South African Case

Afrikaner intellectuals may study South African history and Afrikaner history for purely patriotic reasons, but the contemporary generation of black intellectuals studies the same history for a different purpose: to understand better how the Afrikaner struggle for freedom, often noble in its earliest manifestations, could have turned in so negative a direction by the 1970s.[12] One black observer said recently that the Afrikaner dilemma now consists of Afrikaner nationalism's failure to come to terms with the implied consequences of its own struggles and spiritual history.[13]

The development of Afrikaner *volksnasionalisme* has been compared usefully to "white cultures under siege" in the southern United States and in present-day Rhodesia.

The threatened group envisions a society based on its values and belief system.

Dependent upon the society's structural arrangements and the group's own power compared to that of the threatening group (or groups), the siege culture will pursue diverse strategies (dependent upon its own dominant or subordinate position in society) aimed at the preservation or implementation of its culture and belief system. The siege culture evolves a defensive ideology or belief system that (a) articulates contrasting conceptions that distinguish between "we" (the siege culture) and "they" (the threatening group or groups), (b) serves as the basis for establishing group solidarity in the face of the perceived threat, and (c) provides a rationale or justification for its actions and mobilization efforts. The greater the perceived threat, the greater the possibility that the belief system (reflected thereafter in the behavior of the group) of the siege culture will become more rigid, dogmatic, and closed.[14]

The threats to the Afrikaner culture and belief system arose from changing circumstances in the history of South Africa. The most important perceived threats were the intrusive policies imposed by the British imperial administration after annexation of the Cape in 1806 and the presence of African traditional societies that, apart from being racially and culturally different, challenged Boer expansionism with force.

Afrikaner history bears a close (and alarming) resemblance to classical Aristotelian tragedy. Such tragedy encompasses a charismatic nobility and eminent courage, accompanied by a parasitic *harmatia* (weakness of the great). Is it putting it too strongly to say that Afrikanerdom, at the height of its power, is embroiled in a struggle to resolve this tragic contest between strength and weakness?[15]

If a recent paper by a Stellenbosch philosopher, J. Degenaar, can be a guide, enlightened Afrikaners will find little serious fault with the idea of an Afrikaner siege culture. Degenaar suggests that fear of cultural extinction led to the development of Afrikaner *volksnasionalisme*, a "value-oriented movement" that later became a "closed system" of ideas and beliefs. The myth of a God-given identity was also significant and accounts in part for the continued exclusivity of Afrikaner values.

> Although the myth of the chosen people is not generally applied to the Afrikaner today, the policy of separate development is very much rooted in the idea of the identity of the Afrikaner that should be protected . . . Afrikaner nationalism is still based on this *volksnasionalisme*, in that it cannot accommodate English-speaking whites, Afrikaans-speaking Coloureds, the Indians, and the urban and urbanized Africans. *Volksnasionalisme*, which can work in a homogeneous society, is clearly in a paradigmatic crisis when confronted with a heterogeneous society of multi-ethnic and multi-racial complexity. This paradigmatic crisis is indeed one of the basic problems facing the Afrikaner in South Africa today.[16]

One interesting thought should be noted here. It is meaningless to talk of a country facing a crisis if that crisis is in fact occurring in only one segment of the society. For the Afrikaner, the *volk* ideology has outlived its usefulness as an emancipatory concept by turning into a tool for Afrikaner domination of others. In so doing, it has become an "oppressive concept. . . . also for the Afrikaners."[17]

A natural progression in the evolution of siege cultures seems evident. There are honorable beginnings in the desire of a group for freedom and survival as a cultural entity. Then the group experiences strong psychological, social, and economic pressures to single itself out for a special dispensation in which all the negative attributes in its own identity are projected onto any other groups in the society that are subordinate.[18] But in a heterogeneous society, when any one group develops a strong, exclusive, and oppressive group identity, other groups will also try to do so. As a result, tensions develop in the superordinacy-subordinacy pattern. The dominant group becomes even more oppressive in its effort to squelch the rise of competitive group identities.

South Africa contains several siege cultures. The Afrikaner culture evolved in this general pattern until it reached its current position of dominance. Blacks, on the other hand, have only recently started to articulate an acute perception of threats to their own cultural and group survival. Since the beginning of the 1970s, they have also begun to mobilize themselves into a "value-oriented movement," with similar attributes of exclusiveness, dogmatism, and a tendency toward a closed system.

The development of an urban-black siege culture represents a crisis for Afrikaner *volksnasionalisme,* because this competing group identity and nationalism—despite its emulation of the Afrikaner's historical example—increases Afrikaner perception of threat to their own survival as a *volk.* The present consideration of some kind of Afrikaner incorporation of English-speaking whites, Coloureds, and even Indians, in an effort to forestall the black challenge, paradoxically in itself threatens the Afrikaner *volk.* A heroic reappraisal of *volksnasionalisme* is required to resolve this dilemma.

The ascendancy of an urban-black siege culture does not depend only on the dominant white siege culture. The withdrawal of the Portuguese from Mozambique and Angola generated powerful symbols of African nationalist achievement. The power and proximity of these symbols have important psychological implications. African "front-line" leadership, regardless of the merits of its ideological posture, has emerged more aggressive and more charismatic than the leadership of immediately neighboring black states. Thus the standards against which local black leadership is assessed have been raised, with the short-term result that gaps will develop between some present black leaders and their followers.

Another factor of importance is the issue of formal identity vis-à-vis informal identity now posed squarely by homeland independence and citizenship. Black formal identity is defined by the evolving priorities of Afrikaner nationalist political solutions to South African ethnic problems. Black informal identity is another matter altogether, particularly in the cities: "Has 'deethnization' in Soweto then proceeded beyond the point of no return? The government emphasizes 'homeland links' and tries to propagate 'national' identifications. The evidence suggests that it is too late for this kind of political ethnicity; its place is likely to be taken more and more by black ethnicity."[19] It is this "black ethnicity" that, as an informal rallying point, will create about it the elements necessary for the consolidation of an urban-black siege culture. This new siege culture will face two strong pressures: continued, and perhaps growing, oppression from the Afrikaner siege culture; and a developing cleavage between urban blacks and rural blacks that will pose difficulties for the consolidation of a still-larger black siege culture.[20]

Prophets, Academics, and the "Dustbin" Revolt

The Oxford don A. H. Halsey once introduced an article on research into British race relations this way: "The most obvious question to ask about the black British is: will they revolt? All previous questions seem to lead to this one. And however circumlocutory the phrasing, this must surely be posed. . . . a convincing answer would be fabulously cheap . . . to both social theorists of order and conflict and those directly engaged in race relations practice."[21]

This question, posed so bluntly for Britain in 1970, usually appears in the South African context in muted and "circumlocutory . . . phrasing." Nonetheless, it lurks behind most private and public thinking and action about race in South Africa. White researchers have focused on it. Lever dismisses the possibility of black revolt with a listing of black deficiencies that includes "a lack of motivation to actively oppose the system."[22] Schlemmer gives the question more intelligent and systematic attention. Although he suggests some increase in black resentment and hostility toward whites since the 1957 Biesheuvel study, he legitimately notes that his own data do not entitle him to give a definitive answer.[23]

Black observers tend to be unequivocal in their analysis, because of their personal immersion in subordinate social circumstances. They believe a violent racial confrontation is inevitable, unless major social-political change takes place in South Africa.[24]

The question of black revolt must take on a new form and its answering greater urgency after the 1976 urban black revolt. Instead of "Will they revolt?" the question now must be, "What strategies for change are likely to emerge on the South African scene after the 1976 'dustbin' revolt?"

To what extent will the present urban revolt have consequences in the mobilization of black resources? In the long term (although perhaps not in the short term), the dominant group must consider the self-destructive implications of reliance on oppression to ensure its own dominance. Oppressed groups learn to live with violence, and it then changes from a deterrent to an incentive, especially for the young and rebellious. There is a grim omen in the "dustbin" revolt: unarmed, even apolitical, young men and women found a fierce satisfaction in this baptism of fire. They are unlikely to forget their initiation into revolt through violent means.

The most important lesson of what started in Soweto on 16 June 1976 can best be appreciated as a black challenge to psychological domination by Afrikaner *volksnasionalisme*.[25] Blacks in South Africa recognize the short-term difficulties of changing the pattern of structural dominance, although the inherent power of sheer numbers will prove increasingly effective. Nonetheless, it is the psychological domination of blacks by whites that will diminish first, leaving, after awhile, the underlying issue of structural dominance more apparent.

The 1976 disturbances will also have "demonstration effects." Blacks and Coloureds now have a larger awareness of their capability for mobilization and challenge to the regime. With psychological domination undermined, it will become easier to mobilize group resources for pressure (strikes, boycotts, violence, or even warfare) or competition (by the manipulation of labor and skills required by the dominant group).[26] In this light the 1973 Durban strikes involved an early attempt to use competitive resources to secure change, while the 1976 revolt mobilized both pressure and competitive resources.

The pattern of resource mobilization during the 1976 revolt contains an important lesson about the relative influence of formal and informal leadership in black urban communities. The formal leadership is identified with government-created institutions and policies, and it therefore suffers from a lack of legitimacy and credibility among urban blacks. On the other hand, the informal leadership grows out of the 1970s black renaissance and is closely identified with the growing black siege culture. These leaders are effective, but they lack any status or influence in dealing with the government and easily become scapegoats for government reprisals after crises occur. The danger of effective leadership without influence on government was clearly demonstrated in the 1976 riots. Time and again, informal leaders were able to mobilize young blacks to riot or strike, but these same leaders were then unable to gain any attention from the government for black demands. Formal leaders, the government insisted, spoke for urban blacks. This pattern of noncommunication becomes increasingly difficult to break constructively.

Black-black ethnic-based conflict or black-black conflict between the employed and the unemployed cropped up occasionally in the urban unrest of 1976 and 1977. Bloody clashes took place between migrant workers (Zulus in Soweto and Xhosa in Langa) and students over student demands for work boycotts and the closing of *shebeens*—the illegal drinking places. Such clashes will occur again, given the social encapsulation of migrant workers from the surrounding community of the township and the strong pressure to hold on to any job during the long-term South African depression. But it would be a serious miscalculation to take comfort in these cleavages. In the longer run, the entire black industrial population—including migrant workers and their families left in homelands—is participating in an incipient, but massive, regional economic, social, and political revolution. Independent homelands will contribute to the political socialization of migrant workers and their families; so the urban-rural cleavage will shrink rather than expand. This likelihood makes even more important the development of an informed, articulate, and respected formal leadership among blacks.

Should South African society continue to nurture siege cultures with their dogmatic and exclusive nationalisms, a major racial confrontation would be certain in the not-too-distant future. Such an outcome to centuries-long black-white coexistence in Southern Africa would be disheartening to all but the most politically naive and reckless.

The Future of the Race Supremacist Ethos

Any serious consideration of possible future changes in Southern Africa must take into account the impact of the race supremacist ethos. Can this ethos ever be eliminated? A cynical view suggests that the task involved is tantamount to "washing an ethiope white"—that is, doing the impossible. More rigorous examination of the fate of racist beliefs, behavior, and attitudes elsewhere suggests that, at most, a shift takes place from either dominative racism or aversive racism to meta-racism.[27] When constitutional and legal supports for dominative and aversive racism are ended (as in the United States), such racists find it increasingly difficult to maintain their behavior patterns. Their continued need to maintain racial superiority is converted into terms of class superiority, which partly disguises continued racist attitudes and behavior—or meta-racism.

Jacques suggests convincingly that a "fantasy social structure" underlies racist behavior. The interplay between this social structure (or unconscious) and manifest social organization (believed to be rational) must be grasped if the endurability of racism is to be comprehended.[28]

Thus, in any society the rational justification for social values, norms, and institutions is buttressed by an irrational, unconscious set of values and norms. The dialectical relationship between social reality and social fantasy aids understanding of both a racist social structure and racist individuals.

Changing racist attitudes and behavior can be extremely difficult, even when radical changes are made in the institutions sustaining racism. Why is this so? While it is generally true that any social structure is the embodiment of the deepest human concerns, needs, attitudes, symbolization, and unconscious conflicts—the sum of the subjective universe about each individual—in racist cultures, and with racist attitudes and behavior, the primacy of these subjective factors is the strongest.

Social and political activists usually ignore the primacy of the subjective in their preoccupation with practical means and ends, but, nonetheless, their radical positivism can be constructive in creating the social and material disequilibria necessary for the dismantling of racist institutions. Once these institutions are gone, meta-racism begins to show itself.

The greatest danger posed by the transition to meta-racism is the substitution in the racist individual of a consciousness of class superiority for the earlier consciousness of racial superiority. But the racist, like the conversion hysteric or the hypochrondriac—both masters of symptom substitution—remains enslaved to the primacy of the subjective and his own unconscious. He is like a spider trapped in its own web.

The anxiety of racist individuals confronting potential structural change in racist cultures provides a fascinating opportunity to see the primacy of the subjective at work. Anxiety and even primitive fears emanating from the collective racial and cultural unconscious are understandable. They are even a reasonable response, when drastic revolutionary change threatens the survival of privilege, power, and hegemony by a previously superordinate group. But where the demand is limited to "peaceful" change, however radical its rhetoric, the anxieties are often much greater than the situation deserves.

Why is this so? The unconscious not only prefers metaphor to objective reality and a dialectically ambivalent attitude toward reality, it also holds an obdurate preference for hyperbole. How else account for the superordinate threat of the gun when the subordinate offers the olive branch? In listening to and being guided by his unconscious, the racist—in the grip of an intoxicating delusional system—begins to believe that real death is preferable to the horror of metaphysical death: the elimination of his racial fantasies. Although the material and psychological consequences of this subjective fixation are often dehumanizing to both his victims and himself, the racist holds to his subjective values. He has a kind of childhood disease. A product of his socialization experiences, like all humans, the racist has not outgrown his childhood fantasies about magic, narcissistic self-idealization, and personal omnipotence—all of which, because of parental values and experiences, centered around race.

The supposedly adult racist nonetheless can surprise or even shock the observer with claims, actions, and pronouncements during crises which equal those of a developing child. Racial arrogance? A projection of personal omnipotence. Belief in the innate superiority of whites and white culture and civilization? Narcissistic self-idealization. Even magical thinking—the suspension of larger events to meet personal preferences—seems central to the frequent racist comment that Rhodesian or South African blacks either have no interests in political power or no capacity for it. Will these blacks wait a thousand years, or even a hundred, or even a generation? Only in childlike, racist, magical thinking.

The assault on the race supremacist ethos is now international in scope, and because of that, optimism is in order about the global elimination of racist institutions. Dealing effectively with meta-racism will remain a more difficult problem. It will be necessary to develop social institutions capable of linking up with the fantasy social structure of the society so that racist fantasies will diminish in fervor and persistence. This will not be easy anywhere, and especially not in South Africa.

The "Eclipse of Reason"

The questions raised in this analysis are central to the social-psychological circumstances and prospects of South Africa. Yet for these questions to be thought about, debated, and resolved, South Africans of all colors and all shades of political opinion must unmask the "eclipse of reason"—the irrationality—that dominates South African public life.

One of the cardinal difficulties in unmasking the eclipse of reason in this volatile group-conflict situation lies in the diabolic ability of the superordinate-subordinate social structure—in its preoccupation with the maintenance of social-political equilibrium and its concern that marginal change might become uncontrollable—to stifle systematically individuals and groups who, in the long-term at least, could prove beneficial to the society. Whatever the short-term gains in stability, the long-term cost in political rationality is much greater.

Merleau-Ponty says that a society's public life should be evaluated on the basis of whether or not it is guided by a public, formal morality of principles.[29] What is a formal morality of principles? Here I repeat emphatically what I have written elsewhere:

> Quite simply, it is the kind of morality in which principles such as those of justice and liberty are publicly defended in the absence of a just social order and free men and women.[30]

Paradoxically coexisting with the eclipse of reason in Southern Africa is the embryonic triumph of a formal morality of principles. A new order demands that the gap between these formal principles and objective social conditions be rapidly narrowed.

Notes

1. Morris Merleau-Ponty, *Humanism and Terror,* trans. J. O'Neill (Boston: Beacon Press, 1969).

2. G. Wiendieck, "The Behavioral Relevance of Ethnic Attitude Studies," *Social Dynamics* (Cape Town) 1, no. 2 (1975), pp. 125–142.

3. Marshall W. Murphree, "Sociology and the Study of Race: Contemporary Perspectives for Southern Africa," *Social Dynamics* 1, no. 2 (1975), pp. 111–124.

4. David Welsh, "Social Research in a Divided Society: The Case of South Africa," *Social Dynamics* 1, no. 1 (1975), pp. 19–30; and Harold Lever, "Some Problems in Race Relations Research in South Africa," *Social Dynamics* 1, no. 1 (1975), pp. 31–44.

5. Murphree, "Sociology and the Study of Race"; also see Noel C. Manganyi, *Being-Black-in-the-World* (Johannesburg: Sprocas-Ravan Press, 1973), p. 8; and Philip Mayer, "Class, Status, and Ethnicity as Perceived by Johannesburg Africans," in Leonard Thompson and Jeffrey Butler, eds., *Change in Contemporary South Africa* (Berkeley and Los Angeles: University of California Press, 1975), p. 139.

6. Mayer, "Class, Status, and Ethnicity"; Lawrence Schlemmer, "Black Attitudes: Adaptation and Reaction," paper to the Association for Sociology in Southern Africa, Kwaluseni, Swaziland, 1975; S. Biesheuvel, "The Influence of Social Circumstances on the Attitudes of Educated Africans," *South African Journal of Science,* July 1957; and Melville Leonard Edelstein, *What Do Young Africans Think?* (Johannesburg: South African Institute of Race Relations, 1972).

7. Donald G. Baker, "Race and Power: Southern African Race Relations in Comparative Perspective," paper to the association for Sociology in Southern Africa, Kwaluseni, Swaziland, 1976.

8. D. Kruger, *Psychology in the Second Person* (Grahamstown, South Africa: Rhodes University, 1975), pp. 11, 12.

9. Murphree, "Sociology and the Study of Race."

10. Characterizations of South African blacks by whites often attribute to blacks docility, apathy, compliance, and hedonism. Although the adaptive utility of these

and similar attitudes in the face of overwhelming alienation and dehumanization is sometimes noted, the falseness of the consciousness expressed in these attitudes is often overlooked. I argue elsewhere that this false consciousness is in reality intermediate between a subjective ambivalence — the violent reverie (fantasy) — and violence as a social act under propitious revolutionary conditions. See Noel C. Manganyi, "The Violent Reverie: The Unconscious in Literature and Society," in *Mashungu's Reverie And Other Essays* (Johannesburg: Raven Press, 1977), pp. 53–71.

11. Noel C. Manganyi, cited in *Rapport* (Johannesburg), 25 April 1976, pp. 3, 4.

12. D. Kruger, "Die Ondergang van die Afrikanerdom?" [The downfall of Afrikanerdom?], *Deurbraak* (Cape Town), August 1976, pp. 9–11.

13. Manus Buthelezi, "The Christian Challenge of Black Theology," in Thoahlane Thoahlane, ed., *Black Renaissance* (Johannesburg: Raven Press, 1975), pp. 19–23.

14. Donald G. Baker, "Race, Power, and White Siege Cultures," *Social Dynamics* 1, no. 1 (1975), pp. 144, 145.

15. Buthelezi, "The Christian Challenge of Black Theology," p. 20.

16. J. Degenaar, "The Concept of a Volksuniversiteit," paper to the Conference on the Role of Universities in Southern Africa (Cape Town, 1976), pp. 2, 3.

17. H. J. Brinkman, "Comments on the papers of Profesor J. Degenaar and Professor T. van der Walt," Conference on the Role of Universities in Southern Africa, p. 2.

18. Erik H. Erikson, *Dimensions of a New Identity* (New York: W. W. Norton and Company, Inc., 1974).

19. Mayer, "Class, Status, and Ethnicity," p. 153.

20. Ibid.

21. Murphree, "Sociology and the Study of Race," p. 113.

22. Lever, "Some Problems in Race Relations Research in South Africa," pp. 36, 37.

23. Schlemmer, "Black Attitudes: Adaptation and Reaction."

24. Thoahlane Thoahlane, ed., *Black Renaissance;* and Thoko Mbanjwa, ed., *Apartheid: Hope or Despair for Blacks?* Black Viewpoint no. 3 (Durban: Black Community Programmes, 1976).

25. Baker, "Race and Power," pp. 19, 20.

26. Ibid., p. 6.

27. J. Kovel, *White Racism: A Psychohistory* (New York: Vintage Books, 1970).

28. Elliot Jacques, "Social Systems as Defense Against Persecutory and Depressive Anxiety," in M. Klein et al., eds., *New Directions in Psychoanalysis* (New York: Basic Books, 1955), pp. 478–498.

29. Merleau-Ponty, *Humanism and Terror.*

30. Noel C. Manganyi, "Reassessment Towards a New Consensus on Migratory Mine Labour" (Johannesburg: Proceedings of the International Consultation on the Role of the Church among Migrant Mine Workers, 1976).

Part 6

Black African Governments
in Regional Politics

11

Independent African States and the Struggle for Southern Africa

Ali A. Mazrui
David F. Gordon

The continued existence of white minority governments in the states of Southern Africa has been both a starkly visible challenge to the independent black states of Africa and an indication of their own low level of political and diplomatic power. Ending colonialism and racial oppression throughout the whole of the African continent has been a constant theme of African political consciousness and was an important impetus in the formation of the Organization of African Unity (OAU). Yet, more than a decade after the process of decolonization was completed in the rest of continental Africa, the end of white domination in Southern Africa is still not clearly in sight. The Afrikaner Nationalist regime in the Republic of South Africa steadfastly refuses to bend to any criticism from the rest of Africa. Even when leading African states recognized South Africa's "independent sovereignty" and proffered the olive branch of peace in the 1969 Lusaka Manifesto, the South Africans rejected it with contempt. The liberation of Mozambique and Angola, as well, can be interpreted as another sign of Black Africa's weakness in influencing events in Southern Africa since the impetus for liberation came from the April 1974 coup in Lisbon, which though an outcome of the guerrilla struggle in Portuguese Africa, was not caused directly by the actions of Black African states.

The ostensible weakness of Black African states in influencing change in Southern Africa has been analyzed in different ways. Some observers, both within Africa and outside, see the failure as another indication of the neocolonialist patterns that have developed in Africa since independence. They feel that African states could play a much more active role in the liberation of Southern Africa. A more common interpretation involves two elements. First, the new states of postcolonial Africa face immense problems and challenges in meeting the heightened expectations of their peoples and are, by necessity, most concerned with domestic issues. In addition, white power is so entrenched that Black Africa, if it tried, would be unable to effectively challenge it.

Both of these views oversimplify what is essentially a complex interrelationship between white power in Southern Africa and independent African states. In fact the recent past has seen two contradictory trends emerging: increased economic penetration of Black Africa by South Africa, in terms of investments, skills, and exports; and increased political activity by African states in opposition to minority rule in Southern Africa—reflected in aid to liberation movements, initiatives within international organizations, and opposition to South Africa's "outward policy." What has been the net effect of these contradictory trends for the role of Black African states in Southern Africa? In practice do they share the West's complicity with apartheid and white minority rule?

The answers to these questions cannot be reached simply by looking at the level of aid independent African states have given to the liberation movements. A more important factor is Black Africa's response to the political initiatives of the Pretoria regime, the role that African countries play in the transformation of international institutional values, and the impact that this transformation makes upon the evolution of the struggle for Southern Africa.

The importance of the support that independent African states have given to the liberation movements in Southern Africa is often underestimated. Purely in terms of financial contributions and military or paramilitary assistance the role of independent African states appears relatively modest. But that support has wide-ranging repercussions and has been the source of much of the diplomatic legitimacy that the liberation movements have acquired.

Vincent B. Khapoya has distinguished nine manifestations of support that African states extend to liberation movements:

1. provision of asylum to politically active exiles
2. provision of field offices for the liberation movement
3. provision of facilities for military and militarily oriented activities of the movements
4. irregular payment of assessed dues to the Organization of African Unity's liberation committee
5. regular payment of assessed dues to the OAU committee
6. initiation or participation in efforts to unify liberation movements from the same country—such as attempts to unify ZANU and ZAPU in Zimbabwe or the attempt to unify the three Angolan movements before independence

7. opposition by African states to dialogue with South Africa
8. serving as host to nonpolitical refugees from target areas
9. provision of additional aid to movements in terms of cash, medical supplies, educational facilities, and the like[1]

Khapoya underestimates the significance of Black African diplomatic support at the United Nations and in other arenas of world politics, a form of support that continues to erode the legitimacy of white minority rule in Southern Africa and to increase the legitimacy of those who take up arms against white rule. Khapoya also neglects the role that African states have played in thwarting South Africa's political aims in Africa.

Racial Sovereignty and Continental Jurisdiction

What do Black African states have in common in their attitudes to the problems of Southern Africa? In what ways do these attitudes differ from one Black African state to another?

It would of course be naive to conclude that Black African states are united in support of liberation in Southern Africa because they are united in their commitment to human rights. Many of the states that have been very strong in supporting Southern African liberation, ranging from Amin's Uganda to Sékou Touré's Guinea, are guilty of gross violations of human rights in their own societies.

It would be almost as naive to assert that Black African states are committed to the principle of "majority rule," if by that is meant a system of government that allows the majority of the people periodically to choose their own rulers in free elections. Again, almost none of the Black African states that are committed to Southern African liberation are dedicated to majority rule in their own societies.

What the Black African states *are* in fact committed to are two principles often disguised by varying rhetoric. The first is the principle of racial sovereignty. This does involve a concept of "majority rule," but not a liberal one. Under the principle of racial sovereignty, the people in a given society should not be dominated by a racially alien minority. The rulers of each society should as far as possible be racially or ethnically representative. Foreign rule is not merely rule by a nation-state from abroad but rule by a foreign racial or ethnic minority. White rule in Southern Africa is illegitimate partly because it violates this principle of racial sovereignty.

The second important principle operating in Black African attitudes to problems of Southern Africa is the principle of continental jurisdiction. This is an African Monroe Doctrine, seeking to keep outsiders from interfering in African affairs and aspiring to consolidate the autonomy not only of in-

dividual African states but of the African continent as a whole. Primary initiatives in African affairs, under the principle of continental jurisdiction,
must come from Africans themselves.

Motivated by concern for both racial sovereignty and continental jurisdiction, Black African governments and nationalist movements have attempted
to realize two forms of Pan-Africanism: the Pan-Africanism of liberation
and the Pan-Africanism of integration. Pan-Africanism of liberation seeks to
reduce alien control over African affairs, while Pan-Africanism of integration seeks to encourage Africans to form larger economic communities or
wider political federations. Pan-Africanism of liberation is partly concerned
with keeping outside powers at bay, while Pan-Africanism of integration
seeks to bring Africans themselves together.

On balance, Pan-Africanism of liberation has been significantly more
successful than Pan-Africanism of integration. One African country after
another has succeeded in ending political colonialism and establishing at
least formal sovereignty.

Pan-Africanism of integration, on the other hand, has had one failure
after another. These failures have ranged from the breakup of established
federations—like the 1960 collapse of the Mali Federation—to the 1977 collapse of the East African Community, which once linked Kenya, Tanzania,
and Uganda in an elaborately institutionalized form of regional cooperation.

In short, Black Africans have been far more capable of uniting in order to
keep colonialism at bay than uniting in order to bring each other closer
together.

In Southern Africa the two forms of Pan-Africanism have sometimes
pulled in different directions. For example, the Federation of the Rhodesias
and Nyasaland, while it lasted, was a possible basis for integrative Pan-
Africanism once white control ended. Yet, since white control was omnipresent, Pan-African solidarity was aroused more in the effort to end that
white control than to preserve the partial unification of three colonial territories.

On the other hand, apartheid itself, with its doctrine of separate black
homelands, runs counter to both kinds of Pan-Africanism. It compromises
the freedom of the homeland territories and of their citizens working in
white-dominated South Africa. It also attempts to cause serious fragmentation among blacks at a time when prospects for black solidarity in South
Africa itself are brighter than they have ever been.

Within this region, the "front-line" states have definitely provided a major
impetus for Pan-Africanism of liberation. In their pursuit of that goal, some
of them have also experienced the beginnings of regional integration. The
rail link between Tanzania and Zambia, partly conceived for reasons of
liberation, has become part of the foundation for greater economic and

social intercourse between these two countries. The closure of the border between Rhodesia and Zambia, while diluting the integration between those two countries, has initiated Zambian integration with its northern neighbors.

Relations between Tanzania and Mozambique in the modern period entered a new phase as Mozambique struggled for liberation from Portuguese rule and have now become the basis of greater potential intercourse between the two countries. Some analysts speculate that Mozambique and Zambia might one day be integrated more closely with Tanzania than Tanzania was with Kenya in the first fifteen years of Tanzanian independence. Indeed, Tanzania's initiatives in the events leading to the breakup of the East African Community were possible only in the context of her new partnership with Mozambique. Thus, the struggle for Southern Africa has already had important repercussions for East African regional politics and may have broader geopolitical ramifications for many African states.

The Failure of South Africa's African Policy

Nearly ten years ago South African journalist Anthony Delius argued that the more South Africa involved itself in Black Africa, the more its policies advanced the opportunities for communist influence on the continent.[2] Especially in the 1975 Angolan debacle, the South African "outward policy" set into motion the very forces it sought to overcome. In the period since Angola, South Africa's political isolation in Africa has increased. Although economic expansion into Africa continues, this side of the "outward policy" is now less significant. For example, it is true that South African trade with Nigeria is rapidly expanding (from a very small base). But it is sad self-deception if the South African government believes that such trade will counter the Nigerian inclination to become more active in the international diplomacy that is increasingly isolating the Republic. President Carter's visit to Nigeria in April 1978 and his forceful statements there on the need for fundamental change in Southern Africa point to Nigeria's growing international influence. As a center of international investment in Africa, Nigeria is beginning to use its influence to counter South African influence with giant transnational corporations.

African states and African initiative have played an important role in the failure of South Africa's attempt to create an external environment safe for apartheid. African states have contributed significantly to the growing international illegitimacy of white rule in Southern Africa. More generally, they have been an important component in the rise of the Third World as an international force. This rise, in turn, has been a major factor behind the change in global institutional values—those values that inform the activities of major international bodies such as the United Nations. Opposition to institutional racism and colonialism has become a major international institutional value. As a result, the United Nations and other international organizations are increasingly willing to involve themselves in Southern Africa, while only a generation ago it was generally considered an internal affair beyond the scope of legitimate international organizational concern.

The rise of the Third World has also had an impact on recent foreign policy trends among the Western powers. The appointment of Andrew Young as U.S. ambassador to the United Nations, the weight the Carter administration gave to passing the Panama Canal treaties through the U.S. Senate, and the recent shifts in U.S. policy toward Southern Africa all point to the increased political significance that the Third World has for the United States (and other Western nations). Third World solidarity on the struggle in Southern Africa will continue to reverberate in Western capitals.

Also in the area of international diplomacy, African states have entered into a reciprocal support relationship with Arab countries: African states supporting international pressures against Israel, Arab states supporting actions against South Africa. The fact that out of their growing isolation Israel and South Africa have expanded their own bilateral relations can only lead to a further cementing of the Arab-African diplomatic alliance.

Africa's international diplomatic activity has had concrete results. It is almost certain that without Black African pressure the United Kingdom might have been tempted to reach an accommodation with Ian Smith's Rhodesian regime. Without broad African diplomatic solidarity the United States might have found it more opportune to safeguard the status quo in Southern Africa. And without African pressure the United Nations would not have found the political will to pass the 1977 arms embargo against South Africa.

The Bases of Commitment to Liberation

Black African states vary considerably in their commitment to the Southern African struggle, in spite of their readiness to subscribe to the principles of racial sovereignty and continental jurisdiction. Commitment to those principles themselves is inevitably a matter of degree. How far a particular African state is prepared to go in the shared endeavor of liberating Southern Africa is conditioned by a variety of factors, some of which are peculiar or unique to the particular African state in question.

What are the determinants of the degree of support that an African state gives to the struggle for Southern Africa?

Physical distance from the target areas in Southern Africa is the first important factor. Contiguity to Southern Africa defines the "front-line" states, although location is only one of the elements determining their political activism. Until the Portuguese coup, the most important contiguous countries to white-ruled Southern Africa were Tanzania and Zambia. Both countries are ranked highly by Khapoya's measurements of support.

Since the collapse of the Portuguese African empire Mozambique and Angola—both relatively radical countries—have become critically involved in the liberation of the remaining areas; Mozambique as the base for the most active Zimbabwean guerrillas and Angola as the focal point for the liberation of Namibia.

Physical distance is only one form of distance. There is also cultural distance. For instance, different colonial heritages still divide Black African governments in their attitudes toward international politics. Khapoya argues that the least support for liberation movements comes from French-speaking African states. In the case of Portuguese-speaking Angola and Mozambique, physical nearness is combined with cultural distance (at least between the elite groups, though not necessarily among the masses with their indigenous cultural connections). On the other hand, the apparent cultural distance between Arab Africa and Black Africa reinforced by geographic distance has not resulted in a low level of Arab support for Southern African liberation. Algeria and Egypt have contributed most, surpassed only by the "front-line" states. No Arab country falls within the least-active bottom quarter of African states involved in the politics of liberation.

Ideological distance between Black African states and the liberation movements must also be taken into consideration. Sékou Touré's Guinea —though Francophone—scores higher than such Anglophone countries as Kenya and Sierra Leone. On balance, Black African governments to the left of center ideologically tend to be more committed to the liberation struggle, at least in terms of rhetorical and diplomatic agitation in international forums. When measured against concrete actions, ideological perspective is an important but not necessarily decisive factor. The increasingly combative policies of Zambia and Botswana cannot be explained by their ideological positions, but only by reference to the many immediate economic, political, and social pressures that growing regional conflict imposes on them.

The final factor affecting Black African attitudes toward Southern African liberation is the personality of national leaders. Malawi's relatively collaborationist policies are partly due to geopolitical factors, partly due to Malawi's economic weakness, and partly due to the personality and idiosyncracies of Hastings Banda. Idi Amin of Uganda presents an even clearer case of personality as a determinative factor in regional policy. When he assumed power in 1971, Amin quickly proclaimed his belief in dialogue between Black states and South Africa. But well before he became the OAU chairman in 1975, Amin was already militant about Southern African liberation, at least in rhetoric and diplomatic agitation. The Ugandan policy change that occurred in 1972 was primarily the outcome of Amin's own impulses, including his enjoyment of his newfound reputation as one of the militant voices of Third World anti-imperialism. The personality of Houphouet-Boigny of the Ivory Coast also influences his Southern African policies. He sees himself as the voice of moderation, compromise, and enlightened pragmatism in African affairs. This self-image contributes to his faith in the strategy of dialogue and détente between the Black African states and South Africa.

Southern Africa Relations as Derivative Relations

Some observers deny the centrality of personality, culture, and contiguity in African policy toward Southern Africa. They argue that at the least this policy is sharply constrained by considerations and relationships not directly concerned with the issue of liberation. How much evidence exists for this emphasis on derivative relations? Does Western aid to independent Black African countries affect their relations with Southern African liberation movements? In fact, the presumed inverse correlation between Western aid and support for liberation is weak. For example, Zambia and Malawi have received about the same amount of Western aid in the last ten years; yet Zambia has been one of the major centers of commitment to liberation, while Malawi has tended to collaborate with the white minority regimes.

On the other hand, does aid from the Soviet Union affect Black African relations with liberation movements? Indeed, there is a positive correlation between a high level of support from the Soviet Union for an African state and a high level of support by that state for Southern African liberation movements, but this correlation is more likely due to a prior congruence of ideological predispositions: the ideological considerations that made the country increase its contact with the Soviet Union may be the same that made it support Southern African liberation movements.

Regional policies of Black African states are sometimes affected by their mutual relationships. For example, in 1976 and 1977 Kenya's Zimbabwean policies were affected by Kenya's relations with Tanzania. Impatience with Tanzania — or envy of Tanzania's position as a "front-line" state — for a time reduced the enthusiasm of sections of the Kenya government for the Southern African liberation cause.

Arab support for Southern Africa is also partly derivative, linked both with African issues and with the Arab-Israeli conflict. The Arabs have needed African diplomatic support in their widespread attempts to isolate Israel and they have needed African voting power in international organizations as part of the strategy of gaining greater legitimacy for the Palestinian cause.

Dialectical Relations: Regional and Global

Black African states are increasing their economic ties with South Africa while at the same time stepping up their ideological and political opposition to apartheid and white minority rule in the subcontinent. This dialectical relation arises partly from the tension between the legacy of imperialism still existent in newly independent states and the aspirations of these states for total autonomy. Mozambique is a particularly striking example. There is little doubt that independent Mozambique — under a Marxist-Leninist government — is committed to Southern African liberation, but its revolutionary commitment coincides with the country's increasing absorption into South Africa's economy. The Mozambican government receives support in gold and money for its part in the exploitation of Mozambican workers who work in South African mines. Paradoxically, while Mozambique provides a base for Patriotic Front guerrillas fighting for Zimbabwean liberation, it plays a cautious game with the more racist South African regime.

It is this dialectic between dependence and revolution, between the continued survival of imperialism and the quest for social justice, that constitutes the most agonizing dilemma for almost all the "front-line" states. Mozambique's predicament is repeated in a somewhat different manner in Botswana. Zambia, as it has struggled to reduce its dependence on Rhodesia since UDI, has increased its economic dependence on South Africa. Even Tanzania, just as it has become more important in the final stages of the struggle for Southern African liberation, has embarked on partial deradicalization at home. The revolutionary fervor of the late 1960s is beginning to waver, and a new groping for Western economic support is underway. The dialectical relations between dependence and liberation are almost as omnipresent in Dar es Salaam as in Maputo.

At the global level dialectical relations encompass the superpowers themselves. Competitive imperialism between the Soviet Union and the United States helps to provide liberating potentialities for Southern Africa — potentialities that the oppressed may sometimes succeed in exploiting.

Even Cuba's role in Africa has contradictory implications. Cuba is indeed a revolutionary paradigm, a special model for much of the Third World, signifying the success of a small country that managed to transform itself in spite of the hostility and opposition of virtually all its thirty neighbors in the Western hemisphere. And yet this same regime is beginning to play a subimperial role in other parts of the African continent, although so far in Southern Africa Cuba has helped to prepare for the end of white rule. On balance, the Cuban factor remains part of the calculus of liberation.

Conclusion

South Africa may turn out to be the last historical case of institutionalized racism that mankind experiences. Other forms of discrimination will persist for a long time to come, as will racism in some of its other manifestations. But the idea of teaching children in racially separate schools, forcing adults to use racially separated compartments on buses and trains, forbidding adults from marrying across racial lines, structuring electorates on the basis of segregated voting power — all these forms of institutionalized racism may be experiencing their last stand in South Africa.

Essential to this prospect is the high consensus that the international community has reached against white minority rule in Southern Africa. This is one of the first major contributions non-Western and nonwhite countries have made to international morality and international law. There was a time when racism was acceptable to international law because that body of law was derived ultimately from Western values and orientations. At that time, South Africa apartheid policies were accepted throughout the Western world as strictly a case of South African internal jurisdiction. But the alliance of Black African states, supported by other Third World countries, has gradually forced even relatively conservative Western governments to regard South African racism not as simply immoral in a private sense, but as a matter of legitimate international action.

In this struggle to gain world consensus for the eradication of racism, the part played by independent Black African states has been central and quite indispensable. Theirs had to be the initiative for change; theirs had to be the persistent voice of protest against the status quo; theirs had to be the nucleus of agitation. Thus, the superficial view that Black African states have little influence on events in Southern Africa is shown to be false when placed in a broader international setting.

Nevertheless, the dual character of Black African relations with South Africa, having their roots in the imperial legacy and the continued underdevelopment of Black Africa, is likely to persist. South African economic penetration into Africa will continue. Countries like Mozambique, Botswana, and Tanzania will continue to face harsh choices between ending their own economic dependence and their ability to directly confront South African power. South Africa, moreover, will continue to offer incentives for collaboration, but Black African political unity against white rule and the international impact of that unity will also continue to grow. It is this aspect of Black Africa's role that will become increasingly dominant.

Although the liberation struggle continues, prospects for ultimate victory have grown greatly in the last few years. The Vietnam war weakened the United States and reduced its capacity to maintain the Southern African status quo. Nevertheless, the ultimate will for liberation must come from the colonized themselves. The Southern African struggle is now from bush to bush and from village to village; when South Africa itself falls under the challenge of revolutionary forces, the struggle will be from street to street and from alley to alley.

At that final stage Black South Africans will be the fighters, but Black African states will continue to be supportive, bringing to culmination a prolonged struggle for both racial sovereignty and continental jurisdiction.

Notes

1. Vincent B. Khapoya, "Determinants of African support for African liberation movements: a comparative analysis," *Journal of African Studies 3*, no. 4 (Winter 1976) pp. 469–489.

2. Anthony Delius, "China's Waiting Game in Africa," *Cape Times,* 28 July 1969.

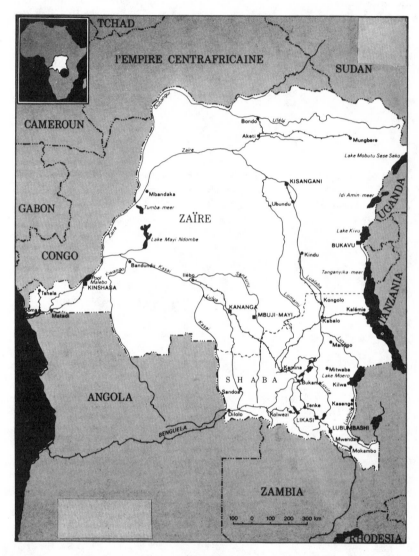

Map 7. Zaire: Shaba Province and the Benguela Railway. Source: The Africa Institute of South Africa, from *Bulletin* 18, no. 3, 1978, p. 113.

12
The Portuguese Coup and Zaire's Southern Africa Policy

Crawford Young

Today, while we have political, economic, and social stability, we cannot feel happy at home while our brothers of Angola, of Mozambique, of Zimbabwe, of South Africa, and of Namibia are yet held under the yoke of the Portuguese colonialists, British settlers, and South African racists. . . . Did not Frantz Fanon say that Africa has the form of a pistol, whose trigger is placed in Zaire? . . . The sons and daughters of Zaire have mandated me to tell you that, henceforward, all of Zaire is mobilized to confront the racists and colonialists of Southern Africa. Zaire stands ready to assume its full responsibilities, with our finger on the trigger of Frantz Fanon's revolver of Africa.

—Mobutu Sese Seko,
president of Zaire,
in a speech to the UN General Assembly,
4 October 1973

In his bold speech delivered to the UN General Assembly a few months before the 1974 Portuguese coup transformed the political parameters of Southern Africa, Zaire's president, Mobutu Sese Seko, laid claim to the mantle of African leadership. Although such ambitions were far from commanding general assent, they could not be lightly dismissed. National size, resource endowment, and pivotal position gave plausibility to a claim of manifest destiny. The apparent stability and unchallenged power of the *Nouveau Régime* had effaced the derision and ridicule that encumbered the First Republic.

Aggressive support for Southern African liberation movements must necessarily be a component of a leadership role. Zaire's finger, declared the president, was on the trigger. But the three years that followed witnessed a steady erosion of Mobutu's position, domestically and internationally. Unhappy circumstance and costly miscalculation conspired to compromise Zaire's standing in Africa, force Mobutu to dependency on the United States, and render impossible a forward strategy in Southern Africa, at the very moment when the fall of the Caetano regime opened new possibilities for rolling back white domination to the south. Bankrupt and isolated, Mobutu has long since quietly removed his finger from the trigger.

Expanding opportunities for political change in white-dominated Africa coincided with a swift contraction in Zaire's capacity to play a major role. Continental leadership, almost within grasp in 1973, receded ever farther over the horizon. The important shifts in Zairian Southern African policy cannot be understood solely within the frame of regional politics, however important Zaire's involvement in the Angolan crisis. Zaire's links with key powers (in particular, the United States and the People's Republic of China), the state of the international economy, and the domestic political and economic situation must also be considered. This chapter examines first Zaire's international role on the eve of the Portuguese coup; then its involvement in the Angolan question; the failure of the twin gambles of domestic "radicalization" and the plunge into the Angolan civil war; and the consequences for Zairian foreign policy of adversity on all fronts.

When the army high command assumed power on 24 November 1965, the source of legitimacy was the claim that no other exit from chaos was possible. As Mobutu told the UN in the same 1973 speech, "We must recognize that anarchy, chaos, disorder, negligence, and incompetence were master in Zaire," adding that "all disorder, in any part of the world, was baptized as 'Congolization.'" Despite Mobutu's close U.S. associations, the *Nouveau Régime* quickly won reasonable acceptance in Africa, symbolized by the designation of Kinshasa as the site for the 1967 annual summit meeting of the Organization of African Unity (OAU). The exclusion of Moise Tshombe from power; the spectacular confrontation with Union Minière du Haut-Katanga in 1967, culminating in the ostensible nationalization of the giant copper mining firm; and the successful battle with mutinous mercenaries the same year all gave a sufficiently nationalist hue to Zairian policy to permit its rehabilitation in the African community.

By 1967 Mobutu had consolidated his power, provided the legal basis for centralized presidential rule in a new constitution, and founded his national single party, the Mouvement Populaire de la Révolution (MPR). His army had put down mutinies by European mercenaries and the units that they controlled, and nothing remained of the 1964–1965 rebellions save one irreducible but isolated redoubt in the mountains near Lake Tanganyika. Mobutu's standing reached a zenith in 1970. The restoration of tranquility facilitated economic restoration, with the gross national product passing preindependence figures for the first time in 1969. The Belgian royal couple made a triumphant tour of Zaire, generating adulatory European press coverage of the *Nouveau Régime*'s achievements. The MPR held its first congress in May 1970, and shortly thereafter Zairian citizens trooped dutifully to the polls to endorse their president. In August 1970 Mobutu paid a state visit to the United States, claiming on his return that he had firm pledges of $1 billion in new U.S. investment.

A massive expansion of the Shaba mining sector was programmed. The Belgian-managed national company, Gécamines—successor to Union Minière—embarked on plans to raise its copper production from 360,000 tons in 1970 to 570,000 tons by the end of the decade. Some extremely rich deposits, previously held in reserve by Belgian interests, were ceded to an international consortium negotiated by Mobutu's close friend Maurice Tempelsman, a U.S. financier previously active in the diamond trade. The major shares of the consortium were held by Standard Oil (Indiana) and Charter Consolidated, a South African company controlled by Harry Oppenheimer, chairman of the giant Anglo American Corporation.[1] This new corporation, Société Minière de Tenge-Fungurume (SMTF), aimed for production of 130,000 tons by the late 1970s and planned an initial investment of over $600 million. A Japanese group, SODIMIZA, was granted a smaller concession, with an anticipated annual output of 50,000 tons. Apparently Mobutu had secured his domestic base and had guaranteed to the state the prospect of a swiftly expanding fiscal and foreign exchange base. The *Nouveau Régime* was now in a position to seek a larger role.

A more vigorous African policy, however, required an alteration of Zaire's image in the Third World. While Zaire was no longer an object of ridicule, its economic recovery was seen as following a neocolonial mode, and Mobutu himself was viewed widely as a U.S. protégé. Many believed that he had served as an informer for the Belgian Sûreté while studying journalism in Brussels in 1959–1960. More important, he was believed to have had a relationship with the Central Intelligence Agency (CIA), at least during the early phase of independence. And finally, there was the closely related issue of Mobutu's suspected complicity in the January 1961 assassination of Patrice Lumumba.[2] The stigma attached to these alleged past associations had not impeded Zaire's acceptance as a member of the African family. However, a claim to leadership was quite another matter. Mobutu needed a more positive Third World image.

Mobutu moved on several fronts to secure this end. His state visit to the United States, highlighted by his effusive National Press Club statement that nationalization was a word unknown in the Zairian vocabulary, was followed immediately by travel to Yugoslavia and Rumania. In the symbolic politics of Mobutism, a pilgrimage to socialist lands signaled the opening of a more broadly based international role. "Neither to the left nor to the right, nor even in the center," an oft-repeated slogan, was given apparent substance by these gestures toward the East.

Mobutu chose the February 1971 congress of the Union Progressiste Sénégalaise as the prestigious forum in which to launch his effort at an original definition of cultural nationalism, or "authenticity." For Third World solidarity to be effective, he declared, each country must accomplish victoriously a return to its own authentic identity.[3] Although "authenticity" seemed on close examination no more than a mere rearrangement of diverse themes Mobutu had described earlier as "authentic Zairian nationalism," it was propagated with vigor. One of the first practical applications of the new doctrine was the abandonment of Christian first names in favor of post names with Zairian derivation. When this and related symbolic manifestations of authenticity led to a confrontation with the powerful Roman Catholic church, many came to believe that the implications of "authenticity" might be more far-reaching than was apparent on first scrutiny. Certainly Mobutu's successful challenge to the Catholic hierarchy conveyed the impression that he was prepared to take on important and entrenched Western institutions.[4] "Authenticity" even acquired some minor converts, in Presidents Eyadema of Togo and Tombalbaye of Chad.

Mobutu also offered himself on the African scene as a conciliator of diplomatic conflicts involving African states. He proposed his services as intermediary to repair the tense relations between Tanzania and Uganda in 1971 after Obote's overthrow, and he was instrumental in the establishment of formal diplomatic relationships between Amin and Nyerere in 1971 (although their relations cooled soon thereafter). He also actively mediated disputes between Burundi and Tanzania created by border violations of Burundi forces in assaults on Hutu refugees.[5] In 1971 he was a member of the OAU team of "elder statesmen" charged with ending the Israeli occupation of Egyptian territory, a conflict then too intractable even for professional mediators.

In addition to mediation, Mobutu embarked on an extremely ambitious program of diplomatic travel. He abandoned an earlier project for regional leadership, in a Union des États d'Afrique Centrale (USEAC), which would have regrouped the Central African Republic (CAR) and Chad under Zairian leadership, when the CAR lost interest. Instead, Zairian diplomacy expanded its horizons to a continental scale. In 1970 Mobutu visited ten African states. In 1972 he made state visits to Togo, Gabon, Ethiopia, Tanzania, and, above all, Guinea. The triumphant reception accorded Mobutu by Sékou Touré, previously one of his most vehement critics, was particularly important. Mobutu was not just tolerated, he was welcomed with deference in Conakry, the symbolic capital of radical African nationalism.[6] Shortly after his return Mobutu greeted eight chiefs of state at an MPR national congress. In 1973 he spent no less than 150 days outside Zaire, visiting twenty-six countries, including fourteen in Africa.[7]

The disability imposed by excessively visible Western associations remained a problem. A warming of relations with the Soviet Union would have provided symbolic balance, but practically was very difficult. Zairian-Soviet relations had been acrimonious since the crisis in September 1960 when Soviet diplomats were first expelled from the country. Soviet backing for the rebel forces in 1964–1965, however ineffective, reinforced suspicions. It was not until April 1968 that a Soviet ambassador returned to Kinshasa. Nonetheless, incidents continued to limit the warmth of relations. Four Soviet diplomats were expelled in 1970 for "subversion," and in 1971 twenty Soviet bloc officials were declared persona non grata, accused of complicity in student disturbances on the Kinshasa University campus. Further, Soviet links were very close with the neighboring Congo-Brazzaville regime with which Zaire had a periodically troubled and always ambivalent relationship.[8]

The People's Republic of China provided a new opportunity for Mobutu. Although the Chinese had given strong moral support and some arms (delivered via Tanzania) to eastern zone insurgents in 1965–1966, this action ceased during the foreign policy paralysis that accompanied the Cultural Revolution. When China resumed its African diplomatic effort in 1970, a new set of premises shaped its actions. Hostility toward Soviet diplomacy was even more marked. Correct inter-state relations became the rule. In any case, there were no genuine Marxist-Leninist movements in independent tropical Africa, and the backing given earlier in Zaire and elsewhere had served neither Chinese state interests nor the anti-imperialist cause. The only consequence was to push incumbent regimes into closer ties with the West.

Informal Zairian-Chinese contacts in 1972 led to Mobutu's dramatic state visit to China in January 1973. He was received with full honors in the heartland of Third World revolution. Six years earlier the Peking *People's Daily* had found it "fantastic" that "Mobutu, the degenerate betrayer of the Congolese people and murderer of Lumumba, has now, as if by magic, made himself look like a different man, waving the banner of the Congolese national hero Lumumba."[9]

That fantastic transformations are indeed possible was demonstrated when Mobutu returned with the Chinese benediction, a commitment for $100 million of economic aid for agricultural development, and pledges of arms and instructors for the FNLA—the Angolan liberation group that enjoyed Mobutu's favor. Mao Tse-tung himself, Mobutu later reported, confided his regret at the funds wasted on the Zairian insurgents.[10] Subsequently, in 1973 and 1974, the Chinese ambassador to Kinshasa enjoyed privileged access to Mobutu. Although these links were apparently not used to influence Zairian domestic policy, they did reflect an altered pattern of intimacies and perspectives and helped to project an image of Mobutu as closer to the Third World mainstream. Although only an indeterminately small fraction of the pledged aid was actually delivered by 1976, Chinese aid teams were quickly and visibly on the scene.[11]

Mobutu's bid for African leadership manifested itself also in the economic realm. Zairian image building vis-à-vis the Third World faced paradoxes in the substantial inflow of foreign investment—stimulated by economic stabilization—in the early 1970s; the earlier Mobutu reputation of pro-Western orientation; the absence of socialism from the political vocabulary; a generous 1969 investment code; and, above all, the vast untapped resources of the country. The flow of Western, and especially U.S., investment was at once the force and the weakness of the regime. It promised to supply the revenue base to maintain the costly patrimonial style of domestic politics,[12] but at the same time validated the claims of the regime's critics that "Zaire, without belonging to NATO, is an important base, both militarily and economically, for American imperialism."[13] In 1973 the moment seemed at hand for a bold move on the economic front to match those in the diplomatic sphere. Copper prices doubled during that year, rising from $1100 per metric ton (an average price level over the fifteen preceding years) to an all-time high of over $3000 per ton in April 1974. Copper provided roughly half of the government's revenue and two-thirds of its foreign exchange.

At the Algiers summit conference of nonaligned nations in September 1973 Mobutu told other Third World leaders that he planned decisive measures to secure economic independence for Zaire in the near future. On 30 November 1973, in a speech to the Legislative Council in Kinshasa, he proclaimed a set of measures on the domestic front that in audacity matched his UN speech on the diplomatic front. Zaire was to recover total economic independence. The plantation sector still in European hands was to be "Zairianized," as were foreign-owned retail and wholesale houses, construction firms, and a number of other kinds of small and medium-sized enterprises. Although the precise scope and procedures of the 30 November measures were not clear at first, it soon developed that the enterprises were to be distributed to Zairians "with the means and the vocation"—criteria that intentionally described the political-administrative elite. New investments were exempted from the measure, which primarily hit Belgian, Portuguese, and Greek business interests. The escalation of rhetoric that accompanied these measures did enhance Mobutu's claim to a more radical posture in the world, as well as at home.

Finally, Zaire needed a more forward position on African liberation issues. Relations with Portugal had been broken, but otherwise initiative was seriously constrained by economic and logistical dependency. Copper smelting operations in Shaba were dependent on Wankie coal from Rhodesia, because north Shaba brown coal was of poor quality and the Zambian coal developed after Rhodesian UDI to supply the Zambian smelters could not be used without costly conversion of existing facilities. The Shaba urban markets and Kinshasa (to a lesser extent) depended on South African imports for many consumer goods, especially food. Replacements could only be found at significantly higher prices. The Benguela railroad carried the largest share of Zairian copper exports (56.6 percent of the 1974 tonnage) and all its manganese. Alternative routes through independent territory had a very limited capacity (Shaba-Kalemie railroad, boat across Lake Tanganyika to Kigoma, rail to Dar es Salaam) or were costly and slow (the "voie nationale," with trans-shipment to river boat at Ilebo, back to rail at Kinshasa, then to cargo ship at Matadi). Finally, a good part of the lower channel for the Zaire River passes through Angolan territory. The regular dredging operations necessary to keep the river open to oceangoing vessels had to be performed by, or with the consent of, Portuguese authorities.

Thus Zairian policy toward Southern Africa had been quite cautious in the early years of the *Nouveau Régime*. Although Mobutu did not openly support the Houphouet-Boigny "dialogue" initiatives in 1968–1970, Zaire did at times abstain on UN and OAU resolutions dealing with Southern Africa and contributed infrequently to the OAU Liberation Committee.[14] Mobutu participated in regular summit meetings with Kaunda and Nyerere and provided sanctuary and support to the FNLA, while opposing the MPLA. Thus, the strong position articulated at the UN General Assembly in September 1973 by Mobutu represented a marked departure from the earlier Zairian position.

A less costly and more sensational gesture in radical diplomacy was available at the northeast end of the continent. Strong denunciations of South Africa were a somewhat debased currency, but a dramatic move against Israel could place Zaire in the front rank of what was increasingly the progressive Third World position. Two days before the 1973 October War began, Mobutu declared,

> Zaire finds itself at the hour of choice; we must stop equivocating and end a kind of ambiguity in the conduct of our African vocation. Thus, Zaire must choose between a friendly country, Israel, and a brother country, Egypt. Between a friend and a brother, the choice is clear. . . . I announce, before the world, the rupture of diplomatic relations with Israel.[15]

At a stroke, Zaire earned itself short-lived gratitude and a more enduring respect from the Arab states. Once the October War began, many African states followed suit, but the Zairian initiative brilliantly outmaneuvered them—especially Nigeria, a major rival for African leadership. The costs of the gesture were not large. Israel had offered a modest amount of aid and

some military training, both easily forgone. More important, while both
Henry Kissinger and Maurice Tempelsman were furious, neither was in a
position to force a confrontation over this issue.

In sum then, on the eve of the momentous changes in Southern Africa
triggered by the Portuguese coup, Zaire's policy seemed on an upward
course. Mobutu was unchallengeable at home. Even some who had been
most suspicious of his underlying motives began to believe that basic
changes were underway. The Chinese embassy apparently had more access to
Mobutu than did the Belgian or U.S. embassies. Sheldon Vance had left his
post as U.S. ambassador in late 1973 and was not replaced until August
1974. A large sector of the economy had been abruptly Zairianized.

As the *People's Daily* had remarked in another context, it all seemed
quite fantastic. As events demonstrated, this surrealistic vision of a radicalized Zaire grasping the mantle of continental leadership was soon sup-
planted by the picture of a bankrupt state, hounded by its creditors, forced
back into demeaning dependency on the United States and international
financial institutions, confronting a massive social malaise in both the urban
and rural sectors for which it lacked the resources—programmatic and
material—to cope. In this equally fantastic transformation, the Southern
African situation served as both cause and effect: regional events, particularly in Angola, created dilemmas and forced decisions that accelerated
erosion of the regime. At the same time the dramatic shift in Zaire's international status from aspirant to African leadership to a client dependent on
Western governments and institutions significantly affected developments
in the fluid situation to the south.

Zaire and Cuba established diplomatic relations on 15 April 1974, just
ten days before the Portuguese coup, whose Angolan aftermath was to en-
tangle Zaire increasingly for the next two years and finally bring Zairian and
Cuban troops into combat against each other. For Zaire, the Angolan question became the central preoccupation, with the rest of Southern African
problems receding into the background. Zaire shared a 1485-mile border
with Angola. It depended on the Benguela railroad and Lobito harbor. The
Zairian government worried about a group of Katangan gendarmes kept in
military readiness by the Portuguese to maintain leverage in relations with
Zaire. Nearly one million Angolan refugees were sheltered in Zaire, thirty-
five thousand of whom had crossed the border in the first months of the
1975 civil war.

Zaire had a large stake in securing a privileged role for the FNLA, with ties
going back to the earliest days of the Angolan revolution in 1961. A number
of leading FNLA figures, including Holden Roberto, are Zairo-Angolans
who have spent most of their lives in Zaire. Mobutu found the Afrocentric,
non-Marxist nationalism of the FNLA far closer to his preferences for

"authenticity" than the more Marxist doctrines of the MPLA.[16] Zaire provided sanctuary, training facilities, and material support for the FNLA forces. When FNLA troops mutinied in a Bas-Zaire camp in March 1972, the Zaire national army quelled the uprising. Finally, Holden Roberto's marriage to a woman from the same village as Mme. Mobutu and often reported to be her sister added a personal link.[17] Roberto, who had for some years received a CIA retainer, held international ties much like Mobutu's.

By contrast, relations between Zaire and the MPLA had been almost uniformly bad. The MPLA was briefly permitted to maintain a Kinshasa office in 1962, but since that time had been denied both access to and transit rights through Zairian territory. The Marxist political culture and mulatto antecedents of some MPLA leaders fostered Zairian distrust. At a personal level, Mobutu and Agostinho Neto of the MPLA harbored a mutual animosity extending back a number of years. The climate of suspicion in Zaire was heightened by the MPLA's Brazzaville links and sanctuary. Tension between Zaire and Congo-Brazzaville was effectively constant, punctuated only by occasional short-lived reconciliation ceremonies. Finally, Soviet backing for the MPLA — in the face of Zairian-Soviet relations that ranged from indifferent to poor — added to Zairian distrust of the MPLA. Zaire came closest to a modus vivendi with the MPLA in 1972, when Mobutu cooperated with an African effort to unify the Angolan liberation movements. The MPLA general secretary, Lucio Lara, later claimed that MPLA pressure against Mobutu led him to push the FNLA into an agreement with the MPLA. The pressure was based on the MPLA charge that Zaire was "sabotaging the struggle in refusing us rear bases and transit facilities," a charge to which Mobutu "was very sensitive."[18] Since the MPLA maneuvers coincided with Mobutu's visits to Guinea and elsewhere in Africa, his sensitivity was understandable.

Although Zaire had little to do with Unita, it did establish links in 1974 with the Cabinda nationalist group, the Frente do Libertação do Enclave de Cabinda (FLEC). Mobutu argued that Cabinda was entitled to self-determination regarding its future relationship with Angola. Despite persistent rumors about a Zairian military seizure of the enclave, the Zairian army lacked the capability to oust the Portuguese army before 1975, or the MPLA units that then took over, or the Cuban units that arrived in late 1975.[19] Whatever the attraction of the $500 million in annual revenue generated by the Cabinda oil wells (roughly equal to the Gécamines contribution to the Zaire annual budget), Mobutu was aware that his military intervention would destroy the diplomatic role he was trying so hard to create.

Throughout 1974 Zaire preferred to see FNLA govern Angola, with Cabinda as an independent mini-client of Zaire. However, some form of coalition regime in which the FNLA held an important voice and retained control of the northern region bordering Zaire would have been acceptable. This preference paralleled that held by the United States and China, which were, for somewhat different reasons, convinced that the MPLA was under Soviet influence. As Angola moved toward civil war, both governments collaborated with Zaire, though not with each other, in reinforcing the FNLA's military capabilities.

While the Angolan political impasse was creating the conditions for the 1975 civil war (the risks of which were certainly underestimated by Zaire), the domestic foundations of Zairian diplomatic power were undermined by a series of unfavorable developments. Zaire was in part the hapless victim of world market trends over which it had no control. However, the impact of trade cycle misfortune was multiplied by serious miscalculations and self-inflicted wounds. The aggressive diplomacy of the early 1970s rested on the premise of unchallenged domestic strength and stability. That premise quickly fell apart.

April 1974 marked not only the Portuguese coup but the collapse of world copper prices. By mid-1974, the price had dropped from $3000 per metric ton to $1900; it dropped to $1200 by the end of 1974. Meanwhile, the Mid-East war sent fuel prices rocketing, and the 1972 Soviet grain crisis had already pushed the cost of food imports to its highest level ever. Inflation, which had been all but contained in Zaire by the 1967 currency reform, gained momentum in 1973, reached 40 percent in 1974, and raged out of control in 1975 and 1976, as a foreign exchange crisis forced restrictions on imports and produced widespread shortages in the cities. The consumer price index, with a 1970 base of 100, reached 350 by mid-1976. The budget deficit in 1974 and 1975 soared. The 1974 operating budget called for a planned increase of 23 percent in outlays; actual expenditures exceeded 1973 outlays by 58 percent and budget estimates by 61 percent.[20] The deficit was financed largely by forced advances from the national bank.

At the same time huge borrowing was undertaken, both to meet short-term exchange needs and to finance several large construction and capital projects:

- phase two of the Inga dam, estimated initially at $250 million, but subsequently more than double that cost
- the Inga-Shaba high-tension power line, experiencing massive extra expenditures against its estimated cost of $350 million
- $220 million for the Gécamines expansion program
- twelve multi-million dollar cargo ships for the Zairian national shipping line
- DC-10s for Air Zaire
- at least $100 million for a steel mill, whose doubtful profitability

       meant 100 percent financing by the Zairian government
- an ambitious airport construction and improvement program

By mid-1976 the overall debt reached a level which neither the Zairian national bank nor its creditors knew precisely, but which was estimated to be about $3 billion.[21] During 1975 Zaire could no longer pay either principal or interest on its foreign debt and was formally in default. The foreign exchange reserves, in surplus during the regime's early years, had been exhausted. During a period when prices rose by 350 percent, wages were permitted to rise by only 20 percent. Shortages of basic commodities—manioc, corn flour, pharmaceutical products—became a resented part of daily life. Officially set prices to producers for many products were at only 20 to 30 percent of their 1960 levels. Frequently villagers were unable to sell their produce because of deficiencies in the marketing infrastructure or were forced to sell at prices well below the already low official prices. From its expansive, optimistic 1973 mood, Zaire nosedived into bankruptcy. The riches-to-rags tale was attributable only in part to the drop in the copper price. Virtually no one in Zaire believed the official protestations that the mishaps of the world market alone explained the dramatic deterioration in the well-being of the general population.

    Joined to these misfortunes were the unhappy consequences of the ostensibly radical economic reform measures of 30 November 1973. What had been announced confidently (at private gatherings of Third World leaders) as a decisive move to economic independence turned into a catastrophe, from every point of view. The principle of Zairianization of the commercial sector was not in dispute. Although the emotional animus against the Portuguese, Greeks, Pakistanis, and Belgians who dominated much of the wholesale, retail, and plantation sector was not as sharp as it had been in Uganda, widespread support existed for forceful measures to assure Zairian control of these sectors, if the measures were carried out without economic dislocation or conspicuous favoritism. However, the distribution of enterprises was an occasion for the patrimonial allocation of goods from the summit, in which the top political-administrative circles took for themselves large sectors of the economy. The improvisation in implementation of these measures, the inability of many beneficiaries to effectively manage their inherited enterprises, and the poorly disguised avarice of many beneficiaries produced—at the worst possible moment—a major dislocation of the commercial sector and fostered a wave of resentment toward the country's ruling elite, believed guilty of profiteering at a time of general distress.[22]

    Mobutu was well aware that new domestic and foreign policy initiatives were required. During 1974 he had already sought to maintain Zaire's position in the forefront of collective African diplomatic efforts. He visited Zambia and Tanzania in May 1974, then took part in the June OAU summit meeting in Mogadishu, received President Numeiry of Sudan in August, and again visited Lusaka in October. In the same period he made a direct approach to the Portuguese, flying to Cape Verde in September 1974 for a secret meeting with Portuguese president Spínola. Although no official clarification was ever given regarding these conversations, it seems likely that they included consideration of the FNLA's future role in Angola and arrangements for Cabinda.[23] Mobutu denied that he was negotiating on behalf of Black African governments or that he had entered into any special agreements. Spínola was ousted soon thereafter, and the radical junta that replaced him was much less sympathetic to Zairian objectives.

As 1974 drew to a close Mobutu made a dramatic gamble to defuse the threatening domestic and foreign forces that were converging upon the regime. His objectives were to

1. maintain Zaire's role as a leading state in African continental affairs and as a significant voice in the Third World;
2. lay claim to a major voice in the diplomacy of Angolan decolonization;
3. develop a capability for armed intervention in Angola by enhancing the military capability of the FNLA and the Zairian army;
4. pursue the option of separate decolonization for Cabinda on terms favorable to Zaire;
5. foster the radicalized image of the regime, both at home and abroad;
6. maintain the confidence of Western capital in order to sustain the flow of investment and to get the short-term bank credit required to overcome the budgetary and exchange crises;
7. allay the domestic social malaise, which was reaching dangerous proportions;
8. ride out the economic crisis without basic alterations in regime priorities.

The mere recitation of these partly conflicting goals makes clear the challenge to policymaking and the temptation to obscure inherent contradictions with lapses into dazzling rhetoric and melodramatic initiatives.

The first step considered was a major state visit to the Soviet Union. The day after the Portuguese coup the official Zairian news agency announced that Mobutu had been invited to the Soviet Union. On 13 November 1974 plans for a December trip were announced.[24] Nothing further was ever mentioned of this visit. The divergent preferences of the Soviet Union and Zaire in the sharpening contest for power in Angola might have been decisive. In any event, the Soviet visit was quietly dropped, and instead Mobutu made a suddenly arranged "study trip" to China and North Korea in December 1974.

The Chinese sojourn did not result in dramatic new agreements comparable to the 1973 $100 million loan, although Mobutu was again received by Mao Tse-tung and top-level consideration was given to the FNLA reinforcement necessary to prevent an MPLA triumph.

The discovery of North Korean friendship and support was the most intriguing result of the trip. Mobutu's party was deeply impressed by the lavish welcome accorded it by Kim Il-Sung. Korean youths put on gymnastic displays involving a collective discipline that left the Zairians envious. Korean schoolchildren sang songs in Lingala praising Mobutu and MPR, to the astonishment and delight of the visitors. North Korean industrial progress, built on a dominant single party and strongly personalized leadership, once its Marxist-Leninist motivation was excised, seemed an ideal model for Mobutu's aspirations. On his return to Zaire he frequently cited North Korea as a model society in which a policy of abundance had defeated the twin legacies of Western capitalism—inflation and recession. Kim Il-Sung's collected works were distributed to many of the Zairian political elite.

Most important, the North Korean tour resulted in military agreements by which North Korea agreed to train a new, elite Zairian strike force, the Kamanyola Division (named after a skirmish in the 1964 rebellions during which Mobutu had demonstrated great personal courage). This large division, designed as a self-contained armored force outside the army's regular command structure, was formed and trained in Kitona, Bas-Zaire, not far from the Angolan border.[25] Chinese instructors also helped, and the North Koreans provided some light armament.

On his return from North Korea Mobutu summoned the MPR's Political Bureau and then, on 30 December 1974, announced a sweeping set of measures intended to "radicalize the Zairian revolution." Taken at face value, the scope of the measures was indeed revolutionary.[26] All MPR cadres[27] were to return to the state those businesses inherited under the 30 November 1973 measures. The public sector's range was to be vastly expanded to include all construction firms, all large production units, all large distribution firms, all enterprises producing construction materials, and all large public transport firms. Only newly established enterprises protected by the 1969 investment code were exempted. Top party leaders were to confine their business activities to the agricultural sector. All bank holdings outside Zaire were to be repatriated, while foreign property owned by Zairians was to be turned over to the state. The "costly and unproductive" army was to grow its own food and otherwise take a larger role in agricultural production. All mission schools—including virtually all the best schools in the country— were to be taken over by the government. All Zairian children enrolled in overseas schools were to be brought home. The secondary school graduating class was to be conscripted for a year of civic service, under the army's direction; subsequent admission to the university was to be conditional on favorable reports by party cadres on "political militancy." Other equally sweeping edicts were promulgated in the following months, among them one cutting all rents paid by Zairians by 50 percent and limiting top salaries to $2000 per month.

Finally, a progressive international image was reinforced by putting visible distance between the regime and its erstwhile U.S. ally. U.S.-Zairian relations had already cooled in 1974, as reflected in the ambassadorial post left vacant by the United States for several months. On the U.S. side there was irritation over the Zairian initiative in the chain of African diplomatic breaks with Israel, over the 30 November 1973 measures, and over the warmth of Zairian-Chinese relations. A further point of friction resulted from Zaire's sudden seizure of Mobil and Texaco distribution and retail facilities in December 1973 (as well as those of Shell and Petrofina) on the grounds that these companies had failed to maintain Zaire's required petroleum supplies. Dean Hinton, who arrived in August 1974 to replace Sheldon Vance as the U.S. ambassador, never established the personal rapport with Mobutu enjoyed by his predecessors and was soon the object of thinly veiled attacks. In January 1975 Mobutu chose the occasion of an African-American Institute conference in Kinshasa (bringing together black and white U.S. leaders with African leaders) to openly denounce Hinton as the author of schemes for "destabilization" in Third World regimes, pointing to Hinton's former service in Chile.

U.S. influence in Zaire reached a low ebb in June 1975 when the U.S. government, and particularly the CIA, was accused of conspiring with elements in the Zairian armed forces to bring about the overthrow and "physical elimination" of Mobutu.[28] While no evidence has yet come to light to substantiate these allegations, the CIA clearly had the ability, disposition, and precedent for doing so. The existent chill in U.S.-Zairian relations does not seem sufficient motive in itself, but there is a suggestive connection between the timing of the alleged plot and the imminent U.S. publication of reports on CIA activities by the Church committee in the Senate and by a special panel chaired by Vice President Nelson Rockefeller. Both bodies had explored in secrecy possible U.S. involvement in Lumumba's assassination and other CIA involvement in the Congo in the early 1960s. If the published reports were to refer to CIA connections with Mobutu, there might have been a considerable impact on Zairian politics. Discovery of a "CIA plot" to liquidate him might have provided Mobutu with a convenient diversion from public reports detailing his own involvement with the CIA. As it turned out, neither report mentioned any specific

Zairian political or military leaders as CIA collaborators.

For Zaire, its involvement during 1975 in the Angolan civil war was in every respect a total disaster. Admittedly, Zaire's original commitment to the FNLA was mediated via North Korean and Chinese advisors and aid, and did not at first carry a neocolonial stigma. Further, until the overt entry of Zairian troops in October 1975 to back up tottering FNLA units, Zaire still clung to the OAU position of support for a coalition regime. But in mid-1975 the Chinese and North Koreans backed out and the scale of Soviet support to the MPLA became clear. Zaire–U.S. rapprochement grew rapidly and, based on their collaborative involvement in the Angolan civil war and U.S. pledges of economic aid to Zaire, Third World governments saw Zaire as firmly placed in the neocolonial camp.

Zaire's de facto alliance with South Africa completed its total diplomatic isolation. Although for the most part the South African incursion into southern Angola and the Zairian–U.S. supported FNLA offensive in the north were separate operations, coordination between them did exist. Zaire was a supply base and (briefly) a staging point for mercenaries bound for both fronts. Further, the July 1975 closing of the Benguela railway forced Zaire to ship the bulk of its copper (some 25,000 tons per month) via Zambia, Rhodesia, and Botswana to South African railways and harbors. At the same time important imports — especially petroleum and foodstuffs — destined for industrial Shaba came from or through South Africa.

By the end of 1975 Zaire's carefully cultivated progressive image lay shattered, its economy bankrupt, its army humiliated, its regime discredited. Zairian ties with China and North Korea, while not cut, diminished in significance, since neither government was in a position to give sufficient diplomatic backing or sufficient economic aid to ease Zaire's plight. Zaire thus found itself in a renewed and increasingly complex position of dependency on the West, especially in the economic realm. Vis-à-vis South Africa, because of its economic dependency, Zaire once more argued for caution. It did not support South African expulsion from the United Nations in 1975 nor the Arab-sponsored resolution that same year equating Zionism and racism.

Zaire had no choice diplomatically but to retrench and set its 1973 ambitions aside for better times. On 27 February 1976 Zaire disengaged officially from Angola, signing an accord with the victorious MPLA delegation providing for "normalization" of relationships. Zaire, Mobutu declared, "had no intention of helping FNLA or Unita crush the MPLA." The Zairian objective, he continued, had been to "support the Angolan people . . . to give a mortal blow to Portuguese colonialism."[29] On the economic side, a painful and embarrassing International Monetary Fund (IMF) stabilization program was accepted (although not wholly applied) as the prerequisite for further necessary financial aid. Demeaning negotiations began with Western governments and the major private banks to seek rescheduling of Zaire's very large debt. With the dual preoccupations of reviving economic stability and achieving mere respectability among its African neighbors, any larger diplomatic ambitions were out of the question.

Any overall assessment of Zairian foreign policy in post-Caetano Southern Africa must account for several interacting elements. First, the U.S.–Soviet–Chinese set of international relationships, involving mutual initiatives and reactions in various international settings, defined and constrained Zairian foreign policy prospects in intricately shifting ways. Second, the international economy, with its shifting market price for copper and its seemingly cyclical moods of capital-peddling and debt-collection, affected the range of freedom available in Zairian foreign policy. Third, changing degrees of stability and Mobutu's changing perceptions of security affected the expansiveness or reticence of Zairian diplomacy. All three factors interacted with each other well before the Portuguese coup, but it was the coup that seemed (falsely, as it turned out) to provide an opportunity for dramatic and massive foreign policy initiatives.

In fairness to Mobutu, his original bid for African leadership in 1973 came at a time when all three factors ran in Zaire's favor: domestic support was high, the copper price was at its peak, Chinese and U.S. support was substantial, and Soviet regional influence was at its nadir. The reversal in all these circumstances could not have been predicted. Zaire's experience suggests that these peculiarly violent fluctuations may be widespread in Africa and that they require a more prudent counter-cyclical diplomacy in which policies at peak times are constrained in advance response to the pressures that will take effect at ebb times. Such a diplomacy may achieve relatively modest enduring gains, but it cannot win the dramatic goals aspired to by Zaire from 1973 to 1975.

Notes

1. SMTF's initial capital participation included Charter Consolidated, 28 percent; Standard Oil (Indiana), 28 percent; C. Tempelsman & Sons, 3 percent; Mitsui, 14 percent; Bureau de Recherches géologiques et minières, 3.5 percent; Omnium de mines (France), 3.5 percent. Zaire received a noncontributing 20 percent share.

2. The most spectacular version of these allegations is Jules Chome, *L'ascension de Mobutu* (Brussels: Editions Complexe, 1975). Also see Stephen R. Weissman, *American Foreign Policy in the Congo, 1960–1964* (Ithaca, N.Y.: Cornell University Press, 1974), pp. 94–98; and Andrew Tully, *CIA: The Inside Story* (New York: William Morrow & Co., 1962). Cleophas Kamitatu, *La grande mystification du Congo-Kinshasa* (Paris: Francois Maspero, 1971) argues Mobutu's close U.S ties,

although he does not specifically allege CIA links. Evidence on the CIA role in seeking to murder Lumumba (although not in his actual death) is provided in U.S., Congress, Senate, Select Committee to Study Governmental Operating with respect to Intelligence Activities, *Alleged Assassination Plots Involving Foreign Leaders*, 94th Congress, 1st Session, Report 94-465, November 1975. (Mobutu is not specifically mentioned.)

3. *Elima* (Kinshasa), 20, 21, 22 May 1972.

4. For a critical view of "authenticity" see N. Tutashinda, "Les mystifications de l'authenticité," *Pensée*, no. 175 (May–June 1974), pp. 68–81. On the conflict with the Church, see Kenneth Adelman, "The Church-State Conflict in Zaire: 1969–1974," *African Studies Review* 18, no. 1 (April 1975), pp. 102–116.

5. This role is well described in Jeannick Odier, "La politique étrangère de Mobutu," *Revue Française d'Etudes Politiques Africaines*, no. 120 (December 1975), pp. 25–41.

6. *Jeune Afrique*, no. 620 (25 November 1972) reported that discussions were held on linking exploitation of Guinean bauxite deposits to development of an aluminum complex near the giant Inga hydroelectric site in Bas Zaire.

7. Odier, "La politique étrangère de Mobutu," pp. 25, 26.

8. Benjamin Nimer, "The Congo in Soviet Policy," *Survey* 86, no. 1 (Winter 1973), pp. 184–210.

9. Alan Hutchinson, *China's African Revolution* (Boulder, Colo.: Westview Press, 1975), p. 148.

10. On the Chinese role, see Bruce D. Larkin, *China and Africa, 1949–1970* (Berkeley and Los Angeles: University of California Press, 1971); Warren Weinstein, ed., *Chinese and Soviet Aid to Africa* (New York: Praeger Publishers, 1975); and Alvin Z. Rubinstein, ed., *Soviet and Chinese Influence in the Third World* (New York: Praeger Publishers, 1975).

11. The most recently published Annual Report of the Banque du Zaire, covering 1974, makes no reference whatsoever to Chinese aid in its national income accounts and government expenditure and revenue statistics.

12. These are well portrayed by Jean-Claude Williame, *Patrimonialism and Political Change in the Congo* (Stanford, Calif.: Stanford University Press, 1971). See also his "Leo 'cles' de la politique Zairoise," *Revue Nouvelle* 62, no. 12 (December 1975), pp. 528–533; and Jean-Philippe Peemans, "L'Etat fort et la croissance économique," *Revue Nouvelle* 62, no. 12 (December 1975), pp. 515–527.

13. Tutashinda, "Les mystifications de l'authenticité," p. 81.

14. On the February 1970 OAU Foreign Ministers Conference resolution calling on the United Kingdom to use force against Rhodesia, see Kenneth W. Grundy, *Confrontation and Accommodation in Southern Africa: The Limits of Independence* (Berkeley and Los Angeles: University of California Press, 1973), p. 111. On OAU financial contributions, see Mononi Asuka-Ngongo, "The OAU Liberation Committee: The Rhetoric of African Liberation" (Ph.D. diss., Indiana University, 1975).

15. *Elima*, 6 October 1973.

16. John A. Marcum, "The Anguish of Angola," *Issue* 4 (Winter 1975), p. 5.

17. Mobutu vigorously denied this relationship in an interview with *Jeune Afrique*, no. 790 (27 February 1976), p. 20.

18. *Afrique-Asia,* no. 110 (31 May–13 June 1976).

19. See the excellent paper by Nzongola Ntalaja, "The United States, Zaire, and Angola," given to the National Conference of Black Political Scientists, Chicago, April 1976. During part of 1975 Congo-Brazzaville also supported Cabinda self-determination.

20. Banque du Zaire, *Rapport Annual,* 1974, pp. 119, 120.

21. *Economist,* 31 July 1976.

22. For convincing documentation on the 30 November measures, see forth-coming Ph.D. dissertations by Michael Schatzberg (University of Wisconsin) and Edward Kannyo (Yale University).

23. Nzongola, "The United States, Zaire, and Angola," p. 13. See official explanations in *Taifa,* 22 September 1974, and *Elima,* 28 September 1974.

24. Agence Zairoise de Presse (AZAP), 25 April 1974, 13 November 1974.

25. On the Zairian armed forces, see Jean Rymenam, "Zaire: Le pouvoir absolu d'un militaire d'occasion," *Le Monde Diplomatique,* December 1975, p. 6.

26. *Elima,* 31 December 1974.

27. The concept of "MPR cadre" was peculiarly murky. At first, it was implicit that it was intended to cover all persons holding authority roles, but its scope was reduced progressively to the near-vanishing point. Indeed, few of these announced radicalization measures were even partly implemented.

28. For the press reports on this affair, see *Elima,* 17 June 1975; all the Zairian press offered abundant commentaries in the next days.

29. *Jeune Afrique,* no. 790 (27 Februaty 1976), p. 20.

13
Independent Mozambique and Its Regional Policy

Keith Middlemas

A newly independent country has few chances to choose a free field for its external policy and Mozambique is no exception: its relations with its neighbors in Southern Africa today can only be understood in the context of its history and the history of Frelimo since the Portuguese revolution of April 1974.

Frelimo came to power unexpectedly. Despite its considerable tactical success in the northeastern province of Tete in 1972–1973 and the deep incursions south of the Zambesi by Frelimo guerrilla columns in the early months of 1974, Frelimo leaders in Dar es Salaam were still talking of a decade of armed struggle, and they assessed General Spínola's book, *Portugal and the Future*, as no more than a renewed attempt to foist a neocolonial "solution" on the country.[1] Even in June, a month after the MFA coup in Lisbon, Frelimo was still short of information and uncertain how to assess the confusing overtures made by different sections of the Portuguese and Mozambican authorities. Apart from a general attack on colonialism, there was no carefully considered plan for assuming power—all the resolutions of the last central committee meeting in 1972 had been concerned with the furtherance of the war in its various aspects, and beyond the twin demands that Lisbon recognize Frelimo as the sole legitimate aspirant and transfer power completely, most other questions remained open for negotiation.[2]

Concentration on these two decisive but uncomplicated demands gave

Apart from a number of government publications and the monthly statistics of the Bank of Mozambique, there is a marked lack of source material for this sort of study on the period since April 1974. The government statistical apparatus has not yet been reconstituted and most departments themselves work on the basis of provisional figures, often six months out of date. Consequently, this chapter has been based almost entirely on interviews with officials, Frelimo members, and Portuguese advisers. Following the practice adopted in my earlier study of Mozambique, *Cabora Bassa, Engineering and Politics in Southern Africa* (London: Weidenfeld & Nicholson, 1975), I have not cited these sources individually.

Frelimo certain advantages in the chaotic summer of 1974. During General Spínola's long rearguard action aimed at retaining a measure of Portuguese influence in Mozambique and Angola, the administration of Mozambique decayed, allowing Frelimo to make rapid inroads against a dispirited and finally supine Portuguese and black Mozambican army; in Lisbon, meanwhile, the MFA was finally forced to exert itself against the president they had, somewhat reluctantly, put into supreme power. In fact, when the Lusaka Agreement was signed on 9 September 1974 in Dar es Salaam, the principal MFA negotiator, Major Melo Antunes, included provisions contrary to the federal concept preferred by Spínola and the civilian foreign minister, Mario Soares. But at the same time, Frelimo's successful stance meant that the disadvantage of its lack of members was compounded by a certain over-confidence in military achievement, which led to over-confidence in its capacity to utilize an essentially rural wartime experience in governing a relatively complicated—albeit colonial—state.

By liberation army standards, Frelimo was a large and unusually well-disciplined force. In 1974 the Front was capable of putting 12,000 men into action, though not, of course, in an outright confrontation with conventional forces. Among its members, standards of literacy, political education, and military training were unquestionably higher than those of the members of Zimbabwean movements or the disorganized groups in Angola. But a group of 12,000 is not large enough to take over the government and provincial administration of a country of nearly 10 million (9.5 million blacks, 250,000 whites, and 15,000 Asians) and to administrate the large cities and ports of Lourenço Marques and Beira, to run the railways with their South African and Rhodesian traffic, and to provide a defense force in lieu of the colonial army.

Frelimo had successfully surmounted the deep internal crisis of 1968–1969, the ideological divisions of the leadership following the assassination of Eduardo Mondlane, and the secessionist bids of the Makonde tribal chief Lazaro Kavandame. But the coherence and single-minded enthusiasm of the movement led to undue optimism about the success of Frelimo's methods in relation to the tribal and separatist problems of a vast area that, with its eight main ethnic groups and five separate languages, could in no sense be called a nation. Frelimo leaders, moreover, were operating on theoretical assumptions appropriate to taking over a colonial state exploited by the metropolis, and they were largely unaware of the effects of Portuguese policy since Caetano's formulation of a new colonial attitude in 1969–1970. These effects included the partly successful attempt to make Mozambique economically independent, which involved the imposition of import substitution, conversion of interterritorial debts to a national debt, and the setting up of financial institutions ready to fulfill the functions of a reserve bank.[3] These economic developments enmeshed the interests of a much larger group than the traditionally narrow circle of investors in Portugal's African colonies: not only South Africa (already deeply concerned with the future of the Cabora Bassa hydroelectric project), but Rhodesia, several West European countries, and of course Mozambique's Black African neighbors. Frelimo's limited acknowledgment that these constraints existed was to have important consequences after the final transfer of power, particularly on those whites who, however sympathetic to Frelimo's aims, regarded recent economic developments as proof of their own importance to a future mixed economy.

The climax of the war effort in the early 1970s and the "hearts and minds" campaign inspired by General Kaulza d'Arriaga had brought a hectic and unbalanced prosperity to Mozambique. The military budget for Mozambique in 1971 had reached 5.5 billion escudos and continued to rise;[4] budgets for the railways and ports for 1974 were 3.3 billion escudos (compared to 2 billion escudos in 1971) and for roads, 540 million escudos (compared to 354 million in 1971).[5] A considerable part of the military budget, perhaps as much as 25 percent, was disguised as infrastructure investment in the north and northeast — in tarred roads, airfields, hospitals, and the grouping of the population into *aldeamentos*, or strategic villages, that by 1974 included roughly one million people, or 12 percent of the population.

Apart from infrastructure and the completion of Cabora Bassa (which Frelimo inevitably accepted, despite its contingent link with South Africa), this massive expenditure, perhaps the largest proportionate injection of capital ever undertaken by a colonial power, produced developments in basic education[6] and in the conditions of certain rural areas (where the *aldeamentos* work had been done by the civilian Overseas Ministry rather than by the army) that Frelimo could accept and build on, even if it did not publicly acknowledge. But the continuation of these improvements, of peak investment, and of export production contingent on the self-sufficiency plan, depended not only on Portuguese public and private capital, which was cut off after 1974, but on the generation of Mozambique investment via savings of white urban middle and skilled working classes and on the will of the white managerial elite to stay. Because the elite largely abandoned Mozambique in the next two years and because black skilled workers eschewed the old pattern of saving, any direct comparison of the present state of the economy (1977) with the 1973 boom is bound to be tendentious and unfair to the new government's capacity for economic management. Nevertheless, in 1974 Frelimo failed to understand the fragile and artificial nature of the boom or to predict the effect of their measures on a white population that had never really understood Africa except as an extension of the Portuguese way of life.

The internal stability of the country was called into question even during the 1974 negotiations, with the spread of administrative chaos and the lack of firm direction from the governor-general in Lourenço Marques. Factions and a separatist movement grew rapidly among sections of the white population, stimulated by the security police, by Portuguese residents in South Africa and Rhodesia, and also by the direct intervention of Rhodesian forces, which had been unofficially permitted to mount military operations since the ZANU (Zimbabwe African National Union) incursions through Tete province at the end of 1972. While some whites joined groups favorable to Frelimo and others (either PCP—Partido Communista Português—members or socialists) worked actively for Frelimo, several provincial governors attempted to foster intertribal rivalry, particularly among the Macua, who had long resisted Frelimo penetration. At the same time, the maverick industrialist Jorge Jardim, having failed to organize a non-Frelimo Mozambican delegation to the peace talks, tried to set up a countervailing force based on Frelimo renegades, members of the splinter group Coremo, and the black paratroop and commando elements of the former Portuguese army. Angry, bewildered, or frightened groups of whites (an amalgam of settlers; small businessmen and traders facing bankruptcy; skilled workers uncertain of a future without job restriction; and poor whites) besieged the Lourenço Marques radio station in a "revolt" in September 1974. The revolt was tactfully suppressed by Portuguese and Frelimo forces, but the first wave of emigration began, reducing the white sector from 230,000 to 80,000 by July 1975.[7] Managerial staff and white artisans were thus drastically reduced even before Frelimo took over.

During the lifetime of the transitional government, Frelimo encountered its own problems. For ten years the movement had been organized as a front for war, political education, and agricultural production in a hostile environment. Suddenly it was required to present itself as a party of government ready to supply ministers, provincial administrators, and civil servants and to take on difficult peacetime duties like combining with Portuguese troops to put down the white revolt in September and the riots of 21–23 October 1974 in the capital.

City life—with its obvious temptations after the long years in the bush—was a profound cultural shock to Frelimo troops, whose proclivity for swaggering about the capital like a conquering army led to tensions and near-hostilities with the remaining Portuguese soldiers. But the real problem of how to convert Frelimo guerrillas into a national army could not be solved until later, when Frelimo was in power, nor could the Front as yet turn itself into a political party. Roughly 5,000 of its membership were placed in government and provincial administration. During 1975 many of the remaining troops were sent out to the *aldeamentos* to supervise the vast hinterland, convert the better civilian-built villages to collectives, encourage formation of new villages to replace the strategic hamlets, and act as the vanguard of political enlightenment and internal discipline until the party apparatus was ready.

This dispersion and diversification of the army probably accounted for the almost complete failure of subsequent separatist movements such as the Makonde-based FCD (Frente de Cabo Delgado) and the exile movement, FUMO (Frente de Unidad de Mozambique), led from Lisbon by Domingos Arouca. But in the towns—and especially in Lourenço Marques—grievances about lack of pay, the absence of ranks and promotion to offset the privileges of those members who had been given government posts, and lack of leave (particularly for the Makonde of the far north) led to discipline problems and finally to the open mutiny of 400 soldiers on 17 December 1975 at the Machava Barracks in Lourenço Marques.

Three days of sporadic attacks by Frelimo were required to put the mutiny down. Decisions in response to the mutiny—about pay and the conversion of Frelimo's liberation army into a conventional defense force allied to but distinct from the party—showed how seriously the mutiny had been taken. During the next six months a new security police unit purged the army dissidents (among them members of an anti-Frelimo organization calling itself Magaia, after an opponent of Machel, murdered in 1971). Then, through recruiting and professional training, the army was brought up to its present strength of 15,000, chiefly to meet the threat of Rhodesian invasion.

Other stresses of the transitional period lasted longer. In an attempt to speed up the mass conversion of the population and inspire genuine dialogue between the swelling numbers of new adherents and Frelimo's central policymaking organs, the *Grupas Dinamizadores* (GDs) were set up in 1975. These varied in style from shop-floor councils to general assemblies of workers in government departments and banks to self-elected meetings of villagers in rural areas. At the start, they lacked any general model or central direction. Representative only in the sense that their discussions reflected the diversity of interest groups, they failed to provide any coherent basis for dialogue. Although they did offer a useful forum for Frelimo exhortations and political education, they almost entirely failed to galvanize production. The huge wage increases lavishly and irresponsibly handed out by the Portuguese to buy off trouble in May and June 1974, and repeated during the transitional period, had undermined the will to work. In turn, intervention by the GDs seriously hampered work patterns and such management as still remained.

In 1974–1975 Frelimo also suffered from the consequences of becoming a party of government without supreme control. The movement worked hard to extend its membership, proselytize in the regions, and prepare new schools for the party cadres. But while the leaders responsible for the party, the army, and the mass movement (including Samora Machel himself, who took no office in the transitional government) were able to remain uncompromised, those who became ministers had to deal continually with the retiring Portuguese over complex questions. These questions included debts; the future of Cabora Bassa; development aid; relations between the Mozambique airline, DETA, and the Portuguese airline, TAP; and the pensions and pay of white civil servants—all matters in which Frelimo's doctrine gave no clear guide. Inevitably, ministers became enmeshed in practical deals difficult to justify to purists. Worse, they were exposed to unaccustomed publicity, not only in Portugal, where the government of General Vasco Gonçalves was felt to be predominantly sympathetic, but in South Africa and Rhodesia. This publicity focused on Prime Minister Joaquim Chissano, an articulate, able, and (to Western eyes) "moderate" figure, in contrast to the "extremist" unknown future president. It created the appearance of a personality cult with effects that disconcerted the Frelimo leadership and revived nightmares of the disputes and assassinations of 1968 –1969 and of Uria Simango's attempt to break up the triumvirate. Against a background of uncertainty among whites in the country, hostility outside, and the collapse of Angola into civil war, all this was enough to create a fear of neocolonialism, Spinolism, and great power intervention. This was unjustified as far as South Africa was concerned, but was sustained by the activity of exiles in Rhodesia and attacks on the left-wing Gonçalves government in Lisbon in the summer of 1975.

There were practical as well as ideological reasons for the "clean cut" from colonialism expounded by Machel in July 1975, just after independence: thus the abrupt takeover of land, communications, and transport; the nationalization of private medicine, schools, legal practice, and church property—far more disturbing to whites; and the stringent surveillance mounted against urban whites in the latter part of 1975. But the price was very high. Of the 80,000 to 100,000 whites who had remained after independence, either as Mozambican citizens or as Portuguese citizens on contract, only 25,000 were still in the country by the end of 1975. More emigrated after the nationalization of rented property in March 1976 and the consequent embargo on the export of any property bought with foreign currency. These measures dispossessed not the administrative and rentier classes (as Frelimo had intended), but the skilled white artisans in the ports, railways, and major industries whose savings had traditionally been invested in property and household goods. By the end of 1976, 90 percent of whites had left. A few were accepted in South Africa, roughly 25,000 in Rhodesia, and the rest, as penniless refugees, in Portugal or Brazil. The majority of those who had taken Mozambican citizenship after independence reverted to Portuguese status during 1976. Many whites who had genuinely sought to live under the new conditions were forced out, even though Frelimo had intended to attack only the exploiters and the ill intentioned. An accurate figure for those remaining in early 1977 is impossible to obtain, but estimates ranged from 12,000 to 20,000 of whom probably three-quarters were expatriates on contract. Following the recent law enforcing a choice between Mozambican citizenship and expulsion, the great majority of this vestigial group fled under chaotic conditions. White society had disintegrated factitiously and ingloriously, with almost irreparable economic loss.

The flight of managers and artisans and the consequent loss of production led to a collapse of the industrial and export sectors in 1975-1976. Export crops — sugar, maize, cotton, rice, sisal, and cashew nuts — fell by between 50 percent and 80 percent of the 1973 figures. Industrial output fell by 50 percent in 1975 and a further 15 percent in 1976, while energy consumption showed a steady decline of 10 percent per year in oil and 15 percent per year in electricity. Although coal production increased (due to a new contract with Japan), it still amounted to only 1 percent of the gross domestic product. Other mining enterprises succeeded only in minimal production, while the ambitious plans for heavy industry in the Zambesi valley were laid aside. Even before the shock caused by the closing of the border with Rhodesia, unemployment in the cash sectors of the economy had risen by 20 percent in a single year, 1975-1976.

Meanwhile, Frelimo-appointed commissions struggled with desperate shortages of trained staff in the enterprises abandoned by Portuguese owners. The remaining private sector managers (whether in small businesses, companies belonging to Portuguese banks, or the great conglomerate, Companhia União Fabril, which had been nationalized in Portugal in March 1975) looked to the government to bail them out of a debilitating liquidity crisis. This the Bank of Mozambique did, using its reserves, rather than risk further bankruptcies and unemployment. Small businesses, garages, and shops collapsed because of abandonment by their owners, shortage of cash to pay inflated wages, or the virtual ban on sacking workers except as a consequence of liquidation.

Having exacerbated these conditions for understandable political ends, Frelimo proved unable to provide short-term remedies. Its leaders and the handful of senior civil servants who staffed the ministries and planning councils were as able and educated as any in Africa, but the next layer down of officials was practically nonexistent. This was not surprising, given the colonial education system in which only 5 percent of university places had gone to blacks and the postindependence disappearance of most of the white teachers in the secondary and technical schools. In the long run, the remedy lay in expansion and remodeling of the education system. The university at Maputo (as Lourenço Marques was renamed) now has nearly 1,000 students and there has been a switch in emphasis from the humanities to practical sciences like agronomy and medicine. Priority is being given to secondary education and teacher training. The share of education in the 1976–1977 budget is $55 million—17 percent of the total—making it the largest item after defense. Moreover, Frelimo has made it a requirement that as part of a higher education course students must undertake an equal term of employment in government service.

The manpower benefits of this policy will not show for several years. Meanwhile, the deficiency has not been met successfully by either promotion or expatriate recruitment. Promotion led rapidly to the creation of a "babu" class, barely competent to fill the minor posts left vacant, battening on to inflated salaries (particularly in the public service), virtually holding tenure for life, and repeating many of the worst features of the colonial bureaucracy. As for expatriate recruitment, campaigns in Portugal produced a small number of qualified staff with linguistic and cultural competence. These became essential to the survival of the railways, harbors, and airways. Otherwise, expatriates recruited from the Soviet Union, Brazil, East Germany, or Western Europe turned out to be ignorant of local conditions and their salaries imposed a severe drain on hard currency reserves. On his 1976 visit to the Soviet Union President Machel was disagreeably surprised at the exacting conditions and salaries required by Soviet technicians. Many of the doctors supplied by North Korea and Bulgaria are unaccustomed to tropical medicine, while Cuban advisors proved unable to avoid a near-disastrous drop in the 1976 sugar crop.

The whole thrust of Frelimo's recent policy has therefore been to prevent further deterioration of the economy. The ambitious hope of working out a national plan was abandoned, replaced by a three-year recovery program covering the years 1977–1979 that was designed to restore production and exports to their 1973 peak. Even this plan was by no means modest, since it was based on the assumption that 1977 would see the bottom of the slump. But the most significant factor was the new pragmatism that the program implied. There would apparently be no more nationalization, apart from taking over a percentage of the shares in companies seeking government finance. Specific guarantees were given to South African and other international businesses with Mozambican subsidiaries that their operations were welcome, on terms somewhat similar to those obtaining in Zambia. The Italian League of Cooperatives set up a joint trading compay with the Mozambique government to serve as the official channel for trade with Western European companies. Mozambique owns 51 percent of the company, which provides a useful defense against Frelimo fears of exploitation by multinational corporations.

The hopes of recovery depend on South African revenue. Mozambique has already received substantial financial and technical aid from South African Railways for the Mozambique railway system since 1974. Revenue from South Africa comes in two ways: from freight and port charges on through traffic and from the 60 percent of wages paid miners by the South African Chamber of Mines. The latter sum is paid—after six months work—directly to the Mozambique government in gold, at the official price, and then paid (less taxes) to the worker's family in Mozambican escudos. Freight and port revenue declined sharply in 1975 but is now reviving; revenue from miners' wages fell in 1976. Nonetheless, on the assumption that the gold is sold for the Mozambique government at a market price of $135 per ounce, the total revenue from South African sources can be computed as 250 million rand in 1975, 225 million rand in 1976, and probably 275 million in 1977.[8] By Southern African standards these are enormous revenues. In 1975–1976 they just about covered the deficit on the balance of payment; deficits of the Mozambique state enterprises; and the deficit in the operating budget; and also allowed a resonable reserve of $60 million at the end of 1976.[9] The consequence has been Frelimo's abstention—almost unique in Africa—from requests for foreign loans. But the South African decision in 1977 to revalue the gold given to Mozambique at its market price has meant much-reduced income, with very serious effects on the underlying assumptions of the recovery program. South African willingness to renegotiate the Mozambique Convention will be a significant measure of its interest in Mozambique.

The planning departments, the Ministry of Finance, and the Bank of Mozambique recognize that recovery cannot be achieved simply by compromise with the remnants of the capitalist sector, even if that compromise has the long-run advantage that Mozambique may be able to choose the best economic bargains. For example, it could choose between East German and South African mining technology and finance in the development of the mineral resources of Tete and the Zambesi basin using Cabora Bassa electricity. Success before 1980 rests largely on Frelimo's ability to achieve the political goal so far unattained by the GDs: to invigorate the population politically and to provide the necessary incentives to increase—or, to begin with, restore—production. It has not proved enough to exhort or even to stigmatize workers' "indiscipline." True, self-criticism, originally inculcated on the Chinese model, has always been an important element in shaping Frelimo philosophy. A typical declaration of a February 1976 central committee meeting referred to the previous year as a period when "moral, material, and ideological corruption began to thrive among us . . . and an atmosphere of anarchy, liberalism, indiscipline, and idleness was created." But the returns on slogans and propaganda have been poor, so that long before the Third Congress in February 1977, the full resources of the government's economic and political policy had been directed to the creation of a socialistic society, based on these adverse economic circumstances.

"There can be no good Mozambican capitalists," the weekly *Tempo* announced in January 1976. The faint, discreet encouragement to foreign enterprises has not been allowed to extend to domestic enterprise. Insofar as the government has freedom of action, policy has been to divert resources to the traditional agricultural sector, with emphasis on collective farms and villages. This commitment, together with education and defense, set the priorities of the 1976–1977 budget exercise. Most UN aid and bilateral aid (not specifically related to losses contingent on the cutting of Rhodesian ties) has been similarly earmarked. As an aid to political policy, and in an attempt within a virtually closed economy to reduce the effective purchasing power of grossly inflated urban wages, deliberate use was made of inflation, then running at 15 percent a year. Note circulation was extended by 60 percent between 1974 and 1977.[10] Given strict import controls, this inflation drove the price of luxury goods to incredible heights. At the same time, many of the unemployed (particularly those thrown out of work at Beira, after the border closure) have simply been "relocated" in rural villages. As part of the drive to reverse the drift to the towns that began in the 1960s, the government has allowed temporary food shortages and has let spiraling prices run largely unchecked, making urban life difficult and often unpleasant. These are the practical aspects of the endless calls for sacrifice, endurance, and struggle and of the restoration, after centuries, of priority to the peasant.[11]

Frelimo's chances of surviving the almost inevitable dissent and resistance to such policies rests clearly on its ability to create a stable political system. Unlike the expanded—albeit unbalanced—economy the Portuguese left, their political legacy held nothing of value beyond the tradition of a one-party state—a tradition Frelimo perpetuated. Faced with the massive problems of effecting the transition from a rural, armed front to a national party, convincing the whole population of the legitimacy of the transfer of power, and reorganizing the army and the GDs, the central leadership in 1975 embarked on a cumulative program of party reform that finally emerged in the resolutions of the Eighth Central Committee a year later—resolutions that were later endorsed by the vast crowds attending the Third Congress in February 1977.[12] Put simply, Frelimo made itself over into a classical Leninist vanguard party in order to lead, discipline, and educate the mass movement. In the process, earlier models of organization linking the party to the mass of the population based on Chinese teaching (of which the GDs seemed most significant) were abandoned, and advice on party structure was sought from Soviet and East German political scientists, as well as from more obvious sources like TANU. A steady purging of the GDs began in order to bring them into line as workers councils, subordinate to the party. The cadre school at Matola was rapidly expanded to train new party workers. Recruitment on a mass basis has now ceased and is carried out through the army or through existing party cadres. The army's relationship to the party has been redefined to fulfill the dual role of guarantor of the political autonomy of the state and embodiment of the Frelimo tradition—a role symbolized by President Machel's regular appearances in uniform, as commander-in-chief. Quite distinct roles were assigned by the Eighth Central Committee resolutions to the police and to the Militia Brigades, a projected national service citizen militia. Thus the army itself is no longer coterminous with the party and—despite its overall quasi-military appearance—the party is no longer dominated by the military leaders. As the war period recedes into revolutionary history, the military tradition is being circumscribed—and this, like the role of the army in the new state, is another instructive example to the Zimbabwean Patriotic Front. Recruitment to the party has been declared to be a privilege rather than a right: "Only those can be members who are ideologically certain, who identify with the people and the revolution, and who are ready for sacrifice," Machel told party cadres in October 1976.[13]

In this way the purity of the party has been institutionalized, leaving the state (government) free to make the necessary day-to-day arrangements and compromises with the outside world. The party has its own responsibilties and finances, but, according to Frelimo theology, it is not the state. The state, however, derives its authority from Frelimo, and democracy "remains an abstraction."[14]

Frelimo's Foreign and Regional Policies

Few of these developments could have been foreseen in 1974. Although the experience of reaction to adverse conditions was not unwelcome (in his speech at Matola on 13 October 1976, Machel directed the party: "Let us kill capitalism, like a crocodile when it is young and lying on the river bank, before it grows huge and swims midstream"), the continuous economic and political crisis enforced a distinction between Frelimo theory and the practice of government that only the abrupt political transformation of the Frelimo movement has been able to contain. It is therefore not surprising that Mozambique's external relations show a divergence between public statements of policy—on South Africa, for example—and the realities of regional coexistence. On the public level, Frelimo has castigated apartheid; recognized the South African ANC as the legitimate political authority; and identified wholly with the condemnations expressed by Julius Nyerere, rather than with the more conciliatory tone of the Lusaka Manifesto. On the economic level, however, it is heavily dependent on South African revenue and regular technical assistance on the railways and ports. Something very close to a tacit bargain was reached following South Africa's carefully correct attitude during 1974–1975. Frelimo deferred any attempts to give the South African ANC Mozambican bases, and the South African authorities in return discreetly watched the Portuguese community in the Republic to prevent active anti-Frelimo operations by FICO and FUMO. Naturally, neither side expected acknowledgment. South Africa's Angolan intervention in 1975 caused Frelimo serious rethinking, even to the extent of putting some political pressure on the Shangaan in 1976 not to allow themselves to be recruited for the mines. Recruiting figures improved later in the year, with the lifting of bureacratic restrictions and Frelimo's acknowledgement that organized contract labor was preferable to illegal immigration. During 1977, however, the figures fell again, to a level of 40,000 in the mines and probably 100,000 overall.

On the other side, South African authorities have done their utmost to ship bulk ore through Maputo in order to replace the lost general cargo, increase Mozambican revenue, and restore employment. The Anglo American Corporation—the principal South African company with Mozambican interests—has reached an agreement on future operations and the safeguarding of its investments. At least in the short term both sides are bound together by mutual economic advantage.

South Africa has also certain long-term hopes, the chief of which is involvement in the development of the mining and industrial complex of the Zambesi basin and the navigation of the river itself. At present these are based on no more than South African corporate experience with Cabora Bassa, but the assumption is that South African technology (if not also its financial aid) will be regarded as politically neutral when the Mozambican economy begins to expand in the early 1980s. Cabora Bassa itself, completed in 1975, has hung fire because the contractors could not guarantee the full output contracted with the South African Electricity Commission (Escom) for the first stage.[15] Power did run for most of 1976 on a test basis, and it was predicted that stage one (800 megawatts) would be completed shortly before stage two (1,250 megawatts) came into operation in 1977.

The complicated legal principles of Cabora Bassa's operation in independent Mozambique had been settled earlier under Portuguese law by the institution of a new company, Hidroelectrico de Cabora Bassa, to operate the dam. An initial 10 percent of the equity was vested jointly in the state of Mozambique and the Reserve Bank. This equity was to be augmented annually by a further 3 percent in lieu of taxes. Thus in thirty years the dam will belong wholly to Mozambique and, at that point, the South African revenue will pass entirely from Portuguese hands. The main contention now lies in negotiations between Portugal and Escom over a price increase from 0.003 rand per unit to 0.006 rand per unit to offset the 60 percent increase in the dam's cost due to the world inflation of the early 1970s. Mozambique will benefit indirectly from these negotiations.

Cabora Bassa's disposition illustrates how tangled was Mozambique's inheritance from Portugal. It took over two years to settle all the outstanding questions, while the harmonious overall relations evident during the Gonçalves government turned to guarded hostility. The effect on Portugal of nearly 200,000 refugees from Mozambique (although not as catastrophic as the effect of 400,000 from Angola) and the often bitter postmortem about whether a more favorable settlement could have been achieved in 1974 by Soares rather than by Melo Antunes soured relations. Frelimo evinced little of the gratitude which the MFA had naively expected and instead alternately bestowed blame and fresh demands that Lisbon, faced with a prolonged economic crisis, could not fulfill. Contact with the PCP, however, became closer the more Frelimo was seen to veer from the Chinese to the Soviet side. Alvaro Cunhal visited Maputo in November 1975, and a triangle of influence developed in the following year in which the PCP played broker to Frelimo and used the resultant credit to enhance its standing vis-à-vis the Soares government in Portugal.

Even before the Angolan war drew the Soviet Union, Cuba, and South Africa into that territory, Mozambique's foreign relations possessed multiple dimensions: economic links with both white and black neighbors; political, economic, and cultural links with Portugal and Brazil; ideological affinities with the communist parties of Portugal and Italy (some of whose members began to fill posts on Mozambican newspapers and in Frelimo cooperatives) and with the Soviet Union and other Eastern bloc countries. (There had never been more than tenuous influence by Western European countries or the United States.[16] Until the 1976 Kissinger talks on Rhodesia, the efforts of these countries were restricted to the time-consuming and often humiliating business of opening formal diplomatic relations. It is difficult to overemphasize the broader cultural isolation of Mozambique from English-speaking and francophone Africa.) As in the cases of Portugal and South Africa, internal considerations dictated Frelimo's responses, which can be separated into two stages: before and after the movement's political problems developed in 1975.

During and immediately after the ten-year war, Frelimo's affinity for China rather than the Soviet Union was scarcely in doubt. While the Soviets continued to supply arms and train skilled personnel, the bulk of guerrilla training went on in southern Tanzania, guided by Chinese instructors.

However careful Frelimo was not to take sides, the movement's style, its collective leadership, its habits of self-criticism and analysis, even its newspapers revealed the appropriateness of Maoist teaching to the Frelimo struggle.[17] Assurances that China regarded itself as a Third World country gained acceptance simply because on past experience Frelimo believed that an identity of interest with China existed that the Soviets could not share.[18] These conclusions seemed to be validated from May through June 1974 when Soviet diplomats in Dar es Salaam tried crude leverage to force Frelimo to settle with the Portuguese civilian emissaries on Spínola's terms—and thus bolster the PCP (and the other established Portuguese political parties) at the expense of the MFA. Similar attempts at coercion in October 1975, relating to the Angolan struggle, provoked an angry retort from Chissano (by then foreign minister) at the fifty-eighth anniversary celebration of the Russian Revolution: "We accepted aid in the past only to gain our independence; and we will continue to accept it only from countries which do not interfere in Mozambique's internal affairs."

At that stage, Frelimo was still emphasizing Mozambique's nonalignment. Even the Chinese, who kept a remarkably low profile, did not escape a measure of criticism. Tanzanian observers remarked on the African nationalist element in Frelimo and on the well-documented mistrust of any outside aid with strings. (As early as 1967 this attitude had led to sharp rebuffs of East German overtures and those of a Cuban mission.) It seemed unlikely that Mozambique would take sides or that it would permit any foreign power to wield greater influence than the supply of arms. But the internal political crisis, the Angolan war, and Frelimo's miscalculation of the costs and dangers of sealing its border with Rhodesia changed the balance. To the dismay of Chinese diplomats, Frelimo shaped itself into a vanguard party and downgraded the significance of the organs of mass movement. The Chinese themselves backed the "wrong horse" in Angola and suffered a grave loss of prestige, just at the moment when the Soviet-Cuban aid to the MPLA presented the Soviet Union and Soviet-style communism in its most favorable light since the early 1960s. Insofar as is known, Mozambique now relies on the Soviet Union and East Germany for its arms supply. In addition, there have been rumors recently that the Soviet Union will build a communications station on the offshore island of Bazarote.

This is not to say that Frelimo has committed itself irrevocably. If foreign ministry statements are any guide, pressure to allow any foreign power military access would be strongly resisted. The small Cuban presence appears to be related more to the vagaries of the sugar crop than to contingency planning for war against Zimbabwe Rhodesia, and there is no evidence of the sort of administrative penetration or military training role adopted by Cubans in Angola after the MPLA-Cuban victory. President Machel's 1976 visit to the Soviet Union did not foreclose relations with Peking, where he had been cordially received a year earlier. Other East European countries have dispensed significant amounts of aid, both civil and military. Most notable is East Germany, which has high hopes of developing mineral resources, particularly the titanium and vanadium in Tete province. The visits of Presidents Podgorny and Castro in March 1977 fitted naturally with Machel's frontline position in the Rhodesian conflict and with the old — though now somewhat formal — links with Angola[19] and should not be given undue weight in the analysis of relations between Mozambique and the socialist countries.

Frelimo is well aware that aid from the Eastern bloc has strings and often costs more than aid from the West. It also appreciates that China has ambitions far less grandiose (and therefore less threatening) than those of the Soviet Union toward Southern Africa. For the economic and political reasons discussed earlier, Mozambique has no immediate reason to identify with the Soviet aim of creating leverage points (rather than actual bases) in countries on which South Africa depends significantly, either for raw materials (Namibia) or manpower (Mozambique). President Machel has been very careful to keep the balance, and Chissano spoke out against alignments at the 1976 Colombo Conference. What concerns Frelimo most is Zimbabwe Rhodesia and the guerrilla war against that country waged from within Mozambique's borders. As early as the 1975 OAU conference in Mogadishu, when summoned to vote on MPLA recognition, Machel was reported to have said, "This vote is crucial. Now we shall discover who will call our friends 'mercenaries' when they come to help us, if we are attacked [by Rhodesia]."[20]

Frelimo's Aims for Southern Africa

Mozambique's borders touch Tanzania, Malawi, Zambia, Zimbabwe Rhodesia, South Africa, and Swaziland. Its economic sectors range from the most primitive agriculture to sophisticated mining and industry. Its service industries depend on South Africa and Zimbabwe Rhodesia. Its railways form a segment of a far wider network. Its rivers could contribute to a navigational system serving landlocked Zimbabwe Rhodesia, Zambia, and Malawi. Its hydroelectric resources could form part of a massive Southern African grid. If Zimbabwe Rhodesia were already Zimbabwe, Mozambique could form part of that middle Africa grouping dreamed of by Julius Nyerere in the early 1970s[21] and put forward again more recently by Tanzania as an alternative to the erstwhile East African Community.

The economic bases of such a grouping already have some political underpinning. These black republics all share a common political model in the one-party state. Although party development is still at very different stages, TANU (Tanzanian African National Union) in Tanzania, UNIP (United National Independence Party) in Zambia, and the Congress party of Malawi have in recent years come to share a number of similar beliefs, one of which is that strong party leadership is the only means to overcome the succession problems of presidential government. In this sense, with the achievements of the Third Congress, Frelimo has already taken the lead. It is regarded by Nyerere, and to a slightly lesser extent by Kenneth Kaunda of Zambia, with a mixture of respect and envy. Close links exist between Frelimo and TANU to their mutual benefit, while Machel and Nyerere weave an elaborate web of friendship and carefully disguised mutual instruction. Nyerere has stated publicly that TANU should learn from Frelimo's discipline, political consciousness, and understanding of the revolutionary process. The thesis that the Zimbabwean movements might be able to discover political consciousness and unity through waging war was based, of course, on the Frelimo example.

Frelimo's consideration of a wider grouping was confined to Tanzania until 1975, in order to avoid compromising future possibilities. But with experience of government, of Mozambique's economic interrelationships in Southern Africa, and above all the impact of the Zimbabwe Rhodesian war and the creation of the "front-line" states bloc, the Frelimo leadership now appears to see Mozambique's future within some form of regional grouping. In the economic sense Tanzania would remain a poor relation, if the bloc also included Zambia, Zimbabwe, Malawi (after Banda's demise), and perhaps Botswana; but Tanzanians remain convinced that historic and ideological ties are far too strong for their country to be excluded. In any case, the breakup of the East African Community leaves them no alternative but to fit in.

It is far too early to ask whether a group of like-minded states with harmonious economic circumstances (only Zimbabwe would have an extensive industrial sector) could form an effective political federation or even an economic community like the East African Community in its heyday. But these governments (with the possible exception of post-Banda Malawi) share socialist perspectives of varying sorts. However ambiguous Zambian economic principles may be, in practice Zambia tends toward state socialism. If Angola and Namibia were to join also, Frelimo would be comfortable with the Marxist-Leninist bent of both the MPLA and SWAPO.

The ideological color of the future government of Zimbabwe is obviously crucial to Mozambican thinking about a regional group of black governments, but until Rhodesia becomes Zimbabwe this planning exercise is no more than dreaming. All of Mozambique's internal and external concerns and fears focus in one way or another on the problem of transition from Rhodesia to Zimbabwe.

The Rhodesian problem first surfaced for Frelimo in 1971–1972 when, for tactical reasons, it cooperated with ZANU in Tete province. In return for giving ZANU a launching pad into the Mount Darwin–Centenary area of Rhodesia, Frelimo gained some relief from raids by Rhodesian security forces (with Portuguese acquiescence) up to fifty miles inside the Mozambican border. Nonetheless, in the subsequent violence, Frelimo lost a considerable number of men.[22] The cost rose even higher after January 1974, when Frelimo mined the Beira-Umtali railway and triggered Rhodesian cooperation with the Portuguese DGS (Direção Geral da Seguridad) and its paramilitary *flechas,* or commando units. Even before the Lusaka Agreement was signed, FICO counted on Rhodesian support. Since Mozambique's independence most attempts at subversion, including the FUMO-operated Radio Free Africa, have depended on Rhodesian tolerance and the support of the 25,000-strong Portuguese exile community in Zimbabwe Rhodesia.

In spite of such interference, Mozambique was compelled to maintain contact—in particular, to continue providing gasoline and other supplies—for nearly a year after independence, because of the revenue from Rhodesian freight and Rhodesian use of Beira harbor. In addition, up to 85,000 Mozambicans worked as migrant laborers in Rhodesia, providing both income and relief from unemployment. On the other hand, Frelimo could not, even had it wished to, avoid harboring the ZANU and ZAPU guerrillas, who by 1976 had coalesced into ZIPA's 12,000 to 15,000-strong force, stationed in the provinces of Tete, Manica, and Gaza. As early as May 1974, Chissano had declared that as a future UN member Frelimo would be bound to observe UN sanctions against Rhodesia.[23] Having themselves relied on Tanzania and Zambia as hosts during the war, Frelimo was inevitably flung into the front line.

Two calculations delayed the closure of the border: the cost to Mozambique's economy and the fear of Rhodesian military reprisals. The economic cost might be partly offset by the United Kingdom's ambiguous statement at the 1975 Commonwealth Conference that it would accept liability up to £15 million.[24] In addition, Mozambique could count on UN aid and large low-interest loans promised by China, the Arab League, and the United States. Avoiding Rhodesian military reprisals required cooperation with Zambia, as the other likely target for hostilities, and the creation of the concept of "front-line" states in order to spread the ensuing risk.

Despite Tanzanian warnings based on Zambia's post-UDI experience, Frelimo calculations made in early 1976 grossly underestimated the cost of closing the border—in lost revenue, in multiplied unemployment, and in bankruptcies of a whole range of businesses only indirectly dependent on the Rhodesian economy. For a start, the railway network (which lacks a north-south axis) was cut in two and Beira port was virtually put out of action. Frelimo's initial figure of $57 million annual losses (reported to the UN in May 1976) increased to $200 million by the end of 1976.[25] The effect of this miscalculation on Frelimo's planning process and on the evolution of the three-year recovery program was substantial. It was arguably beneficial, for it brought the planning ministers face-to-face with the steadily deteriorating condition of the national economy. The contrast between Frelimo's public pronouncements about the war and its increasingly equivocal support for ZIPA grew, however, because in private the government was already deeply worried about the consequences, even before the Rhodesian attacks on ZIPA camps and refugees which began in May and July 1976 and continued through 1977. ZIPA had been rent by factional conflict, leadership clashes, ideological disputes, and tribal murders. In reaction, in mid-1976 Frelimo invited the support of two Tanzanian battalions, to act as a reserve defense in Tete province against the possibility of ZIPA military disorder and to spread among the "front-line" armies the inevitable embarrassment of any required punitive action.

By April 1976, when the Kissinger regional talks revealed how undramatic Mozambique's posture really had become, Frelimo was disillusioned with ZIPA's apparent lack of success.[26] Turning away from its earlier theory of the long war, based on historical analogy, and from Nyerere's vicarious valor, Frelimo found itself at the end of 1976 rather closer to Kaunda's line: If ZIPA was unable to oust the Smith government or keep control of its own ranks, it augured badly for its ability to retain authority in Zimbabwe in the future. Above all, Frelimo did not wish to get involved in future factional fighting *inside* Zimbabwe, having already come under criticism from Bishop Abel Muzorewa for its support of the Mugabe-Nkomo Patriotic Front.

Frelimo might seek to detach itself from total commitment to ZIPA, but it could not safely stand back and ignore the future political composition of Zimbabwe. On the contrary, this was a matter of the utmost economic and ideological significance. It is clear that the party disliked, and distrusted Muzorewa and regarded Sithole as unrepresentative. Yet Mugabe did not fit Frelimo's needs either. Nkomo's substantial claims as an elder statesman and the undoubted strength of ZANU's political machine inside Rhodesia had to be acknowledged by Frelimo. Given the nature of their own party reconstruction, Frelimo leaders naturally enough questioned the strength of the political base commanded by each of these Rhodesian nationalists. The Patriotic Front seemed to provide the best answer to this question. Whether personal antagonism toward Muzorewa clouded Frelimo's perception of his considerable support in Rhodesian townships and whether that attitude can change must remain open questions. But it is perhaps significant that early in 1977 Nkomo began to discuss the possibilities of "scientific socialism" in Zimbabwe, suggesting a radicalization on his part to counter prospective

Mugabe dominance of the Patriotic Front. Muzorewa may also take a sterner ideological stance, in response to Nkomo's and to the continuing frustration of Rhodesian politics. If he does so, Frelimo might have to reconsider its lack of support for his nationalist faction.

More than any other country in the region, Mozambique has a vested interest in the return of peace to Zimbabwe, the reopening of its border with that state, and cooperation with its future government. But with the failure of the 1977 U.S.-U.K. diplomatic overture, Frelimo's attitude changed again. It acknowledged reluctantly that only a military solution was possible, while simultaneously expressing its fear of the consequences for a far less disciplined movement than its own, about to enter a rich country full of administrative and political prizes, with many more qualified noncombatant claimants to a share of power. While a ZIPA military victory would vindicate Frelimo's own long struggle, it might set up tensions inside Zimbabwe that would be destructive of the "front-line" states' unity and Mozambique's own political and economic stability. At the same time, a military victory would threaten Frelimo's tacit economic involvement with South Africa, in which both governments share the same pragmatic perspective about immediate and short-run regional problems. Whether South Africa could ever learn to live with a bloc of black socialist neighbors is another matter, but there can be no doubt that a stable solution to the Zimbabwe Rhodesian problem is crucial for Mozambique. Frelimo fears of subversion or invasion would lessen dramatically, dependence on non-African socialist regimes for aid and weapons would diminish, and the Mozambican government would be free to pursue its long-term interests in regional interdependence.

Notes

1. *Mozambique Revolution*, no. 58, March 1974.
2. Interview with Joaquim Chissano, May 1974.
3. For a fuller discussion, see Keith Middlemas, *Cabora Bassa, Engineering and Politics in Southern Africa* (London: Weidenfeld & Nicolson, 1975), Ch. 10.
4. Ibid., p. 140. The exchange rate was then (1973) 40 escudos to the dollar.
5. Ibid., p. 244.
6. Of 2 million school-age children in 1973, 800,000 were in schools of some sort, compared to 520,000 in 1970 and 418,000 in 1960.
7. Between September 1973 and April 1974 20,000 returned to Portugal. There is also evidence that the administrative class and those with Portuguese residences (roughly 35 percent of the total) had already decided where their priorities lay. See Keith Middlemas, "White Society in Mozambique," *Tarikh*, May 1977.
8. These figures are based on the calculations of the CFM (Mozambique Railways) and the harbor authority, which show approximate totals of 75 million rand (1975)

and 100 million rand (1976); and the statistics of the Chamber of Mines, which show total Mozambican personnel in South Africa as 88,660 (1974), 107,400 (1975), and 70,500 (1976). Twenty percent should be added to the latter figure, for mines which used separate recruiters. Based on an average wage of 101 rand a month, the value of gold can be calculated, after multiplying by three (the difference between official and market prices), as 175 million rand (1975), 125 million rand (1976), and probably 150 million rand (1977). These calculations take account only of monies remitted directly to the government in hard currency or gold; they do not include remittances from men working in other, nonmining employment, nor remittances and freight payments from Rhodesia, which ended with the border closure.

9. Bank of Mozambique, *Monthly Bulletin*, November 1976.

10. Ibid. Part of this was due to the unfreezing of Mozambique escudo deposits by the Banco Nacional Ultramarino in 1974, but two-thirds of the increase represents deliberate policy.

11. The argument for self-sufficiency in agriculture is simple: the census figures for 1972 showed a birth rate rising at 3 percent per year with falling infant mortality (down from 45 percent to 40 percent over the previous decade for most districts). By 1974 55 percent of the 9.7 million population was under fifteen years of age.

12. Government of Mozambique, Ministry of Information, "Resolutions of the Eighth Central Committee." See also Machel's speech to party cadres at Matola, 13 October 1976 (Mozambique Ministry of Information).

13. Speech to the party cadres at Matola, 13 October 1976.

14. Oscar Monteiro, "State and Party," *Tempo*, 14 November 1976.

15. A failure due to delays in commissioning one of the turbines, after a severe rock fall in 1973. The construction of turbine no. 5 was delayed because of damage to a major bridge near Tete by Rhodesian forces during an attack on Mozambique in July 1976.

16. French, West German, and Italian contractors were involved at Cabora Bassa; the British retained long-established investments in Sena Sugar; and Belgium controlled the Moatize coal mines.

17. Middlemas, *Cabora Bassa*, Chaps. 6 and 7.

18. Government of the People's Republic of China, *Hsinhua News Bulletin*, 27 May 1974, p. 19; also Chinese Vice President Teng Hsiao Ping's UN speech, 10 April 1974.

19. Contact between Frelimo and the MPLA in the war years was maintained partly by personal contact and partly by CONCP, the liaison organization for the Portuguese liberation movements. Naturally, Frelimo showed keen concern in the fortunes of MPLA, but since mid-1976 the two governments have grown somewhat apart. Frelimo leaders regard themselves as having far surpassed MPLA in the building of a coherent socialist society and tend to act as mentors rather than allies. There is also a certain distrust of Agostinho Neto's aloof personality and MPLA's excessive dependence on Cuban personnel. The different economies of the two countries preclude close trading links, and Cabinda's high sulphur oil is useless for the Maputo refinery.

20. Private information to the author.

21. "The independent African states need to speak with one voice in order not to

be disregarded by the great powers," Nyerere told an Australian audience in March 1974. "Forty-two states [in the OAU] can meet only rarely, and when they do, our separate sovereignty means that unanimity is required in conference, and then forty-two separate actions are necessary to make the unanimity effective." (*Times of Zambia*, 24 March 1974)

22. In 1973 Rhodesian forces killed 168 men in the northeast, of whom 75 were Frelimo soldiers.

23. Interview with Joaquim Chissano, May 1974.

24. A promise with a deliberately vague cash commitment that later led to some ill feeling between the United Kingdom and Mozambique.

25. United Nations, documents E/5812, 30 April 1976; E/5812/Add. I, 5 May 1976; and A/31/266, 19 October 1976.

26. See also Chissano's interview in *Le Monde*, 30 October 1976.

Conclusion

John Seiler

Despite considerable Western diplomatic effort since early 1977 and despite the remarkable achievement of the U. K. government in concluding the December 1979 ceasefire and transfer of power in Zimbabwe Rhodesia, conflict in Southern Africa has not reached an end. Nor is it likely to do so for the foreseeable future.

In Zimbabwe Rhodesia, the possibility remains high for a massive breakdown of civil order given the animosity among black nationalist forces and the token size of the Commonwealth military contingent. If civil order collapses, neither the United Kingdom nor its Western allies will be free to intervene unilaterally, and international differences about whom to support would be likely to result. These differences would exacerbate the fighting, which might then spread to South West Africa/Namibia and South Africa.

In South West Africa/Namibia, the chances for agreement on a political settlement remain meager. As a result, Angola and Zambia (and perhaps Botswana) will be forced to deal with increasing demands for support from SWAPO guerrillas. In turn, South Africa will be repeatedly tempted to make preemptive raids on SWAPO bases in these territories and extra-regional governments will then be faced with SWAPO demands for even greater support.

Assuming the P. W. Botha government continues its programs of domestic change in South Africa, interested governments will need to appraise with increased rigor the extent to which these changes meet reasonable criteria for democracy and justice. Wholecloth opposition to the South African regime, always easier to espouse from outside the region, will become at least marginally more difficult to justify. Black regimes in the region will find the economic preponderance of South Africa increasingly difficult to resist without the unlikely alternative of massive developmental aid from the United Nations, the West, or the Soviet bloc.

Finally, despite the mutual restraint exercised since the Angolan civil war, the danger of a major U.S.-Soviet confrontation in Southern Africa remains a profound concern. Such a confrontation would be less likely to come from their calculated initiatives than from the sudden escalation of U.S.-Soviet regional involvement in response to military actions taken by the Cubans, the South Africans, or the guerrilla armies. Nonetheless, the results would be catastrophic in the number of lives lost, in the destruction of social stability, in the weakening of fragile political systems, and in the implications for a broader international military confrontation between the superpowers.

But continuing and deepening regional violence is not inevitable. Nor need a modicum of regional peace be bought at the cost of justice and democracy in South West Africa/Namibia and South Africa. The challenge to Western policy remains the encouragement of sustained peaceful change in the region. The United States in particular has genuinely espoused this general goal for two decades, but it has not specified reasonable institutional goals to implement change and has not provided sufficient economic aid to make a continuing impact on regional development. It is now apparent that such goals can be outlined and progress toward them assessed and that the economic resources needed to stimulate their achievement are not extraordinarily high—set against the overall level of Western economic aid and given the urgency of regional stabilization in Southern Africa.

Most importantly, it is now clear that all regional governments without exception want regional stability in order to secure a measure of internal security and the opportunity to concentrate their energies more fully on development priorities. More than any other factor, this common desire—cutting across a wide range of ideological positions without denying the widespread repugnance toward continued racism in South Africa—provides effective leverage for a Western policy aimed at regional accommodation and stability.

To a considerable extent, the desire for regional stability has been used adeptly by Western negotiators to secure "front-line" state support for initiatives in the Zimbabwe Rhodesia and South West Africa/Namibia negotiations.

Unfortunately, no success has come from similar efforts to press South Africa into accommodations. Pressure from the United States in particular has been ineffective because the South African government believes U.S. concern to be mere rhetoric and because South Africa judges its overall economic and military position to be very strong. In any case, given the tentative achievements of constructive change within the Republic since the end of 1978, it would be timely for the United States and its diplomatic colleagues to move away from pressure to a posture of constructive criticism vis-à-vis South Africa.

The first step in such a policy of constructive criticism would involve an acknowledgement of South African bona fides, a simple act that denies the Manichaean moralizing typical of much international criticism of South Africa during the past twenty years. The United States need not accept the inevitability of ethnic-based politics and institutions in South Africa in order to accept using them as a base for the expansion of black political participation and for the facilitation of social and economic justice. One focal point for constructive criticism would be the knotty question of political power sharing. Already acknowledged in the form (but not yet in the substance) of South West African/Namibian political institutions the extension of power sharing to the Republic would be a necessary culmination of the processes of regional devolution and local governance already underway. Another focal point would involve just treatment of blacks in "white" South Africa: in industrial employment, in township homes, in access to cultural and educational facilities, and in control of common services such as electricity, public transport, and water.

The financial cost to the United States of implementing the above suggested policy would not be great. There need be no governmental expenditures toward either South West Africa/Namibia or South Africa once U.S. banks and businesses are encouraged to take a larger role in industrial investment and in urban and rural development projects backed by South African government investment guarantees.

For the regional Black states, however, especially those hit hard by the consequences of the Angolan and Zimbabwean wars—Zambia, Mozambique, Angola, and Zimbabwe—substantial amounts of U.S. government aid (both bilaterally and via the United Nations) should be allocated to reestablish infrastructure and to encourage agricultural production and the training and education necessary to undergird such production.

In its aid for regional development, the United States must follow two principles. First, it will not take sides between the stated developmental goals held by South Africa ("a constellation of states") and those held by the "front-line" states ("balanced growth"). Its entire approach should rest on utilizing areas of tacit agreement between the two views. Second, the United States should not encourage the encapsulation of South African infrastructure and resources or the development of duplicate ones by other countries. Helping Botswana to operate its section of the Rhodesia Railways makes sense. Even building a rail line from South West Africa/Namibia through Botswana to connect with the present Rhodesia Railways line might be justifiable. But projects that ignore the utility of South African rail and port linkages make no economic sense at all. Also, while it would be appropriate to aid in the exploration and predevelopment stages of mineral resources in black-governed states, it would be wrong to put public money into the actual exploitation of such resources. If they are potentially profitable, many

Western and South African companies will then step in, resulting in substantial returns to the host governments in revenue, jobs, and broader economic stimulation.

The outcome of this proposed regional policy would be at best an ambiguous and probably tacit mutual accommodation. Anatagonistic rhetoric would not disappear. Regional institutions would not proliferate. Nonetheless, it is a goal worth pursuing with considerable effort.

The basic concomitant to the continuation of such a regional policy would be demonstrations of increasing black support for, and black participation in, South African political institutions. It is not inevitable that the South African government will have the vision and the determination to carry through a commitment to end racism. Even if the government should be so disposed, it is unlikely that the resultant institutional arrangements would satisfy all blacks. But residual resistance aside, a sine qua non of enhanced social justice would be the step-by-step retrenchment of the elaborate and stifling security legislation and enforcement apparatus built up since the early 1950s.

While U.S. implementation of this new regional policy would require considerable explanation to interested governments and domestic political constituencies, as long as black governments within Southern Africa accept the process of change within the Republic and accept regional mutual accommodation as just and productive, criticisms voiced from outside the region should remain marginally significant and be politically manageable.

Would the regional accommodation and change within South Africa outlined here have been feasible or even perceivable before the 1974 Portuguese coup? I think not. In that sense, despite the costs of the Angolan civil war and the Zimbabwe Rhodesia guerrilla war, there is now hope for Southern Africa's future that did not exist before. The six years since the Portuguese coup have demonstrated vividly the nature of this regional conflict: the mixed motives of all regional governments, the influence of South Africa within the region, and the motives and limited impact of extraregional governments and international organizations. The abandonment of dogmatic rhetoric and the beginning of a long-term process of mutual accommodation will provide no dramatic solutions to the problems of Southern Africa. There are none. But the process itself, however difficult its immediate future, can only be seen as a profoundly encouraging portent for Southern Africa's future.

Index